How to Develop Your Creative Identity at Work

Integrating Personal Creativity Within Your Professional Role

T0349732

Oana Velcu-Laitinen

Apress®

How to Develop Your Creative Identity at Work: Integrating Personal Creativity Within Your Professional Role

Oana Velcu-Laitinen
Helsinki, Finland

ISBN-13 (pbk): 978-1-4842-8679-1   ISBN-13 (electronic): 978-1-4842-8680-7
https://doi.org/10.1007/978-1-4842-8680-7

Managing Director, Apress Media LLC: Welmoed Spahr
Acquisitions Editor: Shiva Ramachandran
Development Editor: James Markham
Coordinating Editor: Jessica Vakili

Distributed to the book trade worldwide by Springer Science+Business Media New York, 1 New York Plaza, New York, NY 10004. Phone 1-800-SPRINGER, fax (201) 348-4505, e-mail orders-ny@springer-sbm.com, or visit www.springeronline.com. Apress Media, LLC is a California LLC and the sole member (owner) is Springer Science + Business Media Finance Inc (SSBM Finance Inc). SSBM Finance Inc is a **Delaware** corporation.

For information on translations, please e-mail booktranslations@springernature.com; for reprint, paperback, or audio rights, please e-mail bookpermissions@springernature.com.

Apress titles may be purchased in bulk for academic, corporate, or promotional use. eBook versions and licenses are also available for most titles. For more information, reference our Print and eBook Bulk Sales web page at http://www.apress.com/bulk-sales.

Printed on acid-free paper

In memory of my grandparents, Maria and Colin, the first creative personalities in my life.

To all the creative personalities who will find guidance in these pages. May you shape the world and improve others' lives like my grandparents uplifted my childhood.

Table of Contents

About the Author

 **Oana Velcu-Laitinen** is a NeuroLeadership coach and speaker with a focus on the importance of creative thinking abilities to improve work performance. Her clients include researchers, change leaders, entrepreneurs, and individuals seeking career growth.

Oana holds a Ph.D. in Economics from Hanken School of Economics in Helsinki, Finland. During her doctoral research on the implementation of Enterprise Resource Planning (ERPs) systems in mid-sized Finnish companies, she repeatedly noticed an underestimation of change management. As a result, she got interested in supporting individuals and organizations to create cultures of creativity and change. So, in 2016, she disrupted her academic career to become a knowledge solopreneur.

The book *How to Develop Your Creative Identity at Work* reflects Oana's curiosity to keep abreast of the latest research on creative identity, mindsets, and beliefs and turn it into actionable principles for ambitious knowledge workers. Her motto is, *"To know fulfillment, follow your creativity."* Originally from Romania, Oana lives with her family in Helsinki.

About the Technical Reviewer

Vlad Glaveanu is Full Professor of Psychology in the School of Psychology at Dublin City University, Ireland, and Professor II at the Centre for the Science of Learning and Technology, University of Bergen, Norway. He has published widely in the field of creativity, imagination, culture, collaboration, social media, perspective-taking, wonder, and human possibility. He is the founder and director of the Possibility Studies Network, editor of the Sage journal *Possibility Studies and Society*, and editor of *The Palgrave Encyclopedia of the Possible*, and of the Cambridge Series in Possibility Studies, with Cambridge University Press. In 2018, he was awarded the Berlyne Award from the American Psychological Association (Division 10) for early career contributions to the psychology of aesthetics, creativity, and the arts.

Acknowledgments

Writers live in a community that facilitates their ability to sit down and write. My community grew as I advanced with the book. And to be fair, I will be expressing my thanks in chronological order as different community members brought their contributions to my commitment to start and finish writing this book.

It all started in 2017 when a friend who had just published his first book told me, "Now it's your turn." I thought, "Me, writing a book while I raise two preschoolers and develop an independent consulting business?"

Yet, this comment, "Now it's your turn," came back to mind. Especially in moments when I facilitated training and could notice how smart people misunderstood their creativity. Also, when I would read some research papers on creativity, I felt that I would want to add my perspective to this topic. So, I thought, "Why not?" Why wouldn't I write a book on the psychology of creativity? I thus thank Oscar Santolalla for prodding me to write about a topic I love.

In 2019, I got down to writing, and like never before, I experienced highs and lows – on the same day! Thousand thanks to my husband, Tero, for the thousand times he interrupted his work to act as my Zen master. Thoughts of gratitude go to my sons, Christian and Alex, for staunchly checking up on my progress, "Mom, how has this day been for you?" They did know I had spent some time managing their conflicts. Finally, I thank my trio of friends, Laura Arranz-Aperte, Sorana Nagy, and Joanna Linden-Montes, for cheerleading the initial writing stage.

You cannot write a book without conducting your own research. I thus thank the charismatic professionals who agreed to spend their precious time to be interviewed by me on their relationship with their creativity.

ACKNOWLEDGMENTS

Matias Kupiainen, Dasha Pears, Vincenzo Cerullo, Helder Santos, John Bates, Harriet Fagerholm, Oscar Santollala, Pamela Thompson, Peter Ivanov, and Tulia Lopes. Their work is not easy, but they handle it with grace.

In 2020 I finished the first drafts of the manuscript. I thank Sara Kuusela for being my beta reader while raising three kids and completing her doctoral dissertation in biomedicine. In addition, I'd like to express appreciation to Nicholas Balcazar for patiently proofreading the second version, which had an academic tone.

I thank my sister, Luiza, for her enthusiastic support throughout, particularly for helping me decide to look for a publisher instead of self-publishing. Next, I thank my mother, Sofia, for being critical and making me think from the readers' perspective. Finally, I thank my aunt Silvia for listening to my updates, withholding her judgment. And I felt she had at least one – "Out of all the things she could do, why write a book?"

When I began pitching the book to publishers, a turning point was when I had my book proposal package reviewed by Paul Roberts, Director of Fifthday and editorial member of the Jericho Writers community. Soon after, I started working with my publication team: Shiva Ramachandran, Jessica Vakili, and Jim Markham. You gave me the energy to tune into the creativity needed for the last mile, the final revisions of the book.

Vlad Glăveanu, a Full Professor in Psychology at Dublin City University, joined the team as the technical reviewer in April 2022. The conversations with him crowned my writing experience, enabled me to fine-tune sections in the book, and opened my eyes to future topics to look into. I am indebted to Vlad for his willingness to take on the project at a moment of change in his career and family life.

Last but not least, I am deeply grateful to the creativity researchers whose work is referenced throughout the book. Their research rocked my world!

Now, when I look back, I am aware that the best parts of the book are the result of my being inspired by each of these fantastic people.

Introduction

Revisit Your Commitment to Your Work Role

Time is precious. We must choose how we go through life.

—Alex, 8-year-old

What are the most critical choices you have made in your life so far?

As a kid, some adults in your life must have asked, *"What do you want to be when you grow up?"* Then, in your teens, you must have explored this question further by looking for answers to *"Who am I?"*, *"What should I do in life?"*, or *"Who do I want to become?"*

Now you are in your thirties and have a status role where you feel something is missing. It's now about prestige or personal wealth. You're content with all that. What you're missing is bringing your total energy to work. You often wonder, *"What other education choices could I have made?"* What is going on? The younger self embraced a higher education track without a strong emotional attachment with the respective choice.

Psychologist Erik Erikson – recognized for his work on the development of identity throughout the lifespan – considered that healthy individuals go through eight psychosocial crises, which are the stepping stones of personal growth.[1] In adolescence, we go through the fourth stage of psychosocial crisis, when we experiment with different beliefs, social roles, and scenarios about the future. The problem is solved when we develop a personal sense of identity. Except that settling upon a work identity is not always resolved in your 20s.

---

[1] Erikson, E.H., (1994), Identity and The Life Cycle, W.W. Norton & Company.

Allowing yourself to explore who you are and committing to who you can become can result into four forms of identity statuses, out of which two are of interest in this book – identity achievement and identity foreclosure.[2]

Have you met professionals who feel they are the right person at the right place? Such individuals enjoy the psychological state of identity achievement. It stems from an earlier identification of a special interest, such as the artfulness in working with their hands or the pleasure in literary skills, math, or science as a pupil. For them it was easier to decide what skills and knowledge to develop at university. From there on, the professional identity was shaped accordingly.[3]

But not all teenagers have the opportunity to explore and develop a sense of self around their creative potential – the combination of cognitive abilities, personality traits, and affinities toward a domain of knowledge that leads to the generation of original products. Psychologists call this identity foreclosure and this may be the identity status with which you've been living for years.[4]

What were your motives for which you selected to specialize in a particular domain? Was it because it was an important and respected job in society? Was it because it would ensure financial stability? Was it because you were infatuated with the idea of the future you in the respective role? Was it because you had no clue what you were doing?

---

[2] Marcia, J.E., (1966), Development and validation of ego identity status, Journal of Personality and Social Psychology, 3, pp. 551–558.

[3] Dollinger, S.J., and Dollinger, S.C., (2017), Creativity and Identity, The Creative Self, pp. 49–64.

[4] Crocetti, E., Monica, R., and Meeus, W., (2008), *Capturing the dynamics of identity formation in various ethnic groups: Development and validation of a three-dimensional model,* Journal of Adolescence, 31, pp. 207–222.
Meeus, W., et al., (2010), *On the Progression and Stability of Adolescent Identity Formation: A Five-Wave Longitudinal Study in Early-to-Middle and Middle-to-Late Adolescence,* Child Development, Vol. 81, No. 5, pp. 1565–1581.

Even for the most independent among us, our educational preferences as young adults were influenced by a family member, a teacher or a friend, with whom you had a special relationship based on emotional connection and admiration. As a result, you settled too fast on a professional competence, which reflects your fidelity to the values of the individual you looked highly upon. You continue to be committed to a line of work while you keep justifying to yourself the choice made, like *"It is too late to turn back. I have to keep going."* Yet, your unconscious is unsettled about who you might become.

What do you want to do when you grow up? This book is an invitation for you to consider customizing your professional role. Your core competence may be in science, engineering, technology consulting, or other fields which are not acknowledged as the topmost creative domains. But if as a child you had a discontinued attraction toward reading, drawing, singing, history, etc., then an important choice you can make as an adult is to **reclaim your sense of creativity as an expert**.

This doesn't mean you should straightaway quit your current job to make room for a new specialization. Instead, you can first bring more of your creative interests in performing your tasks, say, using your acting skills in work presentations. You'll find surprising sources of personal energy when you explore your creative potential in light of current life circumstances. Again, this is about actively reshaping your work environment so that you can close the gap between your sense as a creative person and the emotional attachment to the work you do. Then again, you may develop a taste for a disruptive interest, like talking at TED talks on a theme of interest that cannot be integrated with current work tasks. In this case, you'll prepare for a career shift.

Revisit How Much You Value Your Creativity

It is human to allow ourselves to absorb ideas from those we love or admire. It's human that close people have implicitly shaped your professional choices. As honest and well-intended these individuals were, they may have unconsciously guided you toward their values and away from your creative potentialities.

If the word "creativity" makes you feel equally excited and unworthy, it's a sign that you'd benefit from taking the first steps on the path of self-experimentation as a creative individual.

There is more to your creativity than what past experiences let you believe. On a scale of 1 (*not at all*) to 5 (*very much*)[5], to what extent do you agree with the following three statements?

- "My creativity is an important part of myself."

- "I'd like to work regularly with problems that require creative thinking."

- "I'd like to work on projects for which I feel intrinsic motivation."

Should your average score be three or above, you are ready to explore how you can manifest your latent creativity.

You can look with compassion and gratitude toward the past. And get curious about the future. Your foreclosed identity is not set in stone. Benefiting from a deeper experiential and factual knowledge and updated life situations, **you can be faithful to yourself and explore your neglected creative side from here on**.

---

[5] 1= not at all, 2 = rather little, 3 = intermediate, 4 = rather much, 5 = very much.

Here we are, in the 2020s, when creativity is considered one of the top future skills in the job market, next to originality and initiative.[6] Being creative appears to be an essential ability for problem-solving and innovation, emotional well-being, and overall success in adult life.

Collectively, we seem to agree on the benefits of opening up to our creativity. Yet, the devil is in the details of implicit thoughts and feelings. At an individual level, understanding our relationship with personal creativity is not nearly as deep as we might think, due in part to the preponderance of stereotypes and biases that are perpetuated in various educational and organizational cultures.

In particular, implicit creativity biases drive us toward self-harming acts without realizing that they limit our professional choices. As a result, we deprive ourselves of the possibility of prioritizing our creative potential in the work we choose to do. When personal creativity is misunderstood, the creative drive is blocked.

A sense of disengagement and hopelessness can be symptoms of creative underachievement. You dedicated years to do a kind of work, the value of which you understand at an intellectual level but experience as a compromise at an emotional level. You may be thinking, *'I'd like to bring a touch of improvement to the world. I just can't see where to get started.'*

You'd like to take on an innovative challenge that makes you feel you're helping the world develop. Starting your own business? A leadership position? A central role in an innovation domain? A new specialization in a creative career?

What will it be? What might be the next step that brings you into the stream of creative guardians of life?

---

[6] www3.weforum.org/docs/WEF_Future_of_Jobs_2018.pdf
www.ibm.com/news/ca/en/2010/05/20/v384864m81427w34.html

In every creative person, there is a being and a doer. The being is grounded in the energy of life, which brings creativity, wisdom, and intuition. The doer does practical stuff like setting goals, planning, and taking action.

When the being and the doer are aligned, life feels good. You feel comfortable in your skin and have a deep sense of accomplishment. Conversely, when the doer gets ahead of itself without consulting the being, dissatisfaction, exhaustion, and hopelessness are on the daily menu of emotions.

You may be competent at performing the tasks related to the current role. Yet, performing those tasks leaves you uninspired. Exploring your relationship with your creativity enables actionable insights for your next project. The trick is to discern the new activities where the skills you practice are aligned with the creative being in you.

We are told that creative people tend to be willing to test new ideas at the risk of appearing less competent.[7] Creative people are courageous to go through trial and error until they find the environment that accommodates their creative force. Creative people are motivated mainly by the feeling of aliveness when experimenting with meaningful ideas. The entrepreneurial pursuits of the Leadership Communication Expert John Bates are illustrative.

"For my whole life as an adult, since 1994 basically, I had somewhere in the neighbourhood of 15,000 dollars worth of debt. And I had millions of dollars worth of useless stock that would never get liquid. And I was the evangelist for all these different companies, travelling around the world. Very fun, cool but I was always in massive massive debt. And then that all dried up and I started this business in the face of me admitting I might not make much money, it might not be a good idea, because there were other

---

[7] Lai, E.R. and Viering, M., (2012), Assessing 21st Century Skills: Integrating Research Findings, Pearson, Paper presented at the National Council in Education Vancouver, B.C.

opinions and stuff. But I knew I was providing value because I had seen the value I provided when I was doing the TEDx events for free. And I was like, 'I know that I can make a difference with this. I know I can provide value so I'm gonna do it anyway.' For the first year and a half, I just went further in debt. By year 2, it started to look like maybe it's gonna be ok. Year 3 I made more than I ever made in my life. Year 4 I doubled that. Year 5 I tripled that. We are now in year 7. Yes, it's great to make money. Not having to worry about money. That's such an old story for me. I did that for so long and it takes my attention from the difference I make.

But here's the real thing for me. I realized that when I was solely focused on making money as an entrepreneur, 'Oh, this will make money,' I had debt. When I shifted the focus just a little but to 'how can I provide the greatest value?,' it wasn't all of a sudden but I did start making money.

So, for me one of the happiest things in my life is that I had never felt before that I provided something that was this valuable to other people. And that is tremendously fulfilling, you know? And the money is just the scoreboard. The game is actually down here on the court and making an actual difference. And if I'm doing that, the score shows the money. But that's not the point. This is the point, down here on the ground. Does this make sense?"

As tempting as the prospect of vitality and fulfillment may sound, you may still think you're not a daredevil. Your trust in your ability to develop ideas that make a difference is built when you see what you can do for yourself. This book was written to help you understand and trust your options as a creator. Each choice strengthens your sense of creative competence.

Why Is This Book Helpful for You?

On a scale of 1 (*never crossed my mind*) to 5 (*full of excitement*), to what extent are you willing to prioritize the time to understand the nuanced nature of your creativity?

Generally, books on creativity tackle the question, *"How can we be more creative at work?"* It is the same approach underlying the creativity courses I design. The focus is on cultivating thinking skills – imagination, inspiration, and intuition – that contribute to long-term creativity.

This book explores these questions: *"Why do we not create when we have the potential to create?"* and *"How can we disrupt ourselves to understand what we can create?"* The following comment is made by one of the participants – a medical doctor and researcher in complex disease genetics – in the creativity course.

"Some of the insights I got from the course included that the importance of creating habits that boost creativity cannot be overlooked. I had never really thought previously that habits played a role in the context of creativity. I also got further insight into the consequences of approach and avoidance motivation, the benefits of play in science, and the advantages of sharing your ideas with others."

Indeed, favorable environments are crucial for developing the creative identity of knowledge workers. The challenge for some people with a high level of expertise is that they may feel that the work environment "forces" them to behave in a way that stifles their personal creativity. Others may think that the best way to perform is to feel fear. Therefore, personal beliefs determine the degree to which we see affordances in the environment to exercise our personal creativity.

Beliefs influence habits. Thinking habits – like engaging in a task out of curiosity versus engaging in an activity out of fear of losing something, like your job or a promotion – determine who we become. Who we think we are influences our habits. Our habits affect our beliefs. It's thus a spiral effect between beliefs and work identity, which is mediated by the environment.

The desire to write the book was formed and reinforced during five years of facilitating creativity training sessions. I noticed some cognitive biases that prevent us from developing habits to integrate personal creativity in our work. I couldn't stop thinking about how **each of us could benefit from a more accurate understanding of the versatile character of personal creativity.**

I observed one tendency that most of us have in common – to become attached to patterns of thinking and beliefs. To be creative means to be willing to reconsider some of these patterns. However, for most of us, letting go of a core idea, even for a thinking exercise of a few minutes, may feel like letting go of a rope while crossing an abyss.

Admittedly, in each domain of expertise, there are fundamental assumptions on which existing knowledge is built. Likewise, in each social network, ground rules need to be respected. However, suppose we cannot be flexible to suspend firmly held beliefs only for the duration of an alternative scenario exercise. In that case, we keep the door closed to creativity, and there is little room for creating new knowledge. Not to mention that we deny ourselves the personal experience of creativity – the joy of self-discovery and knowledge discovery.

One of the participants in my courses told me, *"If I do this exercise (hypothetical thinking scenario), I'll start questioning everything I know."* Someone else wondered whether mindfulness meditation would be time well spent. I was glad they were expressing hesitancy toward the creative thinking exercises I suggested. Critical thinking is one of the best abilities we can possess. But what hides behind the criticism? Curiosity to test ideas or the desire to defend particular beliefs and stay comfortable with your worldview?

I thus took on the challenge to review the research on how our beliefs, mindset, and identity affect why and what we create.[8] In addition, I interviewed professional creators from different fields on how they see their personal creativity.

What would you need to do differently to feel like you're a creative person working in the proper role? **To move away from a foreclosed identity to an achieved one**, you may want to explore how you can consciously manifest your creativity in your environment.

In Erikson's work, the achieved identity implies the state of having explored different interests during adolescence and committing to one in early adulthood. Here, achieved identity refers to realizing you're a creative person who deliberately chooses to test your creative potential at a professional level. Three questions will keep up your transformation: "What is possible and what is impossible for me to get involved in?", "What ideas, from what domains, inspire me?", and "What creative behaviors do I adopt in my work role?".

These are the questions that we investigate in this book. The more diverse your creative initiatives, the bigger the chance to understand your personal creativity's protean nature and experience symbiosis between the creative being and the doer in you.

Summing up, this book is an opportunity for inner reflection on what kind of creative person you are, where you are in the creator's journey and what you can start doing differently to evolve.

---

[8] Karwowski, M., Lebuda, I., Wisniewska, E., and Galewski, J., (2013), *Big Five Personality Traits as the Predictors of Creative Self-Efficacy and Creative Personal Identity: Does Gender Matter?*, The Journal of Creative Behavior 47:215–232. Hojbota, A-M., (2013), *Naive theories of creativity and sociocultural factors revisited. The potential explanatory role of creative self-efficacy and creative personal identity*, The International Journal of Creativity and Problem-Solving, Vol. 23, Issue 1. Karwowski, M., and Kaufman, J.C., (2017), *The Creative Self*, Explorations in Creativity Research.

Creativity and Creative Self Biases

To be a human being on planet earth is to accumulate stereotypes and biases, which bring to attention specific information on which we make decisions. Stereotypes are common beliefs shared by the members of a group about other people who are part of different groups – occupational, ethnic, gender, etc. Biases are personal beliefs. They are fed by stereotypes and inflate or deflate the truth about a person or a context.

"I like this solution."

"I don't like this solution."

"This question is useful."

"This question isn't useful."

Similarly, we are partial about the meaning and value of creativity. The challenge is to become aware of the biases that keep us fixated on a particular way of seeing the world and ourselves. All sorts of misconceptions, like creativity is a rare gift,[9] can confuse us about

- Who is a creative person?

- When is creativity needed?

- What are the important problems worth pursuing?

Watching my sons grow, I could notice creative thinking and behaviors coming up spontaneously, such as eating a pita bread to create the shape of a battle blowing horn, a boat, a thumb, etc. I was curious to see their level of awareness of their creativity, and for the first time, I engaged my eldest son – 8 years old at the time – in a dialogue about creativity.

"Who is a creative person?", I asked.

---

[9] Benedek, M., Karstendiek, M., Ceh, S. M., Grabner, R. H., Krammer, G., Lebuda, I., and Kaufman, J. C. (2021). Creativity myths: Prevalence and correlates of misconceptions on creativity. Personality and Individual Differences, 182, 111068: www.sciencedirect.com/science/article/pii/S0191886921004451

"Einstein," he replied without blinking. "He created physics and he was the best in physics."

How did he come to believe that a creative person is a genius? And not any sort of a genius, forgotten in the obscurity of the second best, but one who is remembered by everyone. Really, who has not heard of Einstein and his theory of relativity? Nowadays, we live in a world shaped by his theories which enabled the photoelectric cells and lasers, nuclear power, fiber optics, and space travel.[10]

We thus recognize a creative individual based on their original achievements. And groundbreaking accomplishments necessitate uncanny intelligence. Can a person of moderate intelligence be creative then? Research shows that above an IQ of around 120, personality factors like motivation and wisdom are more important than intelligence to be able to produce an increased number of creative ideas.[11, 12]

"It is important to foster individuality," Einstein said, *"for only the individual can produce the new ideas."*[13] Indeed, individual creativity is seen as the *"seed of all innovation."*[14] So, avoid fretting about not being the smartest person in the room. Focus instead on finding your creative motivation.

---

[10] Isaacson, W., (2008), Einstein: His Life and Universe, Pocket Books.

[11] Jauk, E., Benedek, M., Dunst, B., and Neubauer, A.C., (2013), The relationship between intelligence and creativity: New support for the threshold hypothesis by means of empirical breakpoint detection. Intelligence, 41, pp. 212–221.

[12] Sternberg, R. J., Kaufman, J.C., Roberts, A. M., (2019), The Relation of Creativity to Intelligence and Wisdom, pp. 337–352, The Cambridge Book of Creativity, Second Edition.

[13] Einstein to Carl Seelig, Mar. 11, (1952), Albert Einstein Archives 39-13, Highfield and Carter, 9.

[14] Amabile, T.M., Conti, R., Coon, H., Lazenby, J., Herron, M. (1996), Assessing the work environment for creativity. Academy of Management Journal 39(5), pp. 1154–1184.

How about asking yourself more often, *"What can make me experience wonder?"* Behind Einstein's revolutionary ideas, there was a fascination with the laws of the universe and his belief that the role of the scientist was to discover the fundamental harmony of nature.

A creative person looks at sundry aspects of reality with a sense of mystery and awe. Then they decide what to do about it. Before being a scientist, Einstein was a patent clerk in Switzerland. As is evidenced in his correspondence with his friend Conrad Habicht, in May–June 1905, Einstein was determined to write four academic papers in his spare time.[15]

A creative person is not only more apt to identify the problems worth focusing on, but they also make time to search for the answers. For example, the first paper that Einstein planned to write in 1905 was about the energy properties of light. The second paper was about determining the actual size of atoms. The third paper was about the irregular movement of microscopic particles in a liquid. The fourth idea resulted in a draft on the electrodynamics of moving bodies.

Einstein didn't know when he wrote to his friend about the plan for the four papers that he would produce a fifth paper the same year. It was an addition to the fourth paper. It discussed the relationship between energy and mass, which resulted in the well-known equation in physics: E=mc2 (the energy of a body is equal to its mass times the speed of light squared). Prior to this special relativity formula, mass and energy were considered distinct entities. Creative people transform "What if" questions into concrete projects of experimentation, which open them up to new possibilities of creative achievement.

How did Einstein use his creativity? With his messy hair and eyes brimming with humanity, he was a highly imaginative individual who discovered the principles underlying his theories thanks to thought experiments and not to induction methods applied in the lab. Already as a 16-year-old, he imagined what it would be like to ride beside a light beam.

---

[15] https://einsteinpapers.press.princeton.edu/vol5-trans/42

At best, creativity biases can inspire us. But, if creative people positively change the world, wouldn't you want to be one of the people who enable progress for others?

Continuing the dialogue with my son, I asked, "Who is the most creative person you know personally?"

Silence.

"How about your teacher?" I prompted him.

Silence.

"Or some friend? How about yourself?"

My son remained as mute as a fish.

At their worst, preconceived ideas about what it takes to be creative can prevent us from realizing our creative potential. If creative people are intelligent, self-driven, and imaginative, who dares see themselves as such? In addition to being blind about the creative people we directly interact with, we can be self-biased about our ability to come up with original ideas, in a negative sense like, *"I'm not talented enough to...."*

What might be meaningful to know about your creative capability? Considering how stumped my son was when I asked about the creative people he knows, I must have tapped into his implicit belief about creativity.[16] Could it be that some tasks or people make us feel creative, but we did not have the opportunity to engage with those tasks or people yet?

---

[16] Sternberg, R. J., (1985). Implicit theories of intelligence, creativity, and wisdom. *Journal of Personality and Social Psychology, 49*(3), pp. 607–627. https://doi.org/10.1037/0022-3514.49.3.607

Tang, C., Baer, J., Kaufman, J.C., (2014), Implicit Theories of Creativity in Computer Science in the United States and China, Journal of Creative Behaviour, Vol. 49, Issue 2, pp. 137–156.

Richard W. Hass, Roni Reiter-Palmon, Jen Katz-Buonincontro, (2017), Chapter 12 – Are Implicit Theories of Creativity Domain Specific? Evidence and Implications, Editor(s): Maciej Karwowski, James C. Kaufman, In Explorations in Creativity Research, The Creative Self, Academic Press, pp. 219–234, https://doi.org/10.1016/B978-0-12-809790-8.00012-1.

The question is not whether you are a creative person. What might be the self-biases that prevent you from expressing your creativity? For example, *"I'm not talented enough to write a blog on a topic ...,"* or *"I'm not talented enough to learn to code,"* or *"I'm not talented enough to tell a joke,"* etc. What activities would you engage in if you did the opposite of what the negative creative self-biases direct you to?

Being the best in the respective roles should be the least of your worries. Instead, your focus should be on becoming the kind of person who is fascinated by certain types of creative activities.

Creators Are Drawn by Novelty

I can't understand why people are frightened of new ideas. I'm frightened of the old ones.

—Composer John Cage

Maybe you will not come up with a theory in the same league as the theory of relativity. Then again, you can never know what you are capable of creating until you try. As the above quote says, you can start by taking initiatives to create something at a smaller scale, like a gadget, a book, a speech, a course, or a constructive conversation, which brings novelty to a context. Novelty means introducing a change in perspective to something previously agreed upon. Yet, the human brain has a strong need for certainty. As a creator, you go against others' beliefs of what appears to be possible and appropriate. What pushes some of us to expose ourselves to situations in which we disrupt others' sense of familiarity?

Indeed, it appears that human beings evolved through the development of a nervous system that activates the pleasure centers in the brain when we create things, even small things like drawing, storytelling, or cooking.[17] This is the creator's personal experience.

Let's do the following exercise, shall we? Kindly take one minute to complete the drawing below. Allow your imagination to flow freely.

How did it feel? This drawing is one of my favorite warm-up exercises when I facilitate training. What I enjoy most is noticing the participants' joy when they present their finished images. We all feel joy in discovering new ways to create. But we may not be aware of the enjoyment of creating either because we have not yet had the chance to find suitable environments or because we have a more dominant tendency toward conformity.[18]

Psychologist Mihaly Csikszentmihalyi hypothesizes that we are the descendants of tribes of human beings who appreciated curious children and protected them so that they might grow to adulthood and have children of their own.[19] For example, suppose you enjoy cooking without following a recipe or are willing to taste a new ice cream flavor despite being a bit skeptical, or you walk in a new city without being guided by

---

[17] Flaherty, A. W. (2018). Homeostasis and the control of creative drive. In R. E. Jung and O. Vartanian (Eds.), *The Cambridge handbook of the neuroscience of creativity* (pp. 19–49). Cambridge University Press. https://doi.org/10.1017/9781316556238.003

[18] Piffer, D. (2018). The genetics of creativity: The underdog of behavior genetics? In R. E. Jung and O. Vartanian (Eds.), *The Cambridge handbook of the neuroscience of creativity* (pp. 437–450). Cambridge University Press. https://doi.org/10.1017/9781316556238.025

[19] Csikszentmihalyi, M., (2013), Creativity, The psychology of discovery and invention

Google Maps. In that case, you likely have the prehistoric **"I see the beauty of engaging in new experiences" gene**, which underlines the tendencies of the creator in you. This book will help you grow aware of changes in habits and personal traits that help you discover new interests and nurturing environments.

So far, we have discussed implicit biases as internal obstacles that confuse you about what kind of acts of creation you can kick-start. What qualities might enable you to enact new roles as expert creators?

To Explore Your Creative Potential Requires Responsibility to Take Action and Humility to Learn

On a scale from 1 (*hopeless as a penny with a hole in it*) to 5 (*hopeful like the sun peeking through the clouds*), to what extent do you believe it's within your control to get involved and create in an area of interest?

No need to panic if your score is low. Often, a low level of trust in your resourcefulness to create can overrule the decision to engage in acts of creation.

In one of his notes, humanistic psychologist Abraham Maslow spoke about the *"fear of one's own greatness"* or *"the running away from one's own best talents."*[20] It refers to a general fear of fully developing the potentialities that we glimpse in our most perfect moments.

One day the sun is shining on your street. The first opportunity for aligning your work with your creative potential is within your reach. Imagine that someone offers you a temporary leadership project, the chance to partake in a start-up initiative or a content creation task.

---

[20] Maslow, A.H., (1993), The Farther Reaches of Human Nature, Penguin Compass, pp. 34

You catch yourself trembling inside, feeling comfortable with the ongoing tasks. The dissatisfaction with work-life feels sweet. Maslow called this tendency to avoid growth **the Jonah complex**.

Who was Jonah? The Old Testament tells the story of Jonah, whom God chose to preach to the locals in the city of Nineveh.[21] But Jonah didn't feel up to the task of telling the people of Nineveh that God thought their wickedness had gone too far and some repenting would do good. So what did he do instead? Jonah boarded a ship to escape God, sailing in the opposite direction of Nineveh. During the journey, a storm broke out. Jonah was thrown overboard where a 'great fish' swallowed him.

In the same way that Jonah ran away from his fate, we evade the responsibilities suggested by nature or chance. And if we deliberately shy away from being less than what we are capable of being, by setting lower aspirations, we're resigning ourselves to stagnation.

As for Jonah, he did rise to his potential. After spending three days and nights in the belly of the great fish, praying for deliverance, Jonah was spat out onto dry land, where he committed himself to find a way to Nineveh.

For the rest of us who care to improve or innovate in the world, our destiny may be similar to Jonah's. It takes years of honest dialogue with ourselves until we identify a curiosity – artistic, intellectual, entrepreneurial, scientific, etc. – gain confidence to perform in the respective domain and commit to **unleash the maximum potential as a creator**.[22] It requires the willingness to work with ourselves and negotiate with the world. This is taking responsibility for the creator's call.

---

[21] www.britannica.com/topic/Book-of-Jonah

[22] Pretz, J.E., and Nelson, D., (2017), Chapter 9 – Creativity Is Influenced by Domain, Creative Self-Efficacy, Mindset, Self-Efficacy, and Self-Esteem, Editor(s): Maciej Karwowski, James C. Kaufman, In Explorations in Creativity Research, The Creative Self, Academic Press, pp. 155–170, https://doi.org/10.1016/B978-0-12-809790-8.00009-1.

Along the way, we'll learn **when to be humble and when to be stubborn** about the creative projects we choose to engage in. When to **actively engage in creation and when to be patient, preparing for the next moment to take action.**

For instance, my son put me through a humility test. One day when I was writing new paragraphs in this book, stomping sounds came from the next room. I went to see what was happening. He was jumping up and down on the sofa, doing indoor parkour. Against a background of my discontent with my writing, I admonished him with the authority of a parent who thinks themselves superior, *"Could you please be quiet? I'm trying to write a book here."*

He retorted, *"What happens if you don't write your book?"*

"Someone else will do it," I mumbled, taken aback by the question.

I returned to my writing room, thinking about why I went to such great lengths to focus on my writing. If someone else can do it, then shouldn't I step aside?

I imagine that this is **the experience of other creators** as well. We go through moments of humility which, for some of us, result in stubbornly choosing to create rather than engaging in different professional experiences, endlessly repeating what we have done in the past. As the choice to create is renewed, obstacles appear, big and small, internal and external barriers. Nevertheless, determination to keep creating is a virtue.

"L'homme n'est rien, l'œuvre tout," wrote novelist Gustave Flaubert in his correspondence with George Sand in December 1875.[23] *"The individual is nothing, the work of art is everything."* When a new product – a book, a song, an invention – is finished, it becomes available to the individuals interested in interacting with it. The act of creation ends and the creative engagement of those who consume the product begins.

---

[23] www.etudes-litteraires.com/flaubert-art.php

Let's take a book as an example. From a reader's perspective, it doesn't matter who writes a book that they enjoy and which opens them to new emotions and understandings. And yet, from the writer's perspective, writing is a process of self-transformation and intimacy with the ideas that result.

Irrespective of your aspiration to create, when there's an alignment between the creative personality and the work being performed, there is a process of self-discovery and growth toward the upper limits of personal skills and self-awareness.

Last, committing to becoming a creator is a character-building experience. Triumph and rejection are unavoidable yet valuable experiences. You may want to learn how to avoid becoming intoxicated by praise and, simultaneously, how to protect yourself from harsh criticism. You may never be able to master this skill of humility, but it's worth having it as an ideal for growth.

In one way, Jonah had a smoother experience accepting the mission bestowed upon him. He could hear God's voice, was aware of the role God chose for him to perform, and knew the group of people that he was supposed to serve. Jonah's challenge was to establish his trust in the mission.

We should understand God's message as a metaphor representing the moment the aspiring creator **understands** their **purpose is to create**. The time spent in the belly of the great fish is the process of negotiation and **acceptance**. And being spat out on dry land is the first sign of **trust in your mission**, in your ability to deal with the tasks as best you can.

In real life, establishing trust in your choice to become a creator is more painstaking. In the beginning, the challenge consists in you learning to trust your impulses and intuition even when you don't have objective proof that your act of creation is the wisest choice.

As you accumulate experiences, you train your nose to find the medium for your acts of creation and the people who will benefit. In Jonah's story, the destination is crucial, although it doesn't have a central place. Do you know where your Nineveh is?

Your Nineveh is the place where your creative interests meet the specific needs of a workplace or community. It is not a physical place but an emotional space where you **trust,** with every cell in your body, that your purpose is to bring novelty to an area of interest.

Establishing your space to experiment with what you might create is a creative process in itself, during which **the awakened creator transcends the current self to embrace the full potential of creativity**.

The world is blissfully populated with artists, activists, entrepreneurs, philosophers, scientists, and all sorts of niche experts to address the diverse needs of societal, economic, and cultural development. What if you could freely choose which of these creators you could be? Who would you rather be?

What if you were invited to talk on a TED stage about one aspect of reality where you'd like to bring improvement? What would be the topic you could talk about for 15 minutes without any preparation?

You have two options. To start fresh in a domain where you must acquire new skills and gain validation as a creative professional. Or, to form a creative initiative in a field where you already have a good level of competence and recognition in a particular role.

Three Underlying Assumptions for the Development of the Personal Creativity

The dialogue on creativity, which I initiated with my eldest son, revealed that a creative person is a genius for him. However, he did not acknowledge anyone else from his immediate environment as being creative, so I asked him, "What comes to mind when you think of your creativity?"

"Creativity is that I create my world in Geometry Dash[24] and I became good at it," he replied.

Then, I turned to my youngest son, a six-year-old at the time of the conversation, and asked the same question.

"My creativity is to paint, as I do in day-care," he said in the blink of an eye.

In these concise statements, we can already notice three important beliefs that determine the level of self-awareness of personal creativity. There is an activity, a feeling and a physical place that make us think of ourselves as creative:[25]

- There's an **activity** which makes the kids feel creative and in which they engage repeatedly – the activity of painting or playing a platform game.

- They **see themselves able to perform** the required tasks – my elder son thinks that he is good at combining the elements in Geometry Dash in his unique ways and reacting spontaneously to obstacles in this fast changing game.

- **Awareness of the environment** – the day-care or at home – where they feel safe to access the available resources and use their creativity.

---

[24] Geometry Dash is a fast paced video game in which the player steers an icon through a landscape replete with spikes and other obstacles that can destroy the icon upon impact. The game is created by the Swedish software developer Robert Topala. https://geometrydash.io/

[25] Glăveanu, V.P., (2010), Paradigms in the study of creativity: introducing the perspective of cultural psychology. New ideas in psychology, 28 (1). pp. 79–93. DOI: 10.1016/j.newideapsych.2009.07.007

If you're anything like my son, then you'll find enjoyment when you spend a significant part of your leisure time on a creative outlet, such as performing arts, handicraft, visual arts, creative cooking, literature, music, interior/garden design, and science/technology.[26] Consistent findings in the creativity literature show that people are interested in pursuing a particular creative activity for explicit personal reasons, such as to have a good time, to cheer up, to acquire a sense of competence or to feel recognized.

Moreover, to develop your creative potential in a professional role means to deliberately choose to practice a particular creative activity in a job context. In this case, your motivation can be curtailed by the implicit assumption that there's no creative activity where you'd be able to excel at a pro level or that you see no milieu that would support you – emotionally, financially, or resource-wise – to create. So what could help you recognize the motivational basis for engaging in creative projects at work?

The Structure of the Book

In this book, we'll look into the psychological development of a creator. To this view, we'll shed light on what habits might be helpful to steer your focus to new personal initiatives. This book continues with the following four topics:

1. The fit between your creativity and your activities.

2. Learn to live like a creator.

3. Prime your mind for creative insight.

4. Develop a creative communication style.

---

[26] Benedeck, M., Bruckdorfer, R., and Jauk, E., (2019), Motives for Creativity: Exploring the What and Why of Everyday Creativity, The Journal of Creative Behaviour, Vol. 54, Issue 3, pp. 610-625.

A healthy individual is a right creator, on the right path of creative self-exploration. The journey described in the book is illustrated in Figure 1.

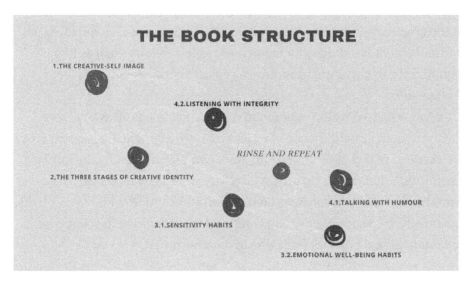

THE BOOK STRUCTURE

1.THE CREATIVE-SELF IMAGE

4.2.LISTENING WITH INTEGRITY

RINSE AND REPEAT

2.THE THREE STAGES OF CREATIVE IDENTITY

4.1.TALKING WITH HUMOUR

3.1.SENSITIVITY HABITS

3.2.EMOTIONAL WELL-BEING HABITS

Figure 1. *Book Structure*

The most common definition of creativity is the ability to make unusual connections, resulting in novel, surprising, and valuable products. In this book, creativity is defined as the flexibility to explore interests in an area of knowledge or experience that awakens your sense of meaning and the resilience to stay involved and produce new artifacts into existence.

In the first part, we'll look into why it matters what you think of your own creativity.[27] The way you understand your creativity defines the kind of life you live.

---

[27] Batey, M., (2012), The measurement of creativity: from definitional consensus to the introduction of a new heuristic framework. *Creativity Research Journal*, 24, pp. 55–65.

When creativity is understood as a way of behaving, it may help to look into what you take for granted about your curiosity, risk-taking, and environments that bring out the best of your creativity.

What if you showed more imagination and curiosity in your current role? What would that look like?

We'll discuss how new beliefs about appropriate work behaviors can inspire new actions, redeeming your creativity, energy, and enthusiasm.

In the book's second part, we'll map out the three psychological milestones in the developmental journey as a professional creator.

There seems to be a consensus among creativity researchers that any significant creative work in scientific and artistic fields requires ten years of developing mastery in a particular domain of knowledge.[28]

The most celebrated creative acts happen in the third stage of development of the creative self, the **being established phase**. Before this, the evolving creative self goes through learning, collecting impressions, and leveraging out-of-the-box thinking. Two moments of a trial are worthy of being mentioned.

First is the moment of encountering the idea or object that arouses your curiosity, *"Oh, this is a fascinating topic! I want to know more about it."*

And second is the moment when the crippling self-doubt gets loud, *"Why do I want to create?"*

To make it to the third developmental stage, connecting with the psychological needs that ground you in acts of creation is essential.

Another way to think of creativity is the ability to see and the desire to do something about what you see. The third part of the book is about

---

[28] Simonton, D. K., (2004), Creativity in Science, Cambridge University Press. Carson, S., (2010), Your Creative Brain, Harvard Health Publications. Csíkszentmihályi, M., (2013), Creativity, the Psychology of Discovery and Invention, Harperperennial.

looking differently at the environment. It's about forming new thinking habits around your creative sensitivities, which will steer your attention toward opportunities to create.

At the same time, emotional well-being is a critical facilitator in the ability to see things which you haven't seen before. Hence, we'll discuss how we can manage the vulnerability of opening up to a new creative process.

Becoming a creator is a matter of social interactions with suitable people as much as it is a matter of personal disruption. Compellingly describing your original ideas is a test of your budding creative identity. The fourth part of the book is about allowing your creative personality to shine in the way you communicate your ideas.

Direct communication is composed of listening and speaking. We'll discuss a specific type of listening, listening for inspiration and imagination. In addition, we'll elaborate on what kind of humor can increase other people's motivation to offer good views on your work-in-progress.

This book is an opportunity for inner reflection on what kind of creator you are, where you are in the creator's journey and what you can start doing differently to evolve.

Let's start with three warming-up questions about the developmental journey of your creative potential:

1. Out of all the professionals you've recently interacted with, who are the individuals you admire most?

2. What was it about them that left a mark on you?

3. What, if any, are the career shifts you lived through?

PART I

The Fit Between Your Creativity and Your Activities

CHAPTER 1

Four Types of Creators

Our beliefs guide our desires and shape our actions.

—Charles Sanders Peirce, Polymath

Who is a creator? The United Nations Educational, Scientific, and Cultural Organization (UNESCO) defines a creator as

> *...any person who creates, or gives creative expression to, or re-creates works of art;* ***who considers his/her artistic creations to be an essential part of his/her life; who contributes to the development of art culture;*** *and who* ***asks to be recognised*** *as an artist, whether he/she is bound by any relations of employment or association.*

This definition emphasizes the engagement in artistic activities as the central aspect of being a creator.

The Merriam-Webster dictionary is more inclusive. A creator is *"one that creates usually by bringing something new or original into being."* Author, establisher, initiator, founder, and generator are synonyms. What does new and original mean? In a nutshell, bringing something new

© Oana Velcu-Laitinen 2022
O. Velcu-Laitinen, *How to Develop Your Creative Identity at Work*,
https://doi.org/10.1007/978-1-4842-8680-7_1

refers to coming up with a solution that didn't exist before or identifying a problem that nobody else noticed before. Bringing something original refers to a surprising solution compared to existing solutions to a problem.

Yes, artists are the most memorable and recognized creators. Besides, there are other types too. A creator is someone who brings into being a product which adds incremental value for the people who buy it. A creator is someone who writes a book on a popular topic but where they add original stories and perspectives. A creator can be someone who starts a change initiative in an organization, drawing on the inspiration from another organization that experienced the change. Finally, a creator is an individual involved in a conversation where they help others have "aha" moments.

To this view, in this book, we broaden the definition of **a creator as an individual who engages in a domain of knowledge or expertise within or outside the industries traditionally acknowledged as creative**. What is essential is that the creator accepts their personal creativity and feels authentic engagement with the domain where they pitch in their fresh perspectives. Equally important, what all these types of creators have in common is their ability to find audiences who approve of the elements of novelty and originality.

For example, **a creator can be a scientist** whose academic career depends on writing research papers that advance the understanding in their area of knowledge. In this book, we'll get a peek into how two university professors view their relationship with their creativity at a point in their careers when they both made it to full professorship.

A creator can be an entrepreneur, whose financial success rests upon their ability to create value for their clients. I interviewed seasoned entrepreneurs, who will share how their understanding of their creativity led to their choice of entrepreneurship as a career.

Last but not least, **a creator can be an individual in an expert role**, such as sales engineer Oscar Santollala, who is committed to standing out in his field as a speaker and author on how to present product demos which wow an audience.

Artists, scientists, entrepreneurs, and technical experts are four breeds of creators who have three common aspects emphasized in the enlarged definition of who is a creator.

(1) **The way you relate with your work**. In UNESCO's definition, the creator sees their artistic creation at the core of his/her life. In this book, a creator can also be an individual who sees **the realization of a mission** – be it scientific, social, entrepreneurial, spiritual – as an inherent part of who they are.[1] Artistic or not, you **love your mission** and the work required to carry it through.

(2) You understand the **central role of your personal creativity** in the way you engage with your work to bring surprising ideas.

You see the importance of creativity in your professional role. For instance, some people in entrepreneurial roles know that their strength is the ability to develop an abundance of ideas to craft new products, marketing messages, and sales strategies.

Being an idea generator thus helps with business development. You may think, "Well, other qualities are essential for the success of a business." And that's true. As an entrepreneur, it's essential to be savvy in networking, persuasion, and the core competencies that help you land a deal and deliver a quality product.

However, in the same way vitamin C strengthens the immune system, your creative thinking boosts the activities essential for thriving in your business. Hence, the more you acknowledge that creativity is a required personal strength and make space for it in your work, the more likely you are to get recognized by clients, bosses, peers, etc.

---

[1] Lebuda, I. and Csikszentmihalyi, M., (2017), Me, Myself, I and Creativity: Self-Concepts of Eminent Creators, *The Creative Self, Effect of Beliefs, Self-Efficacy, Mindset, and Identity*, pp. 138–148.

(3) **Being willing to take the initiative for personal growth and cross-disciplinary learning.**

"In the past I had boyfriends who used to say to me, 'Why do you do all these things, why do you go to all these courses that have nothing to do with what you do?'" says Communication Architect Tulia Lopes. "And I say, 'Well, I don't know, I'm curious.' But life has proven to me that one way or another, in the future, whatever you learn, you'll use it. So, it's never wasted time."

Like Tulia, creators are individuals who take responsibility for engaging with new learning without waiting for external approval. As a creator, you take responsibility for doing more than copying what others have done. As a result, you develop the courage to undertake a new project that no one in your close network may have done.

This book features the Finnish composer Mattias Kupiainen who describes the development of his artistic creativity. More than ten years ago, when he joined the power metal band Stratovarius as a guitar player, Mattias had the option to learn a new skill, composing music. To date, Mattias has over 32 million streams of songs.

Dasha Pears is a photographer who experienced a long journey of inner conflict before embracing her call to become a surreal fine art photographer. Throughout the book, you'll hear her most tender memories and reflections of that time.

So, **creators are pioneers of human experience and knowledge**. They chart territories unknown to themselves, intrigued by how much there is yet to know. They are sincerely curious about learning new skills and rehashing their knowledge in projects that bring something new and meaningful to their environments.

What are you interested in creating today? What will you be interested in creating tomorrow?

When There's Hope, There Are Opportunities to Craft Your Role As a Creator

I never think that I cannot do it. I only think, how can I do it?

—Tulia Lopes, Founder of Speak Up and Lead Academy

Opportunities for creative self-disruption start with initial observation, followed by hope for making change happen.

What are the qualities that you like most about yourself? Is being hopeful one of them?

When you hope to bring something new and meaningful to the world, you **get the inner drive to find solutions to how you can get *"there"* from "here."**[2] *Here* is the present where you feel that something is missing in your work life. *There* can be the next hour when you allow yourself to do something you haven't done before, slowly discovering the ideas that make you a creator.

What does hope mean to you?

The path of self-discovery toward a customized role as a creative expert can take a few years of trial and error. However, being hopeful is not about naively waiting for someone to engage you in a project while you're binge-watching seasons of your favorite series.

Being hopeful is about seeing yourself as the lead actor in your life. It is about seeing yourself as the primary contributor to good events that happen to you in the future. A hopeful person makes plans and is willing to work hard to achieve a better future.

---

[2] Charles Rick Snyder, (1994), *The Psychology of Hope: You Can Get There from Here*, Simon and Schuster.

Tulia Lopes is one of the ten creative experts featured in this book as a professional who has changed from one role as a creator to another. The way from *here* to *there* is certainly not straightforward nor predictable, as we can see from her career journey, which led to her current status as a Confident Communication Architect.

"I always put myself forward to do things. Never thought that I cannot do something. And this is a very good skill to have. You don't doubt yourself. But you burn your hands sometimes because of that. And that's OK. Because also, my training in architecture reinforced that. To be an architect, you have to believe, you have to be convinced that what you have in your mind can become reality."

After graduating from Architecture and Urbanism at Universidade Católica de Goiás in Brazil, Tulia got a postgraduate grant to work in Spain. A few years later, she was involved in IT project management in Ireland. Yet, she felt that she needed to do something creative.

She quit her job to research the jewelry market in Brazil and Spain. In 2005, she opened her jewelry shop in Barcelona. However, when the global economic crisis hit in 2008, Tulia had to close her business and reinvent herself again.

She's learned not to get attached to things, *"Well, that's not what I expected," she said.* So she took courses and learned new skills while wondering, *"What is my calling?"*

There are many possible paths to getting *there, the calling as a creator.* Hope gives the emotional energy and responsibility to put in cognitive effort to figure out the next move daily.

You may behave creatively in relationships with close ones. Your creativity may be essential as a creative outlet. But to become a creator, you need the desire to bring your new or original contributions to the professional sphere and be recognized for that. How do you relate to your present work with the corresponding status and tasks? Each of the following sentences describes possible work orientations that people can have. What is the sentence that most resonates for you?

- For me, work is a 9:00 am to 5:00 pm job. I do the minimum of what's required. I start living after 5 pm.

- For me, work is a career. I do more than what's expected of me. For instance, leadership would fit me well.

- My work has meaning. I can often see the impact of my efforts.

- For me, work is a calling. The skills I exercise in my role are my lifeblood.

How would you like to relate to your work?

When work is seen as a career, a source of meaning, or a vocation, there can be four types of insights that trigger your future as a creator (see Figure 1-1).

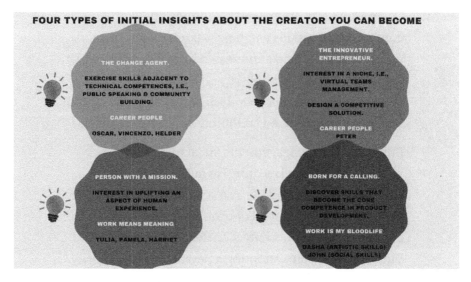

Figure 1-1. *Four Types of Creators*

- Some people who see their work as a career may take the initiative to improve some aspects of the work culture or processes in the organization where they currently work or in other professional communities. As a result, in addition to the technical skills, they develop secondary skills, which propel them to the role of a change agent.

Three of the creative experts featured in this book are individuals on a career path that develops their creative personalities as change agents. Oscar Santolalla is a Sales Engineer at a company specializing in digital identity management software. Vincenzo Cerullo is the head of the Drug Research Program at Helsinki University. Helder Santos is a professor in Biomedical Engineering at the University of Groningen.

Oscar Santollala discovered his interest in communication skills when he was a lecturer. From public speaking, he got interested in writing skills, which led to two published books, *Create and Deliver a Killer Product Demo* and *Rock the Tech Stage*. As a book author, Oscar enjoys enhanced credibility as a sales engineer.

Public speaking engagements are activities for which Vincenzo makes time. He talks about scientific research and life as a scientist to students or his academic fellows. For example, in his talk at TEDxHelsinkiUniversity, *Creativity goes viral!* Vincenzo advocates adopting a perspective of curiosity, openness, and being *"unfocused in a focused way"* on scientific problems.[3]

---

[3] www.youtube.com/watch?v=1btbElPnREI

Helder Santos is one of a kind among his peers. His community-building skills are visible in his Linkedin messages, when he shares his research team's leisure moments or when he's profiling the newcomers. In addition, Helder is a generous leader who encourages his people to work in teams and shows appreciation to individual members.

- Do you have a *new tested solution* that might help more than one organization improve its processes and practices? You could then embrace the entrepreneurial path as an independent innovator like Peter Ivanov, who specializes in delivering management training for international virtual teams. Over the years, Peter has developed an effective method known as – *The 10 Big Rocks* for leading remote, hybrid, or virtual teams. The technique promises to deliver projects faster, reduce costs, and prepare organizations for the future. In 2012, it received the "Global IT Connect Award."

- You may be the *mission kind of person.* In this case, your energy goes to exploring entrepreneurial pursuits with a promise to uplift some aspects of human existence. For instance, Tulia Lopes has found her calling in supporting female leaders to speak up. Pamela Thompson supports heart-centered leaders to embrace change for positive impact. Harriet Fagerholm explores co-creation, guiding people in releasing their creative impulses and conscious evolution.

- The fourth type of insight that drives you to customize your role as a creative expert is the intuition that you were born for *a calling*. When you identify an attraction toward *a set of skills*, you gain the evidence that confirms your intuition. There can be that you realize you want to get involved with developing artistic skills like Dasha Pears, who is committed to surreal fine art photography. On the other hand, you may realize you excel at soft skills, like John Bates' listening ability, which enables him to support top leaders at large corporations and make their speeches "TED-talk"-worthy.

Which of the four ways of exploring your innate creativity are you most hopeful about? To allow more creative thinking in the current role and advance your career? To explore your potential as an innovative or social entrepreneur? Or to focus on specific skills that make you a niche expert?

Could there be a fifth way – your way? What might be the trigger that motivates you to reinvent your role as a creative expert?

Let's look at what creativity means for creativity researchers and the creators featured in the book. Along the way, you'll also clarify why creativity is a multifaceted human ability.

CHAPTER 2

Definitions of Personal Creativity

The Outside-In View: How Researchers Study Creativity

Among creativity researchers, one standard definition is that it is the **ability to make unusual connections** and engage in **specific habits** that lead to **novel, useful**, and **surprising outcomes** (e.g., ideas, projects, initiatives, products).[1] Hence, creativity can refer to a type of thinking, a process, and an outcome. Let's take a detailed look at each of these.

---

[1] Runco M.A. and Jaeger, G.J., (2012), The Standard Definition of Creativity, Creativity Research Journal, Vol. 24, Issue 1, pp. 92–96, www.tandfonline.com/doi/full/10.1080/10400419.2012.650092?src=recsys; Kaufman and Gregoire, 2016, Wired to Create;
Dean Keith Simonton, 2018, Creative Ideas and the Creative Process: Good News and Bad News for the Neuroscience of Creativity, The Cambridge Handbook of the Neuroscience of Creativity, pp. 9–18.

© Oana Velcu-Laitinen 2022
O. Velcu-Laitinen, *How to Develop Your Creative Identity at Work*,
https://doi.org/10.1007/978-1-4842-8680-7_2

Creativity As a Type of Thinking

Creativity is a **type of thinking** which is triggered when faced with an unexpected or new situation. It boils down to making unusual associations of ideas to solve the new problem, generate stories, use analogies, improvise, etc.

Thanks to the emergence of magnetic resonance imaging (MRI) and electroencephalogram (EEG) technologies, we learn that creative thinking does not involve only the right side of the brain, which is creative, passionate, vivid, and poetic.[2] Creative thinking needs the left side of the brain as well, which is analytical, practical, and organized. For example, in a study that used EEG to record the brain waves of 32 jazz musicians during live guitar improvisation, the higher quality performances appeared to be associated with left hemisphere regions.[3]

According to a more accurate description of reality in the brain, creative thinking involves three brain regions, spanning the left and right hemispheres of the brain, and it necessitates the combined activation of cognitive systems (conscious and unconscious) and emotions to work on non-routine and creative tasks. It consists of two modes of information processing: 1) opening up to alternative meanings and interpretations of what is happening and 2) selecting one idea of what might work to fit the context.

The first mode is thus an engagement in an open, divergent, or generative mode of thinking associated with the **default mode network** of the brain, also known as the imagination network.[4] The second mode

---

[2] Kaufman, S.B., (2013), The Real Neuroscience of Creativity, `https://blogs.scientificamerican.com/beautiful-minds/the-real-neuroscience-of-creativity/`

[3] Rosen, D.S., Oh, Y., Erickson, B., Zhang, F., Kim, Y.E., Kounis, J., (2020), Dual-process contributions to creativity in jazz improvisations: An SPM-EEG stidy, Neuroimage, Vol. 213, 116632.

[4] Anna Abraham, (2018), The Forest versus the Trees: Creativity, Cognition and Imagination, pp. 195–210.

of creative thought consists of a closed, convergent, or evaluative thinking mode that activates the **executive network** of the brain. In a study of 25 young adults whose brains were monitored in a functional magnetic resonance imaging (fMRI), it is shown a functional connectivity between these two networks and a third network.[5]

When presented with an everyday object (e.g., brick, umbrella) and asked to come up with unusual and creative uses for it, researchers noticed increased activation of **the salience network,** the third brain network coupled with the default mode network, in the beginning of the task.

The salience network is like a bridge between the imagination and executive networks and it is responsible for the level of motivation to keep searching for original ideas for a creative task. When this brain system detects promising ideas generated by the default brain network, it pushes them forward to the executive network for advanced processing.[6]

In brief, creative thinking means flexibly switching the attention to our inner experience and then outwardly to keep track of relevant external information in order to make progress and to come up with useful and original resolutions to a task. All this is happening preconsciously until the moment when we do arrive at a satisfying idea.

How might your creative thinking express itself in ordinary moments of life? In the summer of 2019, I was walking with my family in a Rhododendron park and stopped to take a close-up photo of an alpine rose.

"Mom, flowers are your best friends," my son said.

I do love flowers and taking photos of them. I hadn't thought of them as my friends, though.

---

[5] Beaty RE, Benedek M, Kaufman SB, Silvia PJ (2015) Default and executive network coupling supports creative idea production, Scientific Reports, 5, Article number: 10964. www.nature.com/articles/srep10964

[6] Jung RE, Mead BS, Carrasco J, Flores RA (2013) The structure of creative cognition in the human brain. Front Hum Neurosci 7:330. www.frontiersin.org/articles/10.3389/fnhum.2013.00330/full

I replied, "Indeed, flowers do make me feel good."

"But how can it be that they make you feel good?" my son asked with the curiosity of an eight-year-old. "They don't have a voice. They cannot talk to you."

The dialogue continued along with the idea of how you know if someone is your friend. Thanks to my son, I am now aware that through their silence, flowers are a source of resilience, gratitude, and beauty. In a relaxed or sad mood, flowers trigger my creative thinking. The tango between the default brain network and the cognitive control network interprets the physical features of flowers. And the outcome is a transient feel-good experience, captured in a little poem, kept for me.

There are real-life situations when engaging in a creative task requires more effort and involvement, like watching your kids fighting or preparing a new presentation at work.

Let's take the first hypothetical scenario. Your kids start a fight. You watch the conflict escalating and decide to put an end to it. Then, suddenly, you have a stroke of insight. *"You know what?! Today, I saw a guy walking in the street when his pants fell,"* you say.

Imagine the other scenario when you have to prepare a new presentation at work. It's the first time you talk about a new topic. It's a topic that excites and scares you simultaneously. How could you create the content so your colleagues can relate to the subject and engage?

In both situations, **your creative thinking will spontaneously recognize the opportunities** when you think of inventive turns of phrase in conversation or surprising twists in creating content. It's your creative thinking that invents humorous remarks and decides the appropriate time to deliver them to distract your kids from fighting. It's the creative thinking that brings up analogies about the concepts and the storyline in your presentation.

As we could see from the neural description of creative thinking, creativity involves connectivity between the imagination network, the executive network, and the salience network of the brain. The higher the strength in the functional connectivity between the three networks, the higher the creative thinking directed at solving a creative task.[7]

Daily, we have the chance to use our creative thinking for positive action. What might be other creative ways of breaking a fight between your children? Shouting does not count.

Next time your boss asks you to make a presentation on a new topic, say yes even if you may have no idea how you'll do it. **Creative thinking starts with being open to a new challenge for which you lack ready-made solutions.** Then, you'll warm up to the challenge by thinking of creative ways to define your core concepts.

Creativity As a Process

Creativity can also mean the **creative process** that leads to an original idea or product. In the two hypothetical scenarios mentioned above – a rising conflict between kids and a new presentation to make – an orchestra of neural processes plays in your brain. If you could turn into a 0.01 mm nanobot and travel inside your head, you would witness the orchestra playing, and you would be able to hear the music of your creative process.

There'd be the inner dialogue between the orchestra members of the three creative brain sets – the default brain network, the cognitive control network, and the salience network. Here's an overly simplified interpretation of the neural processes that the nanobot would hear when you're watching your kids fight:

The "evaluate" member: "What's the problem we're working on? *'These kids can injure each other badly.'*"

---

[7] Beaty et al., (2018), Robust prediction of individual creative ability from brain functional connectivity, www.pnas.org/content/pnas/115/5/1087.full.pdf

The "openness to new information" member: "What solutions do we have?"

The "divergent thinking" member: "Raise your voice."

The "evaluate" brain set: "Is this all you can come up with?"

The "divergent thinking" member: "Go and stand between them."

The "evaluate" member: "You might get a knee in your face. Other ideas?"

The "divergent thinking" member: "Hah! Tell them, 'Today, I saw a guy walking in the street when his pants fell.'"

The "evaluate" brain set: "How do we know this idea is better?"

The "openness to new information" member: "Kids are fascinated by butts."

The "evaluate" member: "Fine, we'll take the risk and deliver this one. *'The guy's underwear had a Darth Vader print.'*"

You deliver your creative response, hoping it will dissipate your kids' fighting mood. The stream of creative thoughts leading to the final response happens within seconds (remains unconscious).

As for the second scenario, working on the content for the new presentation requires a longer creative process. In reality, this is a messy process, but based on a structured description, it develops in six steps, as shown in Figure 2-1.[8]

---

[8] Lubart, T.I., (2010), Models of the Creative Process: Past, Present and Future, *Creativity Research Journal*, Vol. 13, Issue 3-4, pp. 295–308. https://doi.org/10.1207/S15326934CRJ1334_07

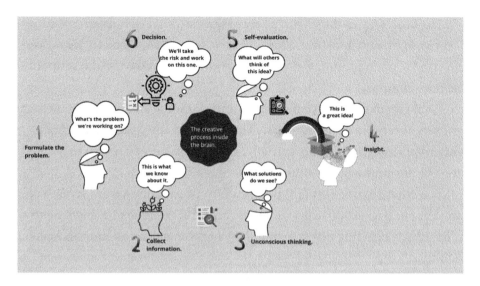

Figure 2-1. *The six stages of the creative process*

The first two steps are the **problem formulation and information collection phases**. You first identify and define the problem that will be addressed. You then acquire information and knowledge about what others have done about the respective topic.

A period of **incubation** follows. At this third step, you are not directly working on the presentation. Other activities may keep your hands and feet busy, but the brain is looking for satisfying solutions. Especially when you do something less demanding, like cleaning your floors at home, the brain processes the relevant conscious and unconscious information.

Incubation is followed by **insight** – the "Eureka" moment when the unconscious connections pierce through the surface of awareness without any voluntary effort. It's when you get an idea about the general structure of the presentation.

In the fifth step, your brain **evaluates** whether the insight is worth pursuing. It is the soul-searching part of the process when you ask yourself, "What will my colleagues think of my presentation?"

The sixth step of the creative process consists of the **implementation** of the insight, and it takes the most time. It's when you need to decide on the visuals and wording to introduce the concepts and write the script of the presentation.

Each creative process can have many iterations, and there can be many loops between the different steps. Depending on the situation we deal with, many insights may be needed, and we may have to return to the first step of information acquisition.

The creative process of preparing a new presentation from scratch can last up to one week, on average. However, other creative processes, such as creating a one-line poem inspired by a flower, can be as short as a few seconds.

When we get an intuition that we have the potential to create, self-discovery takes many years. The immediate milieu, with its people and available resources, can foster or inhibit the creator's mental and personal factors involved in creative self-discovery.

Active engagement and experimentation are the pillars of the creative process of becoming a creator. Yet, now and then, we find ourselves back at the preparation phase. **What might be the next project where I can test my creative potential?**

Creativity As an Outcome

Creativity can be a word we use to refer to what results from coming up with a new idea and implementing it. In this case, creativity becomes liable to judgment. Why would a particular community benefit from new ideas?

When a teacher introduces a new teaching method, does the students' learning experience improve?

When an innovative team designs a smartwatch, who are the people who are willing to pay for it?

When you wrote a humorous message on a birthday card, did it amuse the receiver?

Others in the external environment give feedback on how original, insightful, and valuable your creations are. Significant acts of creation, like an innovative educational method or a smartwatch, or small acts of creation, like writing a fun birthday card to someone you care about, need to pass the test of appropriateness and novelty in the eyes of those for whom they are intended.

From the point of view of the creative person, the usefulness of creative behaviors and products partly consists of seeing the positive impact on the intended audience. For instance, you can quietly celebrate to the extent that your kids get distracted by the Darth Vader print underwear. Your creative intervention paid off. You helped your kids from injuring one another. Moreover, an enhanced sense of competence is another valuable outcome of the creative process for the creator.

Therefore, before expecting your audience's approval, you need your **self-approval to engage in experimental creation**. This is the perspective we take in the book: self-validation gets priority over external validation. However, irrespective of the experimental creation you choose to focus on, it might be good to **be wary of the difference between the usefulness for others and the usefulness for yourself**.

Let's consider the following scenario. You write a poem, and it's a soothing experience for you. Do other people relate to your poetry?

You are joining a virtual reality initiative to treat trauma.[9] People will benefit from the end product. But does your contribution to the project satisfy your need to create?

The experimental creations you engage in necessitate a careful balance between the expected usefulness for others and yourself. A careful balance between generosity toward others and acceptance of the kind of creative person that you are.

---

[9]https://blogs.scientificamerican.com/observations/
virtual-reality-might-be-the-next-big-thing-for-mental-health/

To summarize, creativity researchers define creativity as a type of thinking involving three brain networks connecting the brain's left and right hemispheres. Second, creativity can be viewed as a process comprising six stages, starting with acquiring information about a problem of interest and ending with implementing a novel idea. Third and last, creativity is an outcome that changes your everyday life and brings a change in others' lives.

Let's continue with an inside-out view, through the eyes of professionals who work in fields where they make a living out of coming up with new ideas. How do scientists, entrepreneurs, artists, and engineers understand their creativity?

The Inside-Out View: How Recognized Creators Talk About Their Creativity

In everyday life, most people don't consciously think about when and how their creativity manifests itself. In the best situations, maybe someone else remarks, "Wow! That was creative, the way you managed the conflict between your kids." Or "Congrats! You crafted your presentation in such a creative way." Thanks to others' input, we can gain higher self-awareness about our creative personality and potential. When external feedback is missing, putting into words what creativity means to you is an excellent alternative to discovering your implicit system of beliefs about your creativity.

Let's hear how the professionals featured in this book define their creativity.

> ➤ **As the ability to hear music or write a poem:**

"I hear one thing in my head, I write it down," says Finnish composer **Matias Kupiainen**. *"Then what I'm doing, how I am constructing the whole song together, it's a more technical approach. It has nothing to do with being creative.* **The only thing is the simple melody in my head and that's my creativity."**

"Creativity! There are lots of things that come to my mind," says Leadership Communications Expert **John Bates**. *"The very first thing is that I remember when I was singing in the band and I would consider myself a poet, I would carry around a pencil and a little notebook everywhere with me. Whenever a phrase hit me or I saw or heard something interesting or beautiful, I would stop and I would write it down in the notebook. A lot of that became the songs that I was writing."*

➢   As an ability to change perspective on obstacles:

*"****What creativity means, and helped me, is a way to see,****"* says Communication Architect Trainer **Tulia Lopes**. *"Creativity allows you to see obstacles not as obstacles, something that blocks you to move forward, but you see them as challenges that will require you to have better and more creative solutions. So that's the way I see creativity, it's when you allow yourself to bring different perspectives and different answers for a specific question."*

➢   **As the ability to conceive many new ideas and concepts:**

Let's turn to solopreneur **Peter Ivanov,** who trains virtually remote teams. For Peter, creativity is about *" … **Combining in a new way**, coming up with a new concept. And this is a fascinating process and this is probably what distinguishes us human beings from even smarter learning machines. Apparently we have the capability of imagining something completely new and it becomes something tangible that inspires other people."*

"This is a long time ago, before meeting you, when I started to think that probably, probably I am creative," says **Vincenzo Cerullo**, professor at University of Helsinki and Head of the Drug Research Program. *"I felt like there is one thing that nobody can ever steal, is the amount of ideas that come out anyway, that I cannot stop. It's like sweating when you don't want to sweat. You'll sweat anyway, and the more you think about it, the more you sweat.*

*Another example is the words of my ex American boss who is a great scientist and works with super good scientists. I don't think of myself as a great scientist. I just think that I am somebody that is very curious and wants to learn. But I remember that once he told me: 'Ah, you have been one of the most productive scientists I've worked with!' But he didn't mean in terms of publications, but rather **in terms of idea generating**."*

> ➤ **As the ability to diverge from the habitual ways of doing things and experiment:**

"Yes... Um... I think, to me, what creativity means," says **Helder Santos**, professor in Pharmaceutical Nanotechnology, *"also from the research that we do, means trying to think of a new way to solve a problem. For example, we know that there is a disease. Let's talk about cancer, because it is more familiar to everyone. So we try to look into the problem. What if we use certain kinds of methods? What if we apply our knowledge in a different way that has not been tried, for example, and try to solve this problem? So in a way it is creating a new approach, new ways, to solve in our case a health problem."*

"It's not seeing the boundaries, probably," says surreal fine art photographer **Dasha Pears**, *"And always experimenting and trying new ways, and whatever your field is, whatever you do, if you're a scientist or even if you sew clothes, that's creativity."*

> ➤ **As an ability to express yourself in meaningful ways for yourself and others:**

Pamela Thompson, radio show host "Feminine Leaders Catalyzing Change," describes creativity as *"the ability to tap into my right creative brain and express it through myself, whatever that looks like."*

"I see creativity as a skill." says sales engineer **Oscar Santolalla**, *"I guess everybody has it but some people have developed this skill. You can be a child and you can be already creative and depending on how much you develop, you can be extremely good at that or maybe you forgot and you just don't develop that. Or when you are an adult, you start developing that. So, I see it as a skill.*

I think it's a very important skill. For instance, some people today talk about stories and they say that we people are hungry for stories. You've probably heard that. But the stories that people remember and are passed from generation to generation are stories that are shaped with some creativity. Because something can happen to you in life and if you don't tell it or write it in a way that gets engaging, it just gets forgotten. So, it matters how you craft it, how you write it. So, most stories don't survive for instance because of that."

"It's a very very complex topic. For me, it's the creative impulse of life," says solopreneur **Harriet Fagerholm**, supporting people in releasing their creative sensuous knowledge. *"I have come to learn from myself and through my clients that you need to activate the creative impulse. For example, depression can be the result of that creative impulse so suppressed that you don't understand that that's the source of your life energy. And it's a source of the spirit. The human spirit is creative. We are creative by definition. We are designed to be creative."*

As we can see from the above definitions, the interviewees' creativity is influenced by their work experiences. When you have had experiences in an artistic domain, creativity is understood as artistic creativity. Creativity is perceived as the ability to generate original and practical ideas when you have worked in environments that frequently require solving problems. Creativity is a way of living when you are the kind of person who interacts with the environment through emotional perception and expression.

Self-perceptions are significant at the individual level, because they predict both the creative achievement and the motivation to make an effort to develop a particular creative potential.[10] We thus embrace the following definition of creativity as **self-perceived creativity** :

*"**Personal assessments** concerning the extent to which an **individual** identifies themselves to possess **the traits and processes** required to produce **products** they consider to be creative **as well as perceptions regarding the environments where they feel induce creativity.**"*[11]

Differently stated, self-perceived creativity is the extent to which you see yourself as a creative individual with specific qualities and competencies and the drive to act upon them to improve an aspect of reality. Self-perceptions are shaped by direct experiences. When the direct experiences have not been favorable, you may be confused about your creative potential. Your creative identity develops when you increase the alignment between what creativity means to you, what skills you feel confident in performing, and the places where you contribute (see Figure 2-2).

---

[10] Hughes, D.J. et al. (2013), The structure and personality predictors of self-rated creativity, Thinking Skills and Creativity, 9, pp. 76–84.

[11] Batey, M., and Hughes, D.J., (2017) Individual Difference Correlates of Self-Perceptions of Creativity, in Explorations in Creativity Research, The Creative Self, Effect of Beliefs, Self-Efficacy, Mindset, and Identity, Edited by Karwowski, M., and Kaufman, J.C., pp. 186.

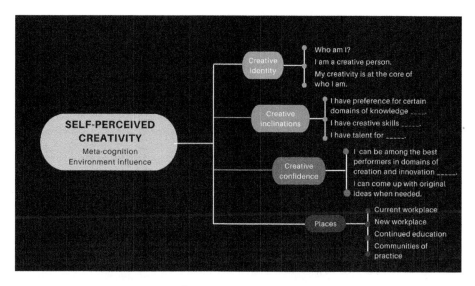

Figure 2-2. *Creativity Defined as Self-perceived Creativity*

In the next chapter, we discuss how social stereotypes might influence the present understanding of your creativity and what kind of habits can open you up to new aspects of your dormant creativity.

CHAPTER 3

For an Updated View on Your Creativity, Make the Implicit Biases Explicit

Two Ways to Relate to Your Creativity

A higher level of awareness of what aspects of creativity matter to you can have enormous implications for the kind of work you engage in and the impact you can make.[1] Communication Architect Tulia Lopes discovered a special interest in drawing as a child. Upon getting into university, she found it easier to apply for studies aligned with her sketching abilities.

---

[1] Barrick, M.R. et al., (2003), Meta-analysis of the relationships between the five-factor model of personality and Holland's occupational types. Personnel psychology, 56(1), pp. 45–74.
Wille, B., and DeFruyt, F., (2014), Vocations as a source of identity: Reciprocal relations between Big Five personality traits and RIASEC characteristics over 15 years, Journal of Applied Psychology, 99(2), pp. 262–281.

© Oana Velcu-Laitinen 2022
O. Velcu-Laitinen, *How to Develop Your Creative Identity at Work*,
https://doi.org/10.1007/978-1-4842-8680-7_3

"I never had this confusion, when you finish high school, to decide, what I'm going to do now with my future," says Tulia. *"I knew I was going to be an architect."*

People like Tulia, who have been practicing their creative skills in industries generally acknowledged to be creative – architecture, design, film, music, video games, visual arts, etc. – are likely to **perceive their creativity to be at the core of who they are.**

"My relationship with creativity is very very close because my background is architecture so you cannot be an architect if you're not creative. And for me creativity was always part of me, is part of me," confesses Tulia.

Later in life, a new stage of creative self-development started when she recognized preferences for new skills.

"I moved from Spain to Ireland to learn English, and with the plan to go back to Spain or go back to Brazil, and I ended up staying in Ireland for 13 years. I got into the IT world because it was the moment there, in 1994 when Ireland was becoming the software hub in Europe. So this was a big opportunity to learn about IT, computers, and things like that. I never went to the very technical area but I was technical enough to understand how certain things work and I started translating software programs for the Brazilian market.

*I got into that as a matter of curiosity and also I saw the opportunity of learning something different, and the money was very good. So, I stayed there for more than 10 years and there I also **discovered a different skill that I had, which was the ability to work with people and lead people.** But that would have come as a necessity but **I felt I had the thing to work with people.***

So I was given more and more responsibilities in my roles, and then I started as a team leader, then project coordinator, then project manager then it was going up and up."

The learning cycle brought Tulia to another professional crossroads when she longed to do something more creative at work. She then took the entrepreneurial path, opening a jewelry store in Barcelona.

When a specific creative ability becomes interesting as you advance through adulthood, it can influence the choice of creative entrepreneurship. For example, creative entrepreneurs and freelancers bring value through their expertise as an illustrator, web designer, graphic designer, photographer, video production, brand communication expert, etc.

In their springtime, other people choose to study skills outside the creative domains. For instance, Peter Ivanov studied mathematics at Sofia University in Bulgaria. He became aware of his creativity in mid-adulthood after years of practice as an IT manager in Germany.

"So it all started with this realisation that actually creativity is my strength. It came through an external source but once you believe it, once you make it believable because you check your past and see it does this, you could create more energy and then it becomes a real strength."

As Peter gained confidence in acting upon his ability as an idea generator, he switched gears to an entrepreneurial life.

"My biggest strength is coming up with new concepts and making them marketable, seeing from your client's point of view … and then coming up with the right messages which would appeal."

When **creativity is recognized as a personal strength**, it shifts your perspective on your professional possibilities, such as entrepreneurial projects requiring a high level of creative thinking.

Where do you stand in the way you relate to your creativity? Are you more like Tulia or more like Peter? People like Tulia, with creative experiences in childhood, are more inclined to see their creativity as an essential aspect of who they are. People like Peter, with analytical training, are more likely to relate to creativity as a personal resource, an extension of their identity, and a psychological tool which enables them to reach their highest performance. Where do you belong? Creative self-development starts when you become aware of the utility that creativity has for you – the psychological force that helps you thrive in life (see Figure 3-1).

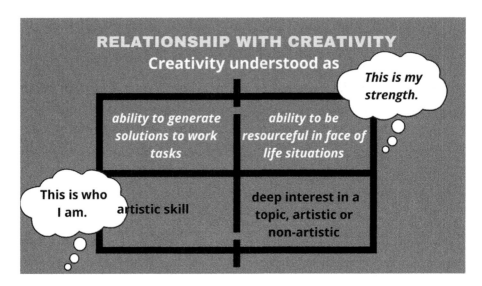

Figure 3-1. *Relationship with your creativity*

As it emerged from the interviews, creativity as a personal strength can be understood in two ways:

1. You are a creative thinker. You enjoy working on new work challenges and being noticed for coming up with solutions to those tasks.

2. You are a resourceful person. You surprise yourself and others with your ingenuity in dealing with life's obstacles.

Which of these two ways to see your creativity do you relate to most? This is the starting point of realizing your creative personal identity. It is crucial for **conscious creative self-development**, comprising two phases of expanded awareness. Some people remain at the first stage when the awareness of their creative thinking abilities and resourcefulness gives them more confidence in engaging in social interactions at work or in their personal life. But for some other people, the realization that their creativity is a personal strength enables the option to reflect it in building their employee brand or in seeking new leadership positions.

Alternatively, there can be a second route that triggers conscious creative self-development when you start to feel that your creativity is a central part of who you are. Thus, you can be in one of the following two situations:

1. You got a few bites of a specific creative skill. You can't wait for the next free time to compose a tune, write, take photos, dance, draw, etc. What is the most recent experience, if any, that reflects your tendency toward artistic creativity?

2. You tap into a topic that turns you into a sagacious learner of the nuts and bolts. You are the kind of person for whom a good life is about having a pet topic. What is your latest experience, if any, that describes your inclination toward intellectual creativity?

At the first stage of discovering an artistic/intellectual interest, you may prefer to develop it as a hobby or a side project. You are the analytical person by day and the artist/avid reader by night. You are content to live your life this way.

For some other folks with higher aspirations, when the learning sinks in, it starts the second milestone of creative growth. After that, they move to the **pro phase**, when they work on projects that bring them emotional, financial, and reputational rewards in the new area of interest.

In the next session, we'll get acquainted with the creativity of scientist Cecilia Payne, as a representative of people with intellectual interests, who pioneered the way for women in astronomy in 1925.

When Trust in Your Creative Capacity Outlasts Authority

Not for the first time I felt I had been passed over because I was a woman.

—Cecilia Payne, Autobiography, pp. 223

When she was 13, Cecilia got involved in many creative activities, which she considered *"the lifeblood of my late childhood."* She acted in Shakespeare's Hamlet for children in less advantaged families, which gave her confidence in public speaking. She made drawings of the plants she found during her walks, which developed her observation and accuracy skills. She practiced different styles of poems, like the sonnet and the rondel, which taught her the craft of writing. Acting, drawing, and writing poetry prepared her for a scientist's life.

When she decided to follow her interest in astronomy, there was the conception that being a woman was not a good fit with life as a scientist. Women in astronomy did the tedious job of data collection and classification so that the men could do the most exciting work.

Cecilia Payne proved that a creative woman could cope with the pressures of family duties and make scientific breakthroughs as much as a male counterpart. What was her secret?

"If my work has been of any value, that value consisted in bringing together facts that were previously unrelated, and seeing a pattern in them. Such work calls for memory and imagination..."[2]

Her trust in her creative capacity paid off. Now, we know that human beings and stars have one thing in common – hydrogen. But it took three years to have her male superiors believe in her findings.

---

[2] Payne-Gaposchkin, C., et al., (1996) Cecilia Payne-Gaposchkin: An Autobiography and Other Recollections 2nd Edition, Edited by Katherine Haramundanis, Cambridge University Press, pp. 172.

In her doctoral thesis, Cecilia made original calculations that showed that hydrogen is more abundant in the stars than on Earth. And yet, when her **proof was received with skepticism** by two authorities in astronomy in the 1920s – Harlow Shapley and Henri Norris Russell – she let herself be persuaded that her data was probably erroneous.

Who were these two men? Shapley showed that the Sun is closer to the edge rather than the center of the Milky Way Galaxy. He was one of Russell's students. Russell's main contribution was in making physics the core of astronomical research, thus establishing modern theoretical astrophysics, at the beginning of the 20th century. [3]

After an exchange of letters with these two giants in the world of astronomy, Cecilia added a paragraph in her thesis stating that the stellar abundance deduced for hydrogen *"is improbably high, and is almost certainly not real."*[4]

Three years later, when Russell himself got the same result but through his own calculations, Payne's findings were acknowledged as a significant contribution to astronomical science.

In spite of allowing herself to be intimidated by male figures and doubting her calculations, Cecilia Payne persevered in making original contributions to astronomy and astrophysics through her **intuition** about what problems were important to look into and solve. This is how she describes her decision to stay connected to the *"fountain-head"* as she calls the source of big ideas, in the essay, *"On being a woman"*:

"As I look over the world of science, I picture most of the many women who are working in that field today in the role of nuns and nurses. They are not allowed – they are not supposed to be fit – to be in direct touch with the

---

[3] www.britannica.com/place/Milky-Way-Galaxy/The-structure-and-dynamics-of-the-Milky-Way-Galaxy#ref956809;
www.britannica.com/biography/Henry-Norris-Russell

[4] C. Payne, (1925), Astrophysical data bearing on the relative abundance of elements, Washington National Academy Proceedings, 11, pp. 197.

fountain-head, whether you call it God or the Universe. (But even as I write, this situation is changing.) Here I have had no cause for complaint. I have always been in direct touch with the fountain-head. No other mortal has made my intellectual decisions for me. I may have been underpaid, I may have occupied subordinate positions for many years, but my source of inspiration has always been direct."[5]

Payne's gender did delay and limit the opportunities for professional advancement. It was commonly accepted that men held the positions of leaders in Harvard Observatory. Eventually, her work was noticed when Harlow Shapley retired as Director of Harvard College Observatory. When Donald Menzel succeeded him, Cecilia felt she was treated as a fellow-scientist and her salary was doubled. Under Donald's leadership, she was nominated as Chairwoman of the Department of Astronomy at Harvard.

In the last 20 decades, the proportion of women who make it to professorship positions has increased altogether with the number of awards that recognize women scientists.[6] However, prestigious science prizes, like the Noble awards, are criticized for **the lack of gender and racial diversity**.[7] Women scientists and scientists belonging to different ethnic groups continue to receive less recognition, which has nothing to do with the quality of their research.

---

[5] Payne-Gaposchkin, C., et al., (1996) Cecilia Payne-Gaposchkin: An Autobiography and Other Recollections 2nd Edition, Edited by Katherine Haramundanis, Cambridge University Press, pp. 221.

[6] www.nature.com/articles/d41586-021-02497-4?utm_source=Nature+Briefing&utm_campaign=484e752263-briefing-dy-20211011&utm_medium=email&utm_term=0_c9dfd39373-484e752263-43655973

[7] www.nature.com/articles/d41586-021-02782-2?utm_source=Nature+Briefing&utm_campaign=484e752263-briefing-dy-20211011&utm_medium=email&utm_term=0_c9dfd39373-484e752263-43655973

Throughout the history of inventions, women too had the motivation to use their creativity to respond to human needs.[8] Except that until the Renaissance period, women in most societies could not own property and were denied the right to education and legal independence. Without knowledge, resources, and support, it's harder to have an extraordinary career in science, technology, and other domains of innovation.

The story of Cecilia's professional advancement teaches us two valuable lessons:

1. Ideas that tease our curiosities can outstand others' prejudices on what we can achieve. Cecilia derived her satisfaction from the sincere fascination with astronomy.

"Undertake it (a scientific career) only if nothing else will satisfy you," advised Cecilia to young people, young women in particular, *"for nothing else is probably what you will receive. Your reward will be the widening of the horizon as you climb. And if you achieve that reward you will ask no other."*[9]

Let's think of the invention of the wheel. Who do you think came up with the idea? Was it a man or a woman? Or a child? Or a family brainstorming around the need to move the harvests faster and smarter? We evolved with biases about who can be a savvy inventor, an acclaimed writer, or a talented barista. The question is, do you see yourself capable of implementing original solutions to existing societal problems?

---

[8] Cropley, D. H., (2020), Femina Problematis Solvendis—Problem solving Woman: A History of the Creativity of Women, SpringerLink https://link.springer.com/book/10.1007/978-981-15-3967-1

[9] Payne-Gaposchkin, C., et al., (1996) Cecilia Payne-Gaposchkin: An Autobiography and Other Recollections 2nd Edition, Edited by Katherine Haramundanis, Cambridge University Press, pp. 227.

2.   The importance of bringing our creativity to perform the work tasks. Cecilia's creativity consisted of her intuition in selecting the problems others failed to notice and her memory and imagination to find the solution.

Where does the trust in creativity start? What anyone of us – within or outside scientific domains – needs is an unexplained intuition that we can bring a positive change somewhere in a tiny aspect of what we call reality.

It's easier to work on projects that others think we should work on. It feels safe to be part of a team where every member has pre-assigned tasks, and there's some clarity about what's expected of you. But are you working on the jobs that match your creativity?

Trust in your creativity starts with trust in your intuition, the feeling of knowing without knowing. You know you are born to be part of something more significant. However, you may be torn between your sense of initiative and the desire to stay in projects that bring a sense of safety. Next, let's look into possible social biases that might hold you back from leading yourself with creativity.

Gender Stereotypes That Confuse You About the Roles That Suit Your Creativity

My youngest son joined a music club. On his first day, I asked him, "How did you like your teacher?"

"It wasn't a teacher." He replied. "It was a man."

This anecdote reflects how early and automatically gender stereotypes can form based on the patterns you notice around you. Truly, until my son joined the bass guitar class, he did happen to have had female teachers without exception.

What if he were in charge of recruiting people for teaching positions in the classes that he attends?

Let's have a quick test for your gender prejudices, shall we? Consider the following domains: technology, business, science, design, and global issues. Imagine you want to listen to a talk so you can learn about the latest trends in each domain. Who would feel more appropriate for you to speak about the latest issues? A man or a woman?

Implicit societal biases influence our convictions on who is competent for a particular role in an organization or who has the credibility to talk about innovative ideas. When it comes to jobs requiring a high level of creative thinking, people are more likely to associate creativity with men than with women. A 2015 paper provides suggestive evidence that there are contexts – TED talks, innovation leadership – where the propensity to think creatively seems to be associated with behaviors that show self-direction and risk-taking, which generally are attributed to men.[10]

In hiring contexts, recruiters can project unconscious mental processes that determine their expectations of **the stereotypical idea of a creative person.** For example, a woman competing for a leadership position may be seen as less innovative than the male candidates. A male architect can be considered more competent than a female candidate. And vice versa, female fashion designers may be viewed as more creative than their male counterparts.

Others' biases are decisive for the evaluation of how we perform in the professional roles that we are entrusted with. The implicit expectations based on gender roles are affecting the **meaning of observed behavior**. A man showing initiative is recognized as an expression of his creativity.

---

[10] www.scientificamerican.com/article/the-creativity-bias-against-women/ Proudfoot, D., et al. (2015). A Gender Bias in the Attribution of Creativity: Archival and Experimental Evidence for the Perceived Association Between Masculinity and Creative Thinking, Psychological Science, Sage Journals, 26 (11), 1751–1761. https://journals.sagepub.com/doi/abs/10.1177/0956797615598739

How would you perceive a woman who takes the lead in a group discussion? There seems to be an unconscious bias toward female and male creativity, which makes others accept new ideas to the extent they perceive a fit between the person and their vision.

Moreover, others' gender prejudices influence our confidence in what we can achieve. For instance, studies show that social cues – words, body movements, facial expressions, intonations, speech rhythm, etc. – become **stereotype threats** that children pick up from teachers and affect the way they perform during class.[11] Stereotypes' negative or positive effect was documented based on a group of Asian-American girls. When the preschool girls were subtly reminded of their ethnic background, they did better in math tests. However, when the same group of girls was reminded of their gender, their performance flattened.

Karwowski et al. (2015) studied how teachers' ratings of middle school students' creativity were significantly related to how students understood their creativity one semester later.[12] Boys perceived themselves more creative in mathematics while girls considered themselves more creative in language tasks. By adulthood, we keep accumulating **embedded attitudes,** governed by the unconscious, that **shape our actions**.[13]

Tierney and Farmer (2004) showed that supervisors' expectations of employees' creativity shape the employees' beliefs that they can be creative in their work roles.[14] While it's realistic to expect that the success of your

---

[11] Regner et al., (2014), Our Future Scientists: A review of stereotypes threat in girls from early elementary school to middle school, RIPS/IRSP, 27(3-4), pp. 13–51, Presses universitaires de Grenoble.

[12] Karwowski, M., Gralewski, J., and Szmuski, G., (2015), Teachers' Effect on Students' Creative Self-Beliefs Is Moderated by Students' Gender, Learning and Individual Differences, 44, pp. 1–8.

[13] John A. Bargh, Our Unconscious Mind, Scientific American, January 2014, pp. 20–27.

[14] Tierney, P., and Farmer, S.M. (2002). Creative self-efficacy: its potential antecedents and relationship to creative performance. Academy of Management Journal, 45, pp. 1137–1148.

initiatives depends on others who have power over the resources you need, when it comes to how you perform in your professional role, clarity about your creativity and trust in your master competencies are more important.

According to a collection of research studies, there does not seem to be any gender difference in how men and women perform in creativity tests, such as divergent thinking, poetry-writing tasks, and story-telling tasks.[15] The age groups varied from pupils in the 5th grade to adults up to their 75s. These findings indicate that both men and women have brains wired for creative functioning and are capable of creative performance.

For healthy functioning in life, both men and women need to be driven by the will to be themselves.[16] Unfortunately, prejudices about what roles are expected of men and women in society are part of life. Hence, the most fruitful way to live with them is to think of them as mirrors that help us identify the contexts when we are inclined to take on new roles as creators.

You may realize inner tension, shame, or doubt whenever new competencies tempt you. However, these feelings are the sign that you can go ahead and test your sense of initiative in choosing the competencies that fit your creativity.

Communication architect Tulia Lopes believes that being creative means thinking flexibly by changing strategies to reach your goals.

"... I believe creativity is, more than anything, the ability and behind this ability, the belief that you can do certain things in several different ways. There is not only one way to reach an optimum result."

Being aware of and comfortable with your creativity is essential for developing an individual's sense of self.[17] The trick is to discern the projects that fit your creative potential. The more you show flexibility in thinking,

---

[15] Baer, J., and Kaufman, J.C. (2008). Gender Differences in Creativity, The Journal of Creative Behaviour, 42(2), pp. 75–105.

[16] Erikson, E.H., (1994), Identity Youth and Crisis, W.W. Norton & Company

[17] Jose de Valverde et al., (2017), Self-Construction and Creative "Life Design," The Creative Self, pp. 99–115.

the more you experiment with different roles to better understand your calls to create. One project at a time, you'll reset the course to the path where you are a creative person in the proper role.

After spending a semester in the company of the male bass guitar teacher, my son forgot that women were his archetype of a teacher. Instead, he has a new dream: one day, he'd like to be a music teacher too. Why music teacher, out of all possible roles, inspired by the hobbies and subjects he studies?

The bass teacher did a simple but impactful thing for learning motivation. He allowed my son to decide what tune he wanted to practice during lessons. Thus, my kid experienced what it's like to have a sense of autonomy in learning to play a musical instrument. Independence inspires self-initiative for anyone else, leading to a commitment to a particular role, at least for a certain period. As my boy grows up, he'll be likely to commit to other roles that he imagines himself to occupy in society.

On a scale of 1 (completely disagree) to 5 (completely agree), to what extent do you associate the following four types of thinking with your creative thinking?

- *Imaginative thinking* – I often think of future scenarios about my life, even if I know that not all of them become a reality.

- *Curiosity* – When I don't understand something, I gather and digest information to satisfy my need to know.

- *Inspiration* – I am an easily inspired person who gets new ideas when talking with people, reading books, or going for a walk.

- *Motivation* – I am the kind of person who is not afraid of challenges in my personal and professional development.

Which are the thinking types that you rated the highest? Can you think of a recent experience where there's evidence of it?

Next, let's examine how your teachers might have conditioned your knowledge of your creativity.

Flexing Creativity Archetypes

What kind of understanding do teachers have of the creativity of the little people they work with? A 1995 study looked into the teachers' views on the personal qualities attributed to a creative pupil.[18]

In the first round of the study, the teachers were presented with a list of personality characteristics associated with high and low creativity. For each quality, they had to answer the following question: *"How characteristic do you think each of the following is of a creative 8-year-old child?"* For example, inventing rules, being impulsive, nonconformist, emotional, progressive, and taking chances were among the most typical creative behaviors. On the other hand, the least familiar of a creative child was to be tolerant, practical, reliable, logical, good-natured, etc.

In the second round, teachers rated the qualities of their favorite and less favorite students. Curiosity and risk-taking were the least appreciated creative behaviors. Moreover, when educators could freely enumerate characteristics of creative personalities, they tended to evaluate their favorite students as their **creativity prototypes**. Could it be that respondents in this study confused a creative pupil for a favorite one?

---

[18] Westby, E. L., and Dawson, V. L. (1995). Creativity: Asset or burden in the classroom? *Creativity Research Journal, 8*(1), pp. 1–10. https://doi.org/10.1207/s15326934crj0801_1 www.tandfonline.com/doi/abs/10.1207/s15326934crj0801_1

A 2019 study found that 15 secondary-school Polish teachers held different views on who a creative boy is compared to who a creative girl is.[19] Who do you think was evaluated as diligent, meticulous, systematic, persistent, calm, acting according to plan, consistent, submissive, obeying all kinds of regulations, and avoiding risk? Who do you think was described as impulsive, independent, rule-breaking, courageous, willing to take risks, capable of defending their opinion, self-confident, individualistic, and spontaneous?[20]

According to this study, the teachers' beliefs fit the **image of the innovator or artistic type of creativity for boys** and the **embodiment of adapter and subordinated type of creativity for girls**[21] (see Figure 3-2).

---

[19] Gralewski, J., (2019), *Teachers' beliefs about creative students' characteristics: A qualitative study, Thinking Skills and Creativity, Vol. 31, pp. 138-155.* www.sciencedirect.com/science/article/abs/pii/S1871187118301718

[20] Most certainly, you guessed that the former set of qualities describes creative girls and the latter set of attributes is assigned to creative boys.

[21] Kirton, M.J., (1976). Adaptors and Innovators: A Description and Measure. Journal of Applied Psychology, 6, (5), pp. 622–629.
Kirton, M.J., (2003), Adaptation-innovation: In the Context of Diversity and Change, Routlege. https://books.google.fi/books?id=FeVlxVHCuNIC&printsec=frontc over&hl=fi&source=gbs_ge_summary_r&cad=0#v=onepage&q&f=true https://files.eric.ed.gov/fulltext/EJ811071.pdf www.researchgate.net/publication/308698479_Subordinated_and_Rebellious_ Creativity_at_School

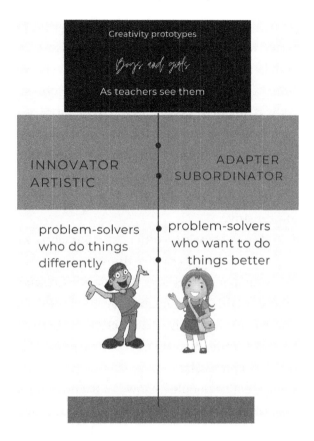

Figure 3-2. *Creativity prototypes boys versus girls*

Innovators tend to do things differently by going against accepted principles in a domain. On the other hand, adapters come up with new ideas within an established framework. Have you met an impulsive woman who stands against an agreed rule? How about a man who likes to obey regulations and is interested in emotions?

You may think, "They are the exception that proves the rule." One of the human brain functions is to process information and place it into familiar categories. This is how the brain copes with the complexity of the surrounding world. When new information comes in, it is unconsciously compared and directed to the "right" category.

One thing is for sure. There is so much complexity and variability within ourselves and outside ourselves. Being a creative person is about solving the tension between fitting in and finding your individuality. Even musicians have their distinguished personalities and thinking styles.[22] For instance, in a study, string players were found to be more often worried, agreeable, conscientious, and controlled themselves more often. In contrast, in another study, woodwind instrumentalists were more extroverted and had more difficulties regulating their emotions. Moreover, keyboard players seemed more introverted, whereas singers were more extroverted, independent, and sensitive.

Since we all tend to put labels on others and ourselves when it comes to the issue of understanding our creative thinking preferences and traits, we might as well invent a new category, *"My Specific Creative Type."* To define the boundaries of this new category, we need the example of some people who are personally inspiring in their creative way. Out of all the people you know and admire, who are the creative ones? What are the qualities that you like in particular?

One of the most creative people I know is a friend of mine who is a chief police officer. He is passionate about what he does. He knows that humor is his strength, and he uses it as a leadership tool to maintain his relationships with his subordinates. His impulsiveness makes him an apt problem-solver in emergencies. Of all these qualities, I see myself in the spontaneity to react to unexpected situations.

---

[22] Haller, C.S. and Courvoisier, D.S. (2010). Personality and Thinking Style in Different Creative Domains, Psychology of Aesthetics, Creativity, and the Arts, Vol. 4, No. 3, pp 149–160.
www.researchgate.net/profile/Chiara_Haller/publication/224045463_
Personality_and_thinking_style_in_different_creative_domains/
links/549849a30cf2519f5a1ddd39/Personality-and-thinking-style-in-
different-creative-domains.pdf

"One part of me says, well, I'm not a creative person," says John Bates, Leadership Communication Expert, *"I don't dress weird enough, you know, like the stereotypical thing of 'You are creative, I'm not."*

John wisely brings to light the myth that creative people are eccentric. Some of us may have this hidden conviction or any other implicit belief about the prototype of creativity. At the same time, you don't see yourself as such. My friend, who is a policeman, describes himself as a non-conformist. He takes pride in being an innovative problem-solver at work. At the same time, he is glad to obey the local culture and traditions in the small town where he serves. In fact, his behaviors are a mix of innovator and adapter types. He is a nonconformist dressed in the clothes of a traditionalist.

To conclude, trying to fit in an innovator or adapter type is a waste of your creativity. Instead, focus on developing your creative style – your creative thinking preferences and habits – centered around **the need to identify a passionate involvement with an activity.**

Touching Base with the Creativity Formed in School Years

Surreal fine art photographer Dasha Pears is a woman who broke away from the mold of a **"well-behaved girl"** out of the desire to look for her happiness.

"When growing up, going to school, I was always following the rules. I was the best student. I was always ready for lessons. I was keen on entering in front of the whole class. I was always the best girl. I was always the best daughter for my mom.

*After that when I started working, I obeyed all the – not the rules, not the orders – but I did everything that my boss told me. And it sort of took a while to break from that and tell myself, '***I can actually create my own rules'***."*

Dasha reached a moment in her life when she decided to take a disruptive turn to engage in photography as you can see in the following image.

The level of awareness of your creative thinking abilities, personality, and career possibilities is determined to a great extent by **the opportunities for creativity you were provided** in the classroom. To this view, **two conditions must have been fulfilled**: (1) there were teachers who helped you to take the role of a creative student in the classroom; (2) the teachers themselves were willing to assume the role of a creative pedagogue and they understood what the role entails.[24]

(1) You took the role of a creative student in the classroom. To turn creative thinking abilities into master skills for the working life, young people would benefit from receiving learning tasks where they can apply their creative thinking. The odds of a fulfilled life are higher when already as a schoolkid, you get used to using your imagination, curiosity, intuition and critical thinking in any of the subjects you study. This is the path of creative self-awareness when students can explore their creative strengths and weaknesses.

---

[23] Dasha's photo, Polka Dots

[24] Beghetto A.B., (2017), Creativity in Classrooms, The Cambridge Handbook of Creativity, pp. 587–606.

What is your earliest memory when you heard the word "creativity"? I was in the third year of high school when the teacher praised my creativity in a test during one of the math classes. It was the first time I heard anyone mention *"creativity"* and *"problem-solving"* in the same sentence. It carried a positive connotation. Even now, I remember my bewilderment, *"What do **maths**, **creativity** and **I** have to do with one another?"*

I didn't know the answer for the next two decades. All I understood back then was that I liked solving math problems. The creativity part was a temporary mystery which I forgot about. Now I know that some of us are born with mathematical creative thinking inclinations.[25]

How about the rest of the people who are not into math? In such cases, to have a chance to see the beauty of math, math can be presented as a source of solutions to everyday problems. In addition, math exercises can be formulated whenever possible to encourage more than one correct answer, such as, what two numbers add up to 5? Finally, when quizzes stimulate divergent thinking, kids have the chance to get more involved in finding solutions.

In any learning subject, children benefit from being offered opportunities to employ their creative thinking. In addition, they can be encouraged to think for themselves and discern when to choose to study subjects at a deeper level on the grounds of innate inclination (**being original**) and when to choose subjects at a beginner level because it is beneficial for life (**conforming**).

---

[25] Adiastuty, N., et al., (2021), Neuroscience study: analysis of mathematical creative thinking ability levels in terms of gender differences in vocational high school students, Journal of Physics: Conference Series 1933 (2021) 012072 doi:10.1088/1742-6596/1933/1/012072

There must be some balance between doing the things you love and see fit and doing those things that are within your responsibility, as a member of society, to understand at a basic level. Maybe math is not your cup of tea, but it can come in handy to understand what height, length, and width are when you buy your furniture.[26]

On a scale of 1 to 5, how much were you supported in exploring your path of creative-self awareness? The higher the score, the more likely that you made it to early adulthood with clarity on the topics you are passionate about. Also, you must have developed the habit of applying your creative thinking to a learning task, and you don't even know it (e.g., a math problem, a history project, writing a report, etc.).

Who were your educators that engaged in creative behaviors during teaching? For example, in a 2014 study, 36 Iranian English teachers were asked if they develop the students' potential revolving around their subject by adopting behaviors such as:

1. *"Guide the students to find new ways of learning, make predictions and solve problems."*

2. *"Provide a stress-free situation to help students foster divergent and creative thinking."*

3. *"Devote a part of the class to students' participation, authentic tasks and discovery."*

---

[26] Kaufman, J.C., and Beghetto, R.A., (2013), www.researchgate.net/publication/262372500_In_Praise_of_Clark_Kent_Creative_Metacognition_and_the_Importance_of_Teaching_Kids_When_Not_to_Be_Creative.
Runco M.A. (2003). Education for Creative Potential, Scandinavian Journal of Educational Research, Vol. 47, No. 3, pp. 317–324.

The teachers' self-perceptions did not match their actual performance in the classroom.[27] They rated the three behaviors high, whereas the observers in the classroom rated them low. Differently said, the participants **created opportunities for creativity less than they thought**.

The blind spot might explain these findings. Sometimes, others can better identify some behaviors that are unknown to us. Or, it can be that the observers didn't recognize the behaviors the same way the teachers intended. This study sheds light on the difficulties of establishing learning environments that foster creativity – the observer can misinterpret creative ideas and behaviors.

Assuming you took the observer role and traveled back to the times of your high school, what were the subjects you felt encouraged to ask *"Why?"* What were the topics where your ideas were praised? By any chance, did you choose any of the respective domains to specialize in?

In the end, even when teachers boost the students' sense of initiative and competence in studying a subject, the student decides to trust their innate interest.

*"What do **maths**, **creativity** and **I** have to do with one another?"*

I was well aware that solving math problems was one of my top favorite activities in high school. But, at the same time, I thought that only gifted children should dedicate themselves to math. And since I wasn't one of those kids, I decided not to take further my interest in math.

(2) The teachers themselves take the role of a creative pedagogue. When educators are motivated to offer their students opportunities to stimulate their creativity in learning, they decide to teach *with* creativity. The educator becomes a role model of applied creativity.

---

[27] Khany, R., and Boghayeri, M. (2014). How Creative Are Iranian EFL Teachers?. *Australian Journal of Teacher Education, 39*(10), pp. 16–28. https://ro.ecu.edu.au/ajte/vol39/iss10/2/

What sort of beliefs do teachers hold about their own creativity? How do these beliefs influence their teaching behaviors? The way teachers perceive their creative abilities shapes the methods they adopt.

In a 2019 study on 53 teachers in five healthcare schools in Taiwan, the authors tested whether the self-perceived levels of creative personality traits – imagination, curiosity, and adventure – could predict the self-perceived creative teaching behaviors.[28] The teachers in this study received previous training in motivating and stimulating creative thinking related to developing healthcare products.

The study measured the participants' perceived levels of personality traits and creative teaching behaviors. The more curious the nursing school faculty thought themselves, the more likely they thought they were to adopt any creative behaviors in teaching. However, they did not believe that their imaginative abilities or adventurous spirit would influence their teaching behaviors.

These findings indicate that the respondents use creative behaviors that they consider appropriate in teaching situations. In the Taiwanese culture, teachers may be more inclined to emphasize the qualities that they think are expected from their role, like being authoritative. Thus, they are less interested in showing their individuality.

Teaching with creativity in any culture around the globe is about teaching a specific subject matter, to a particular group of students, in line with your creative personality. It involves the courage to customize the teaching material. For example, from my high school time, I vividly remember the covers of math magazines where I would find the problems that my teacher recommended to solve. However, I do not recall the book covers we were supposed to study according to the curriculum.

---

[28] Liu, H-Y., et al., (2020), Predictors of self-perceived levels of creative teaching behaviors among nursing school faculty in Taiwan: A preliminary study, Journal of Professional Nursing, Vol. 36, Issue 3, pp. 171–176.
https://reader.elsevier.com/reader/sd/pii/S8755722319301530X?token=11B
0CB3AA5C9C36F8C9E46729C05E1FA57407F2418FC2CED80DFAA039603710DB3E49
A50E4321D840468DE6A267CD47E

I didn't become a mathematician, but what stayed with me from the math teachings is that it's OK to decide for yourself what books to read when you are interested in a topic. Likewise, it's OK to look into different experts' perspectives on the same issue before you choose what feels right. In the same way, the personalized teaching methods that your educators exposed you to may have become part of your implicit or explicit style of collecting information.

Last, teaching with creativity implies spontaneity to explore ideas when unexpected detours occur during class. For instance, spontaneous learning became a part of me. Whenever I find a sudden curiosity, I leave aside the previous plans to follow the unexpected. How about you? What creative learning habits might you have borrowed from your teachers and carried on in your professional life?

Opening Up to Your Inner Creative Diversity

Twenty years after I graduated high school, I paid a visit to my former Romanian language teacher, an imposing figure with a lifelong passion for his subject. During the reminiscences, he stopped and said, *"You were the kind of pupil that could be good at anything you chose to study."*

That was a momentous *"Aha!"* about my sense of autonomy. I had lived with the belief that people in authority see better than myself what I am good at. Hence, others are better equipped to select the tasks that suit me. And I was enthusiastic about coming up with new solutions and initiatives to issues suggested by others. But I hadn't taken the liberty to choose the problems myself. So this is how it is to be an individual with inner motivation but an inhibited sense of autonomy.

Let's do the following test. Let's imagine that your boss unexpectedly offers you a new position in your company. Which of the following reactions is more likely to be yours: 1) Will I live up to the responsibility? (sense of duty); 2) Will the new job be fascinating? (autonomy).

When you are the kind of person with a higher sense of duty, you are used to engaging in activities due to perceived external forces.[29] Hence, you may be a bit confused about your creative choices. It's time to reclaim your sense of autonomy and bring more harmony between your innate creativity and your work.

What does it mean to you to bring more creativity to work? This question is built on two assumptions. First, you are the kind of person who is interested in developing your creative identity in a professional role. Second, you believe that you can freely get involved in new activities driven by your perceived creativity.

When you see yourself as an imaginative individual, bringing more of your creativity to your work means that you are flexible to engage in new thinking habits such as

- Take time to daydream about projects that would have meaning and relevance to you. It would build up your courage toward engaging in topics that you may otherwise miss and which, in fact, can lead to successful outcomes.

- Get into the habit of asking yourself *"What If"* questions by negating the fundamental assumptions of what you know or see. We often focus on finding the right answer and stick to it. By contrast, we train our thinking through problems when we take time to ask basic questions, like *"Is this true?"* and *"Why do I assume it to be true?"* We learn to define and redefine the problems in our minds. We learn to recognize which issues are worth spending time on.

---

[29] Liu, D., Chen, X.-P., and Yao, X. (2010). From Autonomy to Creativity: A Multilevel Investigation of the Mediating Role of Harmonious Passion. Journal of Applied Psychology. pp. 1–16. Advance online publication. doi: 10.1037/a0021294

- Dedicate time to building *hypothetical scenarios* driven by your empathetic thinking. One way to do that is to shift the focus on a particular stakeholder in your project, on their needs and competencies. It gives new ideas about their possible actions and your reaction. Second, when you shift the perspective to technical elements of your problems, you make room for identifying the solutions. Einstein's thought experiments, such as imagining he was watching how lightning strikes from a train in motion or how a person experiences gravity in a falling elevator, illustrate this type of thinking.

The more frequent engagement in these mental exercises, the more open you become to possible versions of yourself and possible realities you can create.[30]

You can see yourself as the kind of person who needs to be refreshed by daily experiences of inspiration.[31] You'll thus be comfortable creating for yourself a ritual of evoking your Muse by enacting one of the following three principles:

- *You are taking a mental distance from the technical problems* you face. It requires that you keep an updated list of information sources you read regularly. When you feel stuck, you play mental games by considering how an idea or concept from outside your field would be used in your line of work. For example, entrepreneur Peter Ivanov wrote his first book by embedding the

---

[30] Glăveanu, V.P., (2022), The Possible as a Field of Inquiry, Europe's Journal of Psychology, pp. 519–530. https://ejop.psychopen.eu/index.php/ejop/article/view/1725/1725.html

[31] Thrash, T.M., and Elliot, A.J. (2003). Inspiration as a Psychological Construct, Journal of Personality and Social Psychology, Vol. 84, No. 4., pp. 871–889.

key tips for leading remote teams in a story about the fictitious character Bernd and his virtual team.[32] In this case, Peter combined the principles of fictional story writing with the real-life challenges resulting from team members' dynamics in different physical offices and time zones.

Alternatively, you can change your view on the technical issues you seek to solve by choosing one of your work's main concepts or objects and contemplating how they can be used in other contexts. For instance, how would you talk about your problem if you had to make an educational YouTube video addressed to your kids?

- *Engage in diverse activities* professionally, as a hobby and as a networking.[33] Studies show that highly creative scientists seem to be able to work simultaneously both on core research projects but also on secondary tasks like evaluating manuscripts and grant proposals. Moreover, they seem to engage more often in creative hobbies and exchange of ideas at conferences or other social events.

---

[32] www.amazon.co.uk/Virtual-Power-Teams-Products-Organization/dp/3981847237/ref=sr_1_1?crid=1ICW2Y87RIOWB&keywords=peter+ivanov+power+teams&qid=1649515220&sprefix=peter+ivanov+power+teams%2Caps%2C75&sr=8-1

[33] Simonton, D. K., (2008), Creativity in Science, Cambridge.
Hany E., (1996), How Leisure Activities Correspond to the Development of Creative Achievement: insights from a study of highly intelligent individuals, High Ability Studies, 7 (1), pp. 65–82.
www.researchgate.net/publication/233078580_How_Leisure_Activities_Correspond_to_the_Development_of_Creative_Achievement_insights_from_a_study_of_highly_intelligent_individuals_1

- *Practice the ability to notice the novelty.* Creative
  scientists are likelier to see something interesting in
  their leisure readings that can be used on a current
  research problem. How can you become more
  receptive to the novelty you are surrounded with?

By frequently reading books from other disciplines, you expose yourself to complementary perspectives on issues that matter. Going for a short walk during working hours can enhance your ability to see, smell, and hear the world around you and get out of your mind. The aim is to allow your brain time for incubation while you train it to be attracted to new aspects in your usual environment.[34]

What else might it mean to bring more creativity to work? Some people's creativity revolves around their ability to exercise a particular creative skill, like drawing, storytelling, or writing. Bringing any of these skills to work means engaging in new techniques to perform and deliver your tasks.

Finally, bringing more of your creativity means allowing more of your creative personality in the form of curiosity for new experiences. You then embark on a personal exploration of new technologies, processes, techniques, or ideas beyond the role expectations.

All in all, bringing more of your creativity at work requires evaluating which of the above-mentioned thinking habits you're most inclined to try under the current work circumstances. Your imaginative tendencies? Inspiration rituals? A particular creative skill? Broadening your expertise?

The central premise of opening up to your creative diversity at work is that *curiosity is the underlying motivational force* that can redeem your sense of autonomy and initiative toward developing your creative potential. We now discuss personal strategies in which you can express this core trait of your creative personality. What kind of curiosities do you allow yourself to show in organizational settings?

---

[34] Carson, S., (2010), Your Creative Brain, Harvard Health Publications.

To Be Creative Is to Think Twice About What You Deem to Be an Appropriate Curiosity to Follow

Teachers in the studies presented in the previous section are not an exception in assuming that not all creative habits are appropriate in teaching contexts. They considered their curiosity suitable but not their imagination or spirit of adventure. Exploring different ways to express your curiosity means becoming aware of what you consider appropriate learning to take on.

According to the componential theory, the individual ability to come up with original and useful ideas is influenced by three intraindividual components, and one external component – the social environment.[35] The intraindividual components are (1) domain-relevant skills, like expertise and technical skill; (2) creative thinking skills such as flexible thinking; personality traits such as openness to experience; and persistent workstyle; and (3) intrinsic task motivation. These components must be present and influence one another, if creativity is to be manifested. The social environment can affect each of the three intraindividual components of creativity – new expertise, creative thinking skills, and internal motivation.

The trigger for creativity is acquiring the necessary knowledge in the area of expertise. For instance, you can take a proactive attitude to learn by indulging in your curiosity about

- *Different professions* – "Whenever I meet new interesting people, I will envision myself in their respective roles."

---

[35] Amabile, T.M., and Pillemer, J. (2012). Perspectives on the Social Psychology of Creativity, Journal of Creative Behaviour, 46, No. 1, pp. 1–25. www.researchgate. net/publication/264251929_Perspective_on_the_Social_Psychology_of_ Creativity

- *Stories of creative resilience* – "Once per week, I look for the story of a creative person who talks about their highs and lows in implementing their ideas."

- *New concepts* – "When I hear of a new concept, I will set a time in my calendar to look it up. I will turn to a person I trust to share my learning."

- *New Ideas* – "Whenever I get a new idea, I take time to write down a possible implementation plan (even though I am not sure I can act upon it right away)."

Which of these four expressions of curiosity is the most alluring to you? Imagining yourself in different status roles and listening to the resilience stories of creative people are the safest choices to start with. The higher the perceived uncertainty of the environment, you'll find it more challenging to engage in openness to new experiences, like taking time to learn new concepts or write notes about developing new ideas.

Mueller et al. (2012) show that despite being open to experiences when the study participants felt motivated to reduce uncertainty, this brought negative associations about creativity, making them less able to recognize a creative idea.[36] This finding indicates that imposed goals can decrease the self-determination to engage spontaneously in creative action.[37]

That's why psychological safety is one of the fundamental requirements of institutions that value creativity. But even in the creativity-friendly cultures, when the brain perceives some environmental threats, it prefers to engage in the same familiar activities rather than new experiences. So, you can motivate yourself to learn something new under less auspicious

---

[36] Mueller, J., Melwani, S., and Goncalo, J.A. (2012). The Bias Against Creativity: Why People Desire But Reject Creative Ideas, Psychological Science, 23(1), pp. 13-17. https://repository.upenn.edu/cgi/viewcontent.cgi?article=1107&context=mgmt_papers

[37] Creative action refers to situations when you are intrigued to find the answer to a problem even when you have no clear or readily identified path to the solution.

conditions by answering the question, *"What's the most beneficial in the long-run? To learn something that leverages the current competences or to take the risk of disruptive learning?"*

When you answer this question, please be cautious of the trap of past performance. It's not only the perceived threats from the environment that bias our preferences for what we know already rather than what we are yet to know. For example, Audia and Goncalo (2007) show that the experience of past creative achievements may be an essential boundary that prevents creative individuals from coming up with disruptive ideas.[38]

Once an individual generates a creative idea, future creative efforts are framed from the perspective of the initial idea. Therefore, for an individual to increase the variety of their creative ideas in the future, it is essential to update the existing knowledge with new expertise from close or distant domains. The dynamic intake of knowledge increases the emergence of original ideas. Thus, you can take up the habit of disruptive learning in the same way as you have the habit of going on a vacation.

What is the expected utility of frequent learning episodes that makes you feel like a novice? Mueller et al.'s (2012) findings also reveal that uncertainty about how well we can perform or what financial rewards we expect to get also makes us associate creativity with the superfluous aspects of life rather than a necessity. Engaging more in your curiosity leads to developing a sense of expertise. It is a question of identity growth and psychological well-being. And it is up to each individual to evaluate it as a luxury or necessity.

Ideas to engage in activities you have not done before, like *"I'll make time to learn about business models"* or *"I'll sign up for an improv class,"* create tension in the creator's mind. The psychological motivator of personal change is the curiosity to challenge the limits of your creative potential. Then again, you may be held back by the fear of missing out on

---

[38] www.researchgate.net/publication/37150341_Past_Success_and_
Creativity_over_Time_A_Study_of_Inventors_in_the_Hard_Disk_Drive_
Industry

the safe and successful activities you have to let go of so you can focus on new learning. When the foreseen emotional benefits are more convincing than the perceived risks, you'll be inspired to do something different in your professional life. But what exactly underlies the emotional drive to do something different?

It's time to look into your patterns of observed impulses that will guide you to new activities as a creative person.

CHAPTER 4

Impulses to Create

Four Possible Temptations Toward Creative Activities

Once I knew that my top strength is input and creativity, I just started to ride on this wave and then my book appeared. I never imagined to be a book author.

—Solopreneur Peter Ivanov

What force coming from within you might push you to a new creative activity which diverges from any other project you've done before in your professional roles?

In the neuroscience literature, there are documented dramatic life changes in people who suffered neurological damage. As a result, they experienced a relentless creative drive to paint, write poetry, or play the piano.[1]

---

[1] Abraham., A (2018) The Neuropsychology of Creativity. Current Opinion in Behavioral Sciences, 21. pp. 71–76. ISSN 2352-1546 DOI: https://doi.org/10.1016/j.cobeha.2018.09.011
Miller, B.L., Ponton, M., Benson, D.F., Cummings, J.L., and Mena, I. (1996). Enhanced artistic creativity with temporal lobe degeneration. Lancet, 348(9043), pp. 1744–1745.

© Oana Velcu-Laitinen 2022
O. Velcu-Laitinen, *How to Develop Your Creative Identity at Work*,
https://doi.org/10.1007/978-1-4842-8680-7_4

Tommy McHugh was an Irish builder who used to suffer from migraines. The day when the stroke happened, he was on the toilet reading the paper when he felt an explosion on the left side of his head. His wife found him lying on the floor and rushed him to the hospital where surgeons operated on Tommy's brain for eleven hours.

When he regained consciousness after the surgery, his behavior, thoughts, and motivations changed radically. He felt a sudden appreciation of the beauty he could see through the window of the hospital ward.[2] A few days later, he felt the urge to rhyme. Afterward, his brain went into overdrive with details, information, and knowledge unbeknownst to his old self, and which his new self couldn't stop from expressing it in writing at first and painting, later.

It wouldn't have crossed the mind of Tommy's old self to pick up the paint brush. Surprisingly, his new self got so absorbed by painting that he covered in layers of paint the walls, floor, and furniture of his home. Painting gave him a sense of well-being.

Although there are some suppositions on what exactly was Tommy's trigger – whether the rich flow of ideas and concepts served as inspiration or the increase in dopamine, which produced the uncontrollable drive toward things that make him happy – what is certain is that the respective triggers turned him into an artist.

Before becoming a painter, the Ukrainian Valera Hrishanin dreamt of playing basketball in the professional league. A nervous system problem affected his movement and coordination, which made it impossible for him to continue his sportsman career. *"Surprisingly, one day I woke up painting. It was like a breath of fresh air and I wanted to live again,"* said

---

[2] Helen Thompson, (2018), Unthinkable, An Extraordinary Journey Through the World's Strangest Brains, John Murray (Publishers).

Valera.[3] He is now ambidextrous, using both hands simultaneously to draw and paint, as he demonstrates in live TV shows. His works are in peoples' homes in many countries.

Tommy's transformation from a builder to a poet and painter and Valera's discovery of his painting prowess make us wonder about our brains, which, as far as we know, we've been lucky to have relatively healthy. What inclinations to create might be hiding in the disinhibited pathways of memory, speech production, and social awareness?

A creative person is a collection of neural correlates of inclinations to bring something new to their physical spaces. Your orientations to create are biologically rooted in the brain's reward system that motivates you to seek out experiences out of the joy of learning.[4] The drive to a personally disruptive activity is determined by the **creative impulse,** which consists of a **sudden and intense emotion,** like awe, excitement, or flusters, to a stimulus you experience in a novel situation. The impulse both intensifies what you feel and drives you into action. As you interact with the external world, your brain absorbs perceptions of others' emotions, behaviors, and events (see Figure 4-1). As a result, for some people, the first impulse is to fix feelings – theirs or others – while for others is to solve a particular external problem.

---

[3] https://twitter.com/vhrishanin
www.etsy.com/shop/ArtMonkeyArt
https://linktr.ee/VHrishanin www.wowbiz.ro/valerii-hrishanin-pictorul-de-la-romanii-au-talent-sezonul-12-ucraineanul-i-a-oferit-andrei-un-dar-nepretuit-20208777
[4] Flaherty A.W., (2018), Homeostasis and the Control of Creative Drive, The Cambridge Handbook of the Neuroscience of Creativity, pp. 19–49.

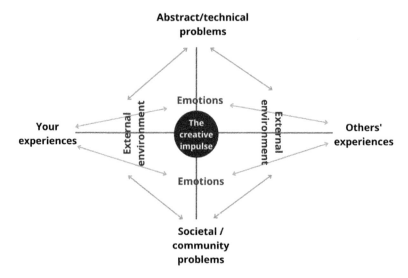

Figure 4-1. *Creative Impulses*

To understand what kind of a creator you can become, you may want to notice the **impulses** that make a particular action more compelling than any other creative activity. The more we allow ourselves to engage in it, the more our occupational identity forms around it, and the next thing you hear yourself saying is, *"I am a creative expert in _____."* We learn how to think and behave like **creators of content, products, or positive change.**

On a busy day, what makes you stop and wonder? Try to avoid overthinking, and instead answer spontaneously

- Details I notice in the physical environment, like

  - The change in the colors of the sky

  - The sounds of the city

  - The formation of ice cubes in my fridge

  - The sound of elevator buttons when pressed

- People's emotions and experiences

- Your own emotions, thoughts, and inner dialogue

- Societal news

Certain aspects can promptly surface to your attention when you partake in events. For example, in the following days, you can realize that your mind keeps returning to a challenge about your personal life, someone else's life, a societal trend, or an impersonal and objective detail in the material world, such as the biological mechanisms of leaves changing color in autumn.

Depending on which emotions about what detail of life become more salient and frequent, you can experience **four types of creative impulses** (see Figure 4-2).

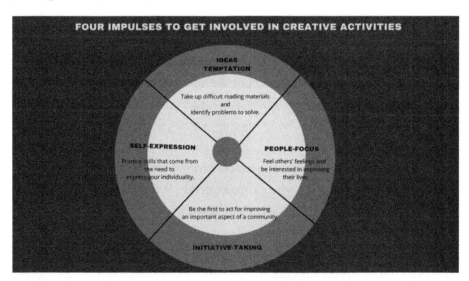

Figure 4-2. *Description of creative impulses*

(1) **Self-expression** – This impulse is behind the artistic output experienced by Tommy Hughes, Valera Hrishanin and other iconic cases of non-artistic people with nervous system illnesses who became obsessed with exercising drawing, writing, or music skills.

67

Healthy brains are wired with an unabated drive for creative expression as well. **Dasha** Pears' surreal photography and **Harriet** Fagerholm's work on conscious co-creation spring from their inclinations toward self-expression. How do you know if you have this tendency in you?

You spend most of your time processing information related to your inner self. For example, you tend to speak about life experiences that touch you deeply, like relationships, work, love, childhood, death, etc.

When you find it soothing to express yourself, your own emotions and experiences provide the source of inspiration to create something to which others can relate and maybe experience catharsis. Therefore, you're drawn by activities that help you develop specific knowledge and skills to express nuanced viewpoints and become an alchemist of words, sounds, or images.

The reward comes from sharing your values and belief system, to feel understood, and connect with the audience. Or quite the opposite, your creative products can signal your withdrawal from the world. The desire for self-expression can ignite different kinds of artistic work and public speaking gigs, embodying messages that you find relevant to communicate.

(2) **Initiative-taking** – During his rehabilitation, Tommy Hughes discovered people like him who experienced brain repair and didn't know how to express or to whom to reach out about what they were experiencing. He got so passionate about this observation that he started giving talks on how to embrace your new mind as a stroke survivor. *"We need to be able to talk about the strange things that happen to us, because getting a bit of support and understanding in recovery can make 100 percent difference,"* said Tommy.[5]

How do you know you have a brain wired with the initiative-taking impulse? You notice your attention frequently goes to an aspect of

---

[5] Helen Thompson, (2018), Unthinkable: An Extraordinary Journey Through the World's Strangest Brains, Ecco, pp. 129.

society or business, which you feel compelled to see improved. You thus volunteer to influence and mobilize people to level up their skills for collective action.

The reward comes from the pleasure of seeing the outcomes of the movement you introduce. This tendency can lead to leadership positions, social entrepreneurship, eco-entrepreneurship, and activism work. For instance, **Tulia Lopes**'s workshops are rooted in the propensity to take leadership for women who need a confidence boost in communicating their ideas.

(3) **Ideas temptation** – You are a thinker, at an abstract, philosophical, or technical level. Solving complex problems – life-related or conceptual ones – is your mind's favorite sport, especially when you anticipate that they might have invention or innovation potential.

The reward comes from the joy of discovering new information to expand the boundaries of what is known as truth in a domain, community, or culture. Philosophers, researchers, and engineers would be defined mainly by this type of impulse, but also science, tech, and knowledge entrepreneurs. For instance, sales engineer **Oscar Santolalla**'s book on pitching technical products stems from his tendency to break geeky ideas into digestible technical information.[6]

(4) **People focus** – It's in your blood to be considerate and supportive of others' well-being and personal development. In the same way a mechanical engineer likes to design, maintain, and improve the movement of a car engine, you want to boost people's lives.

The reward comes from the ability to connect with others and offer them the opportunity to reach their own understanding of themselves. This orientation can lead to professional roles where you work directly with the people whose lives you aim to improve. **Pamela Thompson**'s

---

[6] www.amazon.com/Rock-Tech-Stage-Speakers-Products-ebook/dp/B08PCV3G8Z/ref=sr_1_2?crid=2Q9BO9C5FDWNO&keywords=oscar+santolalla&qid=1649664801&sprefix=oscar+santolalla%2Caps%2C127&sr=8-2

seminars on embracing personal and organizational change with mindfulness about how the body experiences uncertainty illuminate her concern for people's health.

How about you? Which of the four types of impulses are most meaningful to you? As a tip, when you get a tiny sense of liberation as you read the description of a particular impulse, that is an indication of personal meaning. What kind of novel activities might be galvanized?

Let's take a look at the status-quo of actual creative involvement starting from a concise list of activities that are believed to be illustrative of everyday creativity.[7] Out of the following activities, which are the experiences you have engaged in **in your free time**? Kindly circle the activities that you engaged in **at least once, in your adult life**.

Self-expression

- *I participated in a writers' workshop.*

- *I participated in a video editing workshop.*

- *I participated in a painting workshop.*

- *I had an acting role in a dramatic production.*

- *I can play a musical instrument.*

Initiative-taking

- *I like to work for a cause outside of my own skin.*

- *I'm the first to volunteer for new initiatives at work.*

- *I participated in a business ideas generation workshop.*

---

[7] Creative_Behavior_Inventory: Hocevar, D., (1980), Intelligence, divergent thinking, and creativity. *Intelligence, 4*, 25–40.
Dollinger, S.J., (2003), Need for Uniqueness, Need for Cognition and Creativity, *Journal of Creative Behaviour*, www.researchgate.net/publication/260745017_ Need_for_Uniqueness_Need_for_Cognition_and_Creativity, 37(2).
Silva P. et al., (2012) Assessing creativity with self-report scales: A review and empirical evaluation, *Psychology of Aesthetics, Creativity and the Arts, 6*(1), 19–34.

- *I took part in an entrepreneurial program.*
- *I assisted in the planning of a new public event in town.*

Ideas temptation

- *I like deep reading on varied topics outside my main domain of expertise.*
- *I dismantled a computer or other mechanical device only because I wanted to put the pieces back together.*
- *For pleasure, I programmed a primary robotic device.*
- *For fun, I develop experimental designs, like the diet coke and mentos or the ice cubes color experiments.*
- *I use arithmetic to solve practical problems.*

People focus

- *I participated in a workshop to improve my communication skills.*
- *I usually write humorous messages to friends.*
- *I like to make others feel good about themselves.*
- *I like to motivate people to achieve their goals.*
- *When I talk with people, I point out their strengths.*

Please go back to the top of the list and circle the activities you have engaged in in **a professional context** at least once. These activities point to your **current occupational creativity**. The more activities you mark in one category, the stronger the respective creative tendency is imprinted on your work identity.

You may be aware of the creative impulses that drive you at work. However, there's lots of unexplored potential in the creative tendencies you practice in your free time. By contrasting the type of creative activities in your free time with the creative tasks performed at work, you can thus bring light to **your assumptions about what you think you can create and get paid for**.

Taking another look at the preceding list, what would be one activity you'd like to experience in work contexts on a more regular basis? Are you thinking, *"Yes, but ..."*? Do yourself a favor and avoid coming up with arguments about organizational barriers. Instead, imagine you work in a constraint-free culture.

To reach your potential as a creative person, you may want to find ways to allow some creative impulses that push you toward free time activities to become the drivers of work activities.

Software engineers may assume that analytical problem-solving is an essential skill they're capable of and comfortable with. So, to what extent can folks like them consider making a funny video about one day in a programmer's life?

Scientists may have the implicit assumption that research methodologies are their playground. What are the odds that they become an admired science leader? When I asked professor Helder Santos about activities other than research requiring his creativity, he replied. *"If I want to tell you or other kinds of people that are not so familiar with the job we do, we have to be creative in the way that a message gets to the people. Because if we are using the same that we do in the research, they will not understand. So even in the way you communicate, you have to be creative there. You can not just put some kind of graphic there and expect that people will understand. So, in the past several months or even in the past year, one thing I have been interested in is also how to make a very complex field easier to understand. Because, for the public in general, science is still a big box over there, and to take that to their level that they will understand perfectly what we are saying, you have to communicate in the right way."*

Helder's experience is indicative that when creators become aware of secondary impulses – initiative-taking in Helder's case – they'll be motivated to redesign their job tasks of the current role as a creator.

Summing up, watch out for assumptions about new activities you could adopt in your role. On a scale of 1 (*I couldn't care less*) to 5 (*I live for it*), how essential is for your professional life

- Self-expression

- Initiative-taking

- Ideas temptation

- People focus

A clue on the value you assign to possible creative tendencies will open your eyes to new activities that are within reach to do.

Explore Your Creative Drive by Harmonizing the Importance of Creativity for Your Sense of Well-Being and Your Work Role

In the last two years of upper elementary school, I discovered the joy of mathematics. Yet, my confidence in being a good problem solver was somewhat shaky. You see, in the 5th grade, the math teacher thought I had the brains of a pigeon. Then, in the 7th grade, I started attending the classes of another math teacher who would express appreciation of my reasoning. As a result of the boost of confidence, I chose the math and physics study track in high school.

Throughout high school, I represented the school at the mathematical Olympiads, but was not good enough to qualify among the top competitors. In the final examination, I received the highest mark in school, 9.2 out of 10. Yet, I didn't continue with math, seeing myself not sufficiently intelligent for an advanced degree in math.

Above all the interests that astronomer Cecilia Payne had, mathematics was her most loved subject. Ironically, when the family moved to London, the new math teacher drove her into a *"nervous frenzy, and produced a block about the subject that I have never completely overcome."*[8] Mathematics had been her hope, but in the new school, the hope turned into a disappointment.

Cecilia continued to hope for scientific education, through a different route, of botany, physics, and chemistry. Unlike her, not only that I had given up on developing my math skills, I stopped believing I am capable of any other curiosity.

In such situations, the creative drive, the desire to look for activities out of curiosity, is blocked. Creativity experts like Ronald Beghetto call this **"creative mortification,"** which is the loss of willingness to pursue a creative aspiration after a negative performance outcome.[9] As a result, you lose confidence in finding a new interest for which your heart goes pitter-patter, and you're good at. It's like the first time you fall deeply for someone and break up after a while. You think you'll never feel love again.

Your curiosity is an abundant source of possibilities to create. What are the creative impulses that match your current professional skills and interests? Before defying others' conscious beliefs, creative people need to first defy themselves, their self-beliefs, and values.[10]

On a scale of 1 (not at all) to 5 (a great deal), how important is your creativity for feeling good in your skin? How important is it for you to develop your creative potential into a career? Figure 4-3 describes three possible beliefs – cases 1, 2, and 3 – that might prevent you from revving up your creative potential. **Nevertheless, there is the hope of unlocking your creative drive** when you unveil what narrative you tell yourself.

---

[8] Payne-Gaposchkin, C., et al., (1996) Cecilia Payne-Gaposchkin: An Autobiography and Other Recollections 2nd Edition, Edited by Katherine Haramundanis, Cambridge University Press, pp.102.

[9] Beghetto, R.A., (2014), Creative mortification: An initial exploration. *Psychology of Aesthetics, Creativity, and the Arts*, 8(3), pp. 266–276.

[10] Sternberg, R.J., (2018), A triangular theory of creativity, Psychology of Aesthetics, Creativity, and the Arts, 12, pp. 50–67.

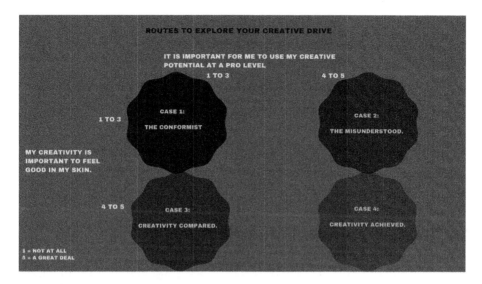

Figure 4-3. *Overcome creative mortification*

Narrative 1: Being a Conformist

You are inclined to think you are not creative and don't see much value in living a creative life. However, conformity is a big part of who you are. Therefore, you will walk on the paths others have opened before.[11] You may have dormant creative interests, but you don't see any reason why to make an effort to explore your creativity, either as a hobby or at work.

Ever since I've known myself, I have admired my grandmother. As a result, in my early teenage, I wanted to make her dream of becoming a medical doctor come alive through me. However, when I randomly discovered my hemophobia, it became as clear as day that I wasn't cut out to become a physician. My potential was somewhere else.

---

[11] Dollinger, S.J., and Dollinger, S.C., (2017), Creativity and Identity, The Creative Self, Explorations in Creativity Research, pp. 49–64.

Conformity can come from a place of wanting to make someone you love happy. Conformity can come from laziness to making an extra effort to stand up for your preferences. Conformity can come from fear of being punished. There are many reasons, sometimes intertwined, why we choose professional roles in line with the expectations of parents and influential caretakers.

No matter the cause of your tendency to conform, as long as you stay unconsciously trapped in it, you'll miss the opportunity to know the creative side of yourself.

Narrative 2: You Feel Misunderstood

You know you are a person who never runs out of ideas. But, sadly, you may have received more skepticism than you could handle. As a result, you are stuck in frustration, fixated on your ideas and blaming others. This is the sales trap of creativity.

Creative experts face others' unconscious or conscious beliefs upon communication of novel ideas. For example, during one of the training sessions I facilitated, I mediated a discussion between a product manager who pitched an innovative idea and the country managing director. The air got so thick with frustrations on both sides that you could cut it with a knife. *"Why don't you pitch the idea to the headquarters?"* the country manager suggested at some point.

Can you guess what the product manager did? Since upper management had nixed his previous innovative ideas, he chose not to communicate the latest one to the board of directors. Similarly, you may have grown disappointed with the people around you for not being open to your improvement ideas. *"Fools, what do they know?!"* or *"Why am I bothering?"* When you grow a sense of superiority or inferiority, you lose your sense of well-being and desire to think differently.

"What could be different this time?" you may be thinking. Creative ideas don't sell by themselves. And who can be the best seller of your ideas if not you? So, next time you get excited about a sparkling idea, how about thinking carefully about **when, to whom, and how you talk about your ideas**?

The story of the astronomer Cecilia Payne shows how the environment – expert groups, company culture, leadership, the available resources – can accelerate or delay your creative achievements. However, she overcame the obstacles thanks to her conviction that she was the right person to investigate stars' properties and her ability to find new ideas to research.

To begin with, Cecilia was well aware that she could not have a career as a scientist in the UK, which is why she moved to the USA. You may also want to explore your role in other contexts, teams, and organizations. Like Peter Ivanov, moving from a managerial position to entrepreneurship. Or, like John Bates, changing the entrepreneurial focus on leadership communication.

Narrative 3: You Compare Your Creativity with Others' Creativity

You value creativity in work contexts and life in general. You recognize the benefits of progress, new perspectives and experimenting, starting from how things are currently done. But you are not confident about having the required personality, intelligence, and competence yourself to be one of the people who challenge the status quo.

"I'm not good enough to become a mathematician," I told myself when I was 18. *"I'll never be like Henri Poincare."* Similarly, you may lose heart when you compare your abilities with the abilities of the greatest minds in your domain of interest.

In this case, we may want to revisit and calibrate **our expectations of creative achievements**. When we perform activities requiring our creative thinking, there can be four outcomes: **Big-C creativity**, **Pro-C, little-c** and **mini-c creativity**.[12]

Big-C Creativity

The Big-C Creativity is what the majority, my eldest son included, think of when they answer who a creative person is. Big-C rests upon the expectation of notable works, Einstein types of contributions, that disrupt a specific domain and bring progress across societies worldwide. This creative achievement results from someone's **ability to notice a necessary but not urgent problem in the environment** and dedicate themselves to finding solutions. When the answers are found, they shift the underlying assumptions in a domain of knowledge, the status-quo in a culture, or cause a radical change in people's lives, in the way the Internet transformed our lives.

"And of course, another thing that I always try to teach or to say to my students, let's be triggered by problems rather than by solutions," says professor Vincenzo Cerullo. *"What problem do you want to solve? Forget about what you are good at. The majority of scientists are very solution-driven. I have the solution, let's see what kind of problem I can solve with my solution. I know how to write, what can I do with that? Instead, I think I need to write a book on creativity. Let's see if I am good at writing.*

That's a completely different thing, the results might be completely different, because there you come up with a problem. While this is a problem, I don't even care whether or not I am good at it, I will find a solution later."

---

[12] Cotter K.N., et al., (2019), Creativity's Role in Everyday Life, The Cambridge Handbook of Creativity, second edition, pp. 640–651.

Some people capable of Big-C Creativity have their statues raised in cities and their work included in school books. We live in their shadows. Yet, even for those people, the performance they are most famous for was likely to appear after decades of working on core and secondary ideas.[13]

Think of creativity as a gift. What do you do when you receive a gift in a smaller package compared with others around you? Do you accept it or reject it right away? You may or may not be capable of Big-C achievement. What matters more is your ability to find an interesting problem that makes you curious to investigate.

Pro-C Creativity

"I think there are different aspects of creativity," says Leadership Communication Expert John Bates. *"Like I think when I hear creativity, something that comes to my mind is something out of nothing.* **It has to be a really big deal.** *Whereas, there are other aspects of creativity. Like maybe you didn't create all those pieces but if you* **put them together in a unique, special way**, *that's creativity too."*

John's intuition is up to something. He describes **Pro-C creativity** when he talks about putting all pieces together uniquely. It results in practical solutions to an identified problem within a community or area of expertise. Moreover, some of these solutions can result in incremental growth in knowledge, as described by Helder Santos, professor in biomedical engineering at the University of Groningen.

"... you create a new way to tackle a certain kind of problem. So, it is creating a new approach to solve, in our case, a health problem."

A shift in my view on what I'm capable of creating happened after graduating from a Master's program in Financial Accounting Information Systems. I was unexpectedly offered a position for doctoral studies. A Ph.D. was something I considered way out of my league.

---

[13] Simonton, DK, (2008), Creativity in Science, Cambridge University Press.

"I bet you can do it," the professor said as if reading my mind. And I spontaneously accepted the bet, still wondering, *"Is it true? Can I really do it?"* As I entered the challenge of Ph.D. studies, I learned to stop being obsessed with being the best. Instead, I challenged myself to find interesting topics.

In sum, when you feel disarmed by the prospect of the Pro-C type of creative achievement, do the opposite. Give yourself the benefit of the doubt and engage in a learning process despite the hesitation of not being intelligent or competent enough.

Little-c Creativity

The third kind of creative achievement, **little-c** or everyday creativity, is manifested in creative hobbies such as playing music, acting, writing, cooking, drawing, do-it-yourself home improvements, etc. This form assumes a keen interest in something, a basic level of related technical skills and some spontaneity and freedom of action. The outcome is surprising, fun, and meaningful both for creators themselves and their small audiences.

"And then the other thing that was the feeling of creativity for me was playing music live with the band," adds John Bates. *"That's a really amazing thing. We played for a long time together, we actually got to a point when we were really good at playing the songs."*

My script-writing hobby also reflected the little-c creativity. The plays were put on the stage by an amateur theater group which performed for small audiences of English-speaking theater fans in Helsinki.

The little-c creativity is triggered by the dominant tendency to express your emotions or others' emotions. For example, out of the following situations, where would you see yourself:

- I sometimes experience feelings that are best managed if I recycle them in a poem, song, blog post, or fictitious story.[14]

- Sometimes others' experiences touch/frustrate/amuse me so much that I spontaneously get ideas to write a poem, song, blog post, or fictitious story.

- My emotions fuel living a creative life in the most ordinary moments of the day.

- A creative hobby would give me the energy to cope with life.

- I need to arrange the physical space of my home in an inspiring way.

Passive participation in creative activities like visiting a museum, going to concerts, or watching a play do not count as little-c creativity. Suppose you do not see yourself experiencing any of the previously noted activities. In that case, you may be more the type of person with tendencies of practical creativity manifested in solving engineering, scientific, or technical problems.

Mini-c Creativity

Very close to little-c, we have the **mini-c** creativity, the fourth type of creative outcome at the personal level, which is about *"the novel and personally meaningful interpretation of experiences, actions and events."*[15]

---

[14] Trnka, R., Zahradnik, M., and Kuška, M. (2016). Emotional Creativity and Real-life Involvement in Different Types of Creative Leisure Activities, Creativity Research Journal, Vol. 28, No. 3, pp. 348–356.

[15] Beghetto, R.A. and Kaufman, J.C., (2007), Toward a broader conception of creativity: A case for 'mini-c' creativity, Psychology of Aesthetics, Creativity and Arts, 1, pp. 13–79.

Mini-c creativity is about recognizing opportunities to improvise in different situations, such as conversations or playing music in the band, as John Bates describes.

"We were reading each other ... We were really tight as a band. That's an absolutely amazing feeling, like a high mind or something. The closest you get to mind melding with somebody that I know. That was an absolute blast, it felt very creative."

Mini-c creativity is about tuning in the present with the people around you and acting upon uninhibited remarks that release energy, joy, and inspiration to yourself and others. **Strengthening your mini-c creativity is the key to unlocking your creative drive** and increasing the chances of engaging with a new learning activity. This means you become an **active observer** of your impulses to create.

Have you recently been in a conversation when you thought to yourself, *"Yes, me too! Me too. I'd like to create something similar"*? What were the topics about?

- Tools

- Data

- Abstract ideas

- A group of people

Some years ago, I passed by the window of a book shop where I noticed the following announcement: *"Every Saturday at 1 pm, we organize a discussion group on spirituality for people from all walks of life"*. I surprised myself with the thought, *"Yes, me too! I'd like to create a group of my own on a topic of my choice."*

The more you notice the tendency to copy others' projects but to transform them into your unique initiatives, the more you create for yourself opportunities for **more knowledge and involvement in an area of interest.**

Narrative 4: Creativity Achieved

You may be one of the people who consciously exercised your creative thinking, skills, and interests for years. Now, you settled upon a creative aspiration which is the core of your professional identity. At this stage, most of the time, you **create on demand** when someone comes to you with a problem, and you provide the solutions.

"I think there is so much space and need and room for creativity that I didn't fully recognize before and didn't validate before, if you will," reflects Leadership Communication Expert John Bates. *"The creativity in what's the product? The creativity in how we market it. How do we tell people about it? The creativity in how we are going to provide customer service. The creativity in how are we going to structure this deal? How are we making a contract that keeps both sides happy to keep going? That's all creativity." (sic)*

In addition, established creators can adopt **a proactive attitude to creative action** by opening themselves up to secondary creative impulses, like initiative-taking in the case of the Finnish composer Matias Kupianen.

"Nowadays, it's a bit more difficult for a musician to have the income from doing just one thing. For me, playing the guitar is not paying my bills. I have to do many other things on top of it.

The music industry is changing drastically because of the internet and other stuff like that. You have to be creative in that kind of manner, you have to be able to get income from different kinds of sources."

Once the choice for a particular role as a creator is made, your relationship with your creativity continues to be shaped by interpersonal relationships and economic and societal events.

In this section, we uncovered ways to reframe our thinking on the mojo to develop creative potential at a professional level. The following section discusses three strategies to find new creative impulses in work contexts.

CHAPTER 5

Three Pathways to the Discovery of New Creative Impulses

At a particular stage in adulthood, the development of **personality traits**, **creative preferences, interests,** and **environmental influences** may realign to motivate us into a more harmonious integration of our potential to create with our work. For example, entrepreneur Harriet Fagerholm was in her 40s when she transitioned from her teaching position to entrepreneurship.

"I nourish the creative part of me," adds Harriet, who has a creative impulse of self-expression. *"Because I now know it gives me the most joy and freedom and meaning. Of course, I don't know what else could come out of my work. How much creativity can I express? I don't know what my limits are. My main teacher in conscious evolution, Barbara Marx Hurbbard, she expanded up until she was 88 and then she died."*

The more you create, the more versatile your creative potential as an entrepreneur, artist, scientist, leader, etc. So let's put on the **detective hat** and start tracing the **signs of creative impulses** in you, shall we?

© Oana Velcu-Laitinen 2022
O. Velcu-Laitinen, *How to Develop Your Creative Identity at Work,*
https://doi.org/10.1007/978-1-4842-8680-7_5

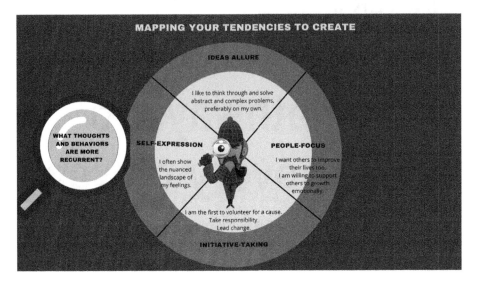

Figure 5-1. *Thoughts and Behaviours Associated with Creative Impulses*

Emotional Availability Is Not Only for Artists

Creativity continues to be understood chiefly as artistic creativity in societies.[1] For instance, The *Artist's Way*,[2] by Julia Cameron, is one of the most read books on discovering and recovering your creative self by strengthening the sense of identity as an artist – aspiring poet, writer, painter, dancer, etc. This art bias of creativity empowers people with self-expression impulses but can represent a mental block for non-artists. The implicit association of being creative with art immersions and artistic talent may lead many of us astray from embracing our personal creativity reflected in proclivity toward initiative-taking, people focus, or ideas allure.

---

[1] Glăveanu, V.P., (2014), Revisiting the "Art Bias" in Lay Conceptions of Creativity, Creativity Research Journal, 26:1, pp. 11–20, DOI: https://doi.org/10.1080/10400419.2014.873656

[2] www.amazon.com/Artists-Way-25th-Anniversary/dp/0143129252/ref=sr_1_1?crid=1VNZJSMXGNV6A&keywords=the+artist+way&qid=1649760543&s=books&sprefix=the+artist+way%2Cstripbooks-intl-ship%2C155&sr=1-1

"If I'm not mistaken, the words 'art' and 'artist' did not yet exist during and before the Renaissance," said M.C. Escher when he received the Culture Prize of the City of Hilversum on March 5, 1965.[3] *"Architects, sculptors, and painters at the time were simply considered practitioners of a craft."*

Yes, painters, musicians, fiction writers, architects, and designers are the artists among us. Yet, they are one community of creators among the more inclusive family of creators where we can find scientists, entrepreneurs, and niche experts. Non-artistic people can have creative personalities, like stubborn commitment, ambition, and impulsivity, except that different environmental factors cause them. Feist (2001) argued that natural selection pressures led to forms of creativity applied in technology, science, and engineering, while sexual selection influenced artistic creativity.[4] It is thus worth wondering. How can we open ourselves up and trust the creative impulses underlying non-artistic creativity?

How essential is it for experts in technology, science, and engineering to possess artistic skills for them to come up with original products and initiatives in their communities?

"Now I'm thinking very broadly and allowing these associations to come," says entrepreneur Harriet Fagerholm. *"Of course, creativity has to do with art. Creativity is also related to artistic expression. But it's not necessarily art per se. That's the outcome. But creativity can be about innovations, new thinking, whatever."*

When I asked composer Matias Kupiainen about other areas of life where he sees the outcomes of creativity, he replied:

---

[3] Escher, M.C., Ford, K., & Vermeulen, J.W., (1989), Escher on Escher: Exploring the Infinite, Harry N. Abrams, pp. 22.

[4] Feist, G.J., (2001), Natural and sexual selection in evolution of creativity. *Bulletin of Psychology and the Arts,* 2, pp. 11–16.

"I have a good example, this Chilean friend who had basically nothing when he came here to Helsinki. He rented a small 2x2 warehouse kind of thing and he was building pedals. Now he is running one of the biggest pedal industries in the whole world, 3.5 million net last year. He made it in less than ten years.

He had a clear vision of what he wanted and he executed it. It was in the long-term what he wanted to do. Does it have to do anything with creativity in this kind of case? Yes it has, you need to have a product and you need to be creative to do the actual product and you have to believe in your product.

You can't sell just nonsense. But when you have the product ready and have to sell it, then it's more like a business and technical approach again. And of course, you need to be lucky.

Product development is the creative, artistic process. Sure," concluded Matias.

What do artistic expression and process refer to? The artistic expression refers to the expression of emotion by works of art.[5] Artists contrive the emotional expressiveness of their works – say, love, sadness, nostalgia. The better the emotions are captured in the final work, the stronger the impact on the audience. Hence, artistic expression is a criterion for the quality of the creations in art, music, dances, and writing.

The artistic process is, in fact, the creative process when artists open up to their own emotions and allow their feelings to guide them in the implementation of their vision. Artistic expression and process may thus be terminologies recognized by artists as requirements for achievement. However, these are two concepts which other professionals, like sales engineer Oscar Santollala, may not identify themselves with.

Oscar thinks he developed his creativity at a good level of 7 on a scale of 0 to 10. Yet, he does not perceive that his main work activities require creativity.

---

[5] www.rep.routledge.com/articles/thematic/artistic-expression/v-1

"What are the activities you would label as creative activities?" I asked Oscar.

*"Everything that is **art**, it requires a lot of creativity,"* replied Oscar. *"Probably it's the field that requires [the] most creativity, but it's not only that. There are other fields. One is **advertising**. It's clear that you need a lot of creativity to do good advertising. The same, people remember only the good ones. Some are really extremely good but it requires a lot of work. Also, in music, writing. Also, if you pay attention to a speech, like a **politician's speech**, there is a lot of creativity to stand out. The majority of speeches are boring, people don't remember. But the ones that stand out have good creativity."*

To Oscar, creativity seems to be mainly associated with communication contexts in arts, advertising, and public speaking. He emphasizes that the most outstanding works are those where creators play with words, with order, and cadence so that people get emotional.

When you don't think of yourself as an artist, you risk inhibiting your creativity, which can be a unique blend of interest in an activity and emotional expressiveness. Hence, you may overlook impulses to create and miss out on original achievements.

Oscar may not think of himself as an artsy person, but he does recognize his creative potential in public speaking on the tech stage. And any other non-artistic creator can find their potential in a domain of interest where they can contribute with personal initiatives and incremental innovations.

Any field of expertise needs innovation. For the diffusion of innovation, the new products need to make an initial impression and a lasting impact on adopters. We could thus talk about the affective impact of original products on the target audience. And of equal significance, we can raise the importance for non-artistic creators to tap into their emotional abilities in order to come up with a significantly improved product or an innovative service.

Emotional ability refers to the capacity to think and reason about and with emotions during the creative process. It's true, the emotional expression and passion of artists is more evident in their works. In reality, all types of creative people, including scientists, engineers, leaders, and entrepreneurs, **need emotional ability and passion for their interest if they are to make a difference in their chosen domains.**[6]

How are emotions used and managed in the creative process? Professor Vincenzo Cerullo needs to create positive emotions that get his creative juices out when he prepares for a public talk. He describes how he generates emotions in himself by envisioning himself in front of the audience.

"I don't know where to put the emotion and I have been trying also to talk before the TEDx talk to other people who are supposed to be experts on creativity," says Vincenzo. *"I don't know where to put emotions, but I have to say, I think to me, it works very well to try to bring up emotion.*

Let's say that I will have a keynote lecture in the university, something big that they are arranging and I am going to give a lecture there. A way for me to come up with something original, nice or a way to get my creativity out a little bit is, if I put myself there. Preparing the lecture, I'm actually already physically there and I can already see the people, they are looking at me, I can see the attention (or tension). It's a positive emotion and I think that positive emotions give me the colour or the thing I want to see."

Sometimes, it can be that negative emotions such as frustration or boredom direct the attention and thinking toward problem-solving aspects of the environment. And then, cognitive flexibility helps us see familiar objects or information differently. For instance, Tulia's calling as a communication entrepreneur was initiated thanks to her ability to act upon her frustration with the format of the networking events that she started attending after she had moved to Zurich.

---

[6] Mayer, J.D., Roberts, R.D., and Barsade, S.G., (2008), Human abilities: Emotional intelligence, Annual Review of Psychology, 59(1), pp. 507–536.
Ivcevic Z. and Hoffmann J., (2019), Emotions and Creativity, The Cambridge Handbook of Creativity, pp. 273–205.

"So when I got to these events in Zurich, there was one thing that I noticed. They had a format, a typical networking event. There's the speaker, usually a woman, with the topic, they come, they present it, there was usually a nice dinner and that was it. And I felt many times when the speaker, the presenter had a nice topic, something interesting that I wanted to talk to the person afterwards.

I felt there was a huge gap and I started observing that this was happening in several different events. There was the speaker, the expert was there and you, the audience, you're there, so there was not a bridge. And that bothered me, because I felt like, well, if you come and you deliver something, the people enjoyed it, people of course want to talk to you. And if you leave, this is kind of half done work."

The new direction in Tulia's entrepreneurship started from her desire to create a different speaker-audience connection.

"So long story short, this became my signature event, the Awe Summit which I've been doing since 2014, I did it in Zurich four times, then we went to Barcelona twice and we went to Porto in Portugal once and I want to do it in Munich, next year, let's see."

Yes, artists need artistic expression. But creators from all walks of professional lives must recognize three ways of working with their emotions (see Figure 5-2).

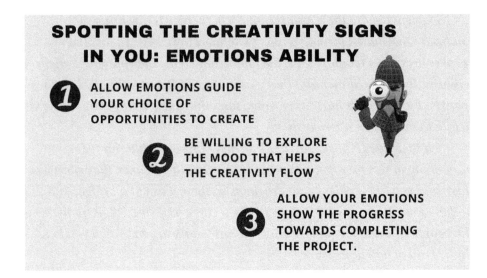

Figure 5-2. *Emotions ability*

First, they need to understand how their **emotions** represent **signals** about novel opportunities to create. For example, feeling positively challenged can be a good sign to take up a new project different from anything you have experienced.

Second, they need to recognize **which emotions** (i.e., happiness, fear, or anger) to activate to manage their **creativity flow** once the creative process is initiated. For instance, positive emotions can increase cognitive flexibility – the ease of switching between different ideas. But on the other hand, negative emotions can enhance perseverance in coming to a solution.

Third, they need to understand how their **emotions** represent cues about the **effort** required to **achieve an outcome**. Positive moods indicate that a new milestone in completing the goal is about to be reached. Negative moods signal that more action is needed toward reaching the next milestone.

In sum, it is not necessary to think of yourself as an artist when you aspire to contribute to the fields of science, technology, engineering, entrepreneurship, etc. However, you do have to understand your emotions and their contribution to the selection and quality of your creative process.

Disrupt Your Patterns of Curiosities

My high school math teacher liked one of my classroom habits in particular. He said I'd often ask, **"Why?"** Depending on our specific motivational, cognitive and neurobiological processes, we are all curious in our unique ways, in what we choose to learn and how we manage everyday contexts. Notably, creative people are curious people, which is reflected in their creative achievements, personality, and professions.

There are curiosities and curiosities. Think of the following imaginary action: you go uninvited to your neighbor's home as soon as they have just received the delivery of a new piece of furniture. This behavior can be motivated by the **nosiness type of curiosity**, rooted in states of boredom caused by mundane information gaps. Yet, this is not the curiosity we talk about in this book.[7]

There is a second type of curiosity, which arises from the need to grow and learn. The itch to understand the work of a person whom you think highly of. The joy of learning new topics, in new areas than the ones you're competent in. The courage of accepting new projects knowing that you'll have the opportunity to know yourself better, your time management skills at the very least. These are **creative curiosities** which steer onwards the learning cycles.

---

[7] Silvia, P.J., (2012). Curiosity and Motivation, The Oxford Handbook of Human Motivation, Edited by Richard M. Ryan, pp. 157–166.
 Litman, J. A. (2005). Curiosity and the pleasures of learning: Wanting and liking new information. Cognition and Emotion, 19, pp. 793–814.

Researchers start to understand that there's a nuanced reality about how creative people can manifest curiosity.[8] Some creative individuals can display high degrees of openness to the world, like Tulia Lopes's inclination toward new social experiences.

"As I was growing up in my teens it was a very difficult time. It was when my creativity was very very high and I wanted to explore things. … It doesn't matter if people tell you, 'Oh this is not going to work,' 'You should not do this.' But if you feel a certain kind of attraction towards something, you have to try."

In adulthood, she continues to be curious and **receptive to sensory inputs**.

"Everything shines and I feel like sometimes I'm like a child and my husband says to me I don't only look at things, I have to touch them, and sometimes I have to smell them. I'm very touchy."

The need to know and understand drives other creative people. For people like Vincenzo Cerullo, a professor of immunology who researches new cancer vaccines, the tendency to experiment reflects his curiosity.

"Of course creativity has helped me a lot. I like to explore ideas..." says Vincenzo. *"Actually very recently I remembered that once when I was 6, I was in my father's pharmacy and my plan was to generate sulfhydric acid to make a hole in the floor so that I could have access to a toy store, which was underneath our house. I thought it was a very creative thing for a 6-year-old boy. I didn't succeed but still, many other things are like this."*

---

[8] Kaufman, S.B., Quilty, L.C., Grazioplene, R.G., Hirsch, J.B., Gray, J.R., Peterson, J.B., and DeYoung, C.G., (2016), Openness to experience and intellect differentially predict creative achievement in the arts and sciences, Journal of Personality, Vol. 84, Issue 2, pp. 248–258.

Hughes, D.J., Furnham, A., and Batey, M., (2013), The structure and personality predictors of self-rated creativity, Thinking Skills and Creativity, Vol. 9, pp. 76–84; www.researchgate.net/publication/233795671_The_structure_and_personality_predictors_of_self-rated_creativity

DeYoung, C.G., Quilty, L.C., and Peterson, J.B. (2007). Between facets and domains: The aspects of the Big Five. Journal of Personality and Social Psychology, 93, pp. 880–896.

When you deliberate on a conceptual problem, the frustration of not having all the information motivates you to try to arrive at a solution. I used to ask *"Why"* during my math classes because I was sincerely interested in understanding the reasoning behind the solutions. In the same way as it feels good when listening to a favorite melody, there was a sense of accomplishment when all the pieces of information fell in the right place.

Considering the professional experiences accumulated over the years, each one of us might have grown aware of **the curiosities that are useful in driving our professional achievements**. Creative people with backgrounds in the arts are more likely to be willing to live through their bodies and explore sensory experiences. Creative scientists are more likely to live in their heads and be driven by intellectual curiosities. Also, the rest of us who perform in professional roles unrelated to arts or science, we are a mix of the aforementioned **patterns of curiosity**.

The first pattern is made up of emotions and sensations that originate from **new experiences,** like social interactions or physical places.[9] To the extent that you see beauty in the smell of the coffee in the morning, feel the need of a creative outlet, or like to muse on what happens to you, you may have a propensity to explore the environment through senses and intuition.

The second pattern is made up of **the new ideas** of improvement and innovation, which you see everywhere, even when you go on vacation.

Throughout the college years in Newnham, Cambridge, Cecilia Payne studied, driven by the desire to be a teacher and share with others the joy of scientific learning. In 1917, when she was about to graduate, she happened to read a newly published book, *The compleat schoolmarm:*

---

[9] Batey, M., and Hughes, D.J., (2017), Individual Difference Correlates of Self-Perceptions of Creativity, Explorations in Creativity Research, pp. 185–218.

a story of promise and fulfillment, by Helen Hamilton.[10] This volume of satirical verse about women's education, small-minded jealousies, and limited career possibilities made Cecilia feel that life as a teacher was *"a fate worse than death."*[11] Her fate was decided when she understood that her interest was in research and not in teaching science.

Each one of us may have more creative curiosities than the ones we are currently aware of. To push the boundaries of curiosity, we look into **three possible sources that may trigger an unexpected impulse to create**: childhood activities, new colleagues, and the less used senses.

Childhood Activities

You may have lost your childhood but not your curiosities. What kind of a child were you? The youngster who enjoyed dancing and singing at family gatherings? The kiddo who was content being solitary and reading books? The child who was the most popular among peers? What were the subjects that made you ask *Why*? Can you search for possibilities in the present life circumstances that are a replacement of the respective pastimes.

Writing seems to be the activity through which I express different curiosities at different stages. As a 14-year-old, I funneled my fantasy into short stories and poems. In my mid-20s, I wrote academic papers that described the use of information systems in companies. In parallel, I joined a writers' group of folks of different ages and professional experiences who would meet weekly to write poetry and fiction. And now, in my early 40s, I am writing this book.

---

[10] www.amazon.com/compleat-schoolmarm-story-promise-fulfilment/dp/B0041N3XB0

[11] Cecilia Payne-Gaposchkin et al., (1996), An Autobiography and Other Recollections, Cambridge University Press, 2nd edition, Edited by Katherine Haramundanis, pp.124.

What was the childhood activity that struck your fancy? Revamping the respective experience requires you to know about the suitable communities of practice in town. What might be the ones you'd like to visit?

Step Outside the Professional Sphere

Open up to new social interactions even if you may have some reservations.

"I always had my nose looking down at business because you know, everybody is just money grabbing," says Leadership Communication Expert John Bates. *"I had no idea until I tried it myself how absolutely creative and fun and interesting business is. It is one of the ultimate creative acts."*

John overcame his negative bias against business activities. However, you may also hold some unfavorable beliefs about a few other professions. For instance, in a large organization, there are specific jobs like "business development," "sales," "accountant," "human resource," "assistant," etc., that can carry unconscious prejudices in the eyes of other experts.

Such biases can affect the quality of interactions and the openness to socializing with others with less valued roles. For example, accountants are boring and introverted, right? What if you met an accountant with a cool hobby that, by comparison, it makes you feel you have a dull life?

Let's do an exercise, shall we? First, think of a job role directly connected with what you do in your company. Now think of a job role that is remotely connected with what you do.

If you are to have lunch with one of these persons, whom and why would you invite?

What if you made time for a **curiosity lunch** in your schedule for people in both roles? Assuming your invitations get confirmed, you have the chance to get closer to new areas of specialization through a person that you may not otherwise meet. Maybe your empathy will awaken before your curiosity. Opening up to the taste of empathy is a valuable driver in connecting with interesting people who may be a source for new ideas, in the form of continued learning, for example.

How about making a list of five expertise roles you hold in high regard within or outside your company? And a list of five expertise roles you have a terrible opinion about?

What if, twice per month, you made time for a **curiosity lunch** in your schedule for both types of professionals?

Use More of the Less Used Senses

What do you use most in your current professional role: your head or your senses? If the former, choose one of the four senses – visual, sounds, taste, and touch – to direct you to learn a new skill. If the latter, choose another sense or, even more daring, get interested in an area of knowledge you hardly know anything about.

There is so much more under the sun to see and experience. What if a photographer falls head over heels with the neuroscience of emotions? What if a scientist got intrigued by an acting course? In light of these curiosities, what would change in how they handle their core tasks? What disruptive activities would there be room for?

To sum up, you might want to unearth your preferred childhood activities to discover your impulses to create. Seek new interactions with colleagues, especially those in roles you initially think little of. Say yes to the less used senses or the intellect. (See Figure 5-3.)

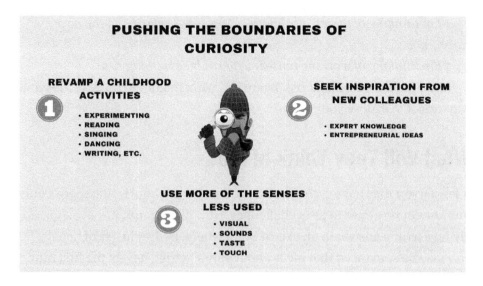

Figure 5-3. *Sources of curiosities*

Take the Risk to Invest Time in Disruptive Activities

"So, when I made the decision to become an entrepreneur, to leave my safe position at school, my salary, and all those benefits, I jumped into nothing but trust in my own self," says entrepreneur Harriet Fagerholm. *"And I must say it hasn't been an easy journey, not at all. Because I faced all my limitations. I had to find the trust in my own creativity. ..."*

Before committing to a new role as a professional creator, there are many moments of micro-decisions to do activities that disrupt your life. For example, let's assume that you announce your life partner something along these lines:

"I took on a freelancing project in addition to my work. It will keep me busy on the weekends."

"I'm thinking of taking a sabbatical to get more clarity on the next career move."

"I'm thinking of working part-time to study something new."

Creators are emotional risk-bearers.[12] What might be the risks that you can expect to expose yourself to?

What Will They Think of Me?

A legacy you may have gotten and forgotten from school is that there's only one correct response to life's challenges. How many times have you feared giving a wrong answer in an exam? Somewhere, in the cluster of beliefs, you may be convinced that life is about either getting it right the first time or being punished for the rest of your life.

My youngest son is nowadays learning to play the trumpet. His band took part in a concert in the pop & jazz conservatorium he attends. During one of the songs, he had two moments when he started playing a few seconds before the rest of the band members. On both occasions, he did get his act together and continued to play as he had rehearsed. But after the concert, he had a mental breakdown. *"Everybody thinks I am an idiot,"* he said, and cried for an hour. Can you think of a time when you had a similar experience?

You are a novice at performing an activity, and you share what you learned with an audience. This is the first challenging emotional risk for a creative person. Luckily for my son, his teacher came to talk with him. She said, *"Would you like to know how many mistakes I made when I played in the latest concert?"* He nodded, and she whispered into his ear.

"What will they think of me?" is the painful and frequent question for a person who takes up new curiosities. Mistakes will inadvertently happen even when you become an acknowledged creator. The faster you learn how

---

[12] Nicholson, N., et al. (2005), Personality and domain-specific risk taking. Journal of Risk Research, 8(2), pp. 157–176.

to live with yourself each time you feel you failed, the less mental baggage to drag in the following creative process. I like to think of mistakes as tests of how much you care to turn a new skill into a master skill.

When to Expect That Your Actions Will Get the Validation of Your Loved Ones

Who doesn't want to feel safe, sound, and accepted by those you care about? But, doing something more rebellious, breaking the mold, as photographer Dasha Pears would put it, may shake up some of the relationships with loved ones. For example, when you tell your partner, *"Honey, I won't be home for the next two weekends. I'll go study at the local library,"* to your partner's ears, it may sound more like, *"Honey, I'm going to travel to Mars in the next two weekends."*

You may wish to have a magic trick of persuasion to convince everyone around you on the spot. The most important question is if you validate your mini-decisions to acquire knowledge in a new area. In time, as you share the joys and sorrows of your discoveries with the close ones, they'll come round to grant their support. Especially when they see you succeed.

Balance Your Long-Term Personal Benefits with Others' Short-Term Benefits

What are the essential activities that you do? What are the urgent ones? What is the time ratio of essential/urgent activities you do in a day? 50/50? 40/60? 60/40?

Answering these questions will enable you to organize a daily structure of activities with a more careful balance between long-term personal benefits and others' immediate benefits, between saying **"Yes, I can help with that."** and **"No, this is not a good time for me."** To gain a more profound understanding of your impulses to create, you may want to make room for the important but not urgent activities, which are the disruptive activities you're interested in.[13]

"I really ask myself, when opportunities come up, 'Is this going to be really where I want to put my energies now?'", says consultant and coach Pamela Thompson. *"I'm really conscious at this point in my life to create space, because what I've found, Oana, is in order for creativity to be fostered, we need space, we can't be busy, busy, busy, programmed up all the time.*

... And this recent opportunity really made me sit back and think, 'What's my priority right here?' And you know, there were challenges with it, that's a challenge to let go of that old pattern."

When you recognize the potential of a new activity to make the difference you hope to see inside and around yourself, you need to say "Yes" to the opportunity. Admittedly, saying "No" to projects that are no longer part of who you want to be, it means losing income streams in the present. Saying "Yes," they take time away from skills you can develop in the long run. More money in the present or a content creator in the future? Which one shall it be?

The Goal Is the Internal Shift

Some of the new projects will result in the expected external impact but not in the internal shift toward the creator that you are. Such projects are the experimental creations we volunteer to experience in search of the harmonious blend between the tendencies of self-expression, people-focus, initiative-taking, and ideas allure. This mix defines the creator in you.

---

[13] Sternberg R.J. et al., (2019), The Relation of Creativity to Intelligence and Wisdom, The Cambridge Handbook of Creativity, pp. 337–352.

Therefore, the fourth risk is to dedicate the time to experimental creations that bring you closer to the feeling of being an engaged creator. With each project, you get more information to reassess what you can create and who is the particular audience you address, as witnessed by Pamela Thompson, in whom there's a balance between the people-focus and self-expression orientations.

"Recently I was asked to contribute to an initiative. That's someone whose work I value. She approached me to be part of a new platform that she's developing and to submit master classes on an ongoing basis, and be part of that community. I had to sort of really sit back and say 'How much of my time is this going to consume?' And I had to think 'Is this really the target, my primary target market right now?' I found within the last 6-8 months I really changed my target market to be heart centred leaders and changemakers and helping them embrace change."

And that's why the time spent on experimental creations is worth it. The process will reveal unimagined insights about your role or your audience.

"Creativity also means that you are active, you are not passive," muses entrepreneur Harriet Fagerholm. *"You're an actor. At the most, you realise that* **'I am a creator.'** *Therefore, when I want to inspire people to get in contact with the creator in them, I ask, 'What do you want to create? What are you creating now?'*

We are creating all the time. But the question is, are we consciously doing it or are we unconscious about what we are creating?"

To what extent are you ready to assume the risk for a new experimental creation?

- On a scale of 1 (not at all) to 5 (extremely), how **confident** are you of the existence of a problem in the environment and to which you can bring your perspective?

- On a scale of 1 (it can wait) to 5 (top priority), how **eager** are you to address the respective problem?

- On a scale of 1 (not at all) to 5 (ready), how **willing** are you to overcome the ambiguity of figuring out the solutions?

To conclude, the decision to enact a new role as a creator does not happen miraculously. Instead, it is preceded by a series of mini-decisions about:

- Spending enough time on a new activity to turn it into mastery, despite the mistakes along the way.

- Standing up in front of your loved ones for what you believe is good for you.

- Carefully guarding your long-term interests versus short-term monetary rewards.

- Maintaining the dialogue with the creator inside you.

CHAPTER 6

Toward the Workspaces Where New Curiosities Take You

The environment is where we all meet; where all have a mutual interest; it is the one thing all of us share.

—Lady Bird Johnson

So far, we've been like detectives following strategies to uncover creative impulses and think again about what kind of a creator you are. Now we turn the attention toward the types of environments where your creative orientations can be fostered. Let's assume you become aware of an unexpected curiosity toward self-expression, people well-being, conceptual problems, or societal challenges. How can you recognize the institutional settings where you could consolidate your knowledge and practice the new skills?

© Oana Velcu-Laitinen 2022
O. Velcu-Laitinen, *How to Develop Your Creative Identity at Work*,
https://doi.org/10.1007/978-1-4842-8680-7_6

John Holland developed one of the most researched and applied theories for career decision-making.[1] Starting from the premise that personality factors affect professional choices, the theory predicts that the higher the harmony between the individual aptitudes and work characteristics, the higher the achievement, persistence, and satisfaction in work. As a result, there can be six areas of match: realistic (R), investigative (I), artistic (A), social (S), enterprising (E), or conventional (C) environments.

Let's have a quick game. Which of the following activities do you relate to most (think more in terms of what activity would suit you and not what you are good at): "promote a product," "fix a computer," "prepare the budget for a new project," "take a human resources course," "develop a product," or "play in a band."[2] To what extent does it fit in your current role? The lesser the fit, the higher the need to look for the role that accommodates your creativity.

Engineering jobs belong to realistic careers. Investigative occupations are based on interests such as biology, mathematics, philosophy, psychiatry, and physics. Artistic jobs include actors, designers of all sorts – interior, graphic, fashion – and journalists. We find coaches, consultants,

---

[1] Holland, J.L., (1997), Making Vocational choices: A theory of vocational personalities and work environments, (3rd ed.). Psychological Assessment Resources. https://psycnet.apa.org/record/1997-08980-000

Bullock-Yowell, E., Leuty, M., To, Y.M., and Mathis, E., (2015), Self-Directed Search Response Project, Journal of Career Assessment, 25 (2), pp. 1–16. www.research-gate.net/profile/Melanie-Leuty/publication/291016202_Self-Directed_Search_Response_Project/links/5beb43ce299bf1124fd0e33f/Self-Directed-Search-Response-Project.pdf

Sheldon, K.M., Holliday. G., Titova, L., and Benson, C., (2020), Comparing Holland and Self-Determination Theory Measures of Career Preference as Predictors of Career Choice, Journal of Career Assessment, Vol. 28 (1), pp. 28–42. https://journals.sagepub.com/doi/pdf/10.1177/1069072718823003

[2] "promote a product" (E), "fix a computer" (R), "prepare the budget for a new project" (C), "take a human relationships course" (S), "develop a product" (I), "play in a band" (A)

managers, psychologists, and teachers among social professions. Business owners, leaders, investors, and salespersons are the enterprising ones. And the sixth and last category, conventional roles include accountants, financial analysts, and statisticians.

Over time, these occupations develop a habitual way of thinking, main skills of competence, and a set of beliefs you keep subscribing to. A new creative curiosity will bring you to the situation when you can ask yourself, *"What if I can become someone I never envisioned?"* and *"How can I create the opportunities to test new skills?"* The more disruptive a new curiosity, the more important it is to try new related roles on a smaller scale before commitment to a different path as a creator.

The awakening of an impulse to create offers you the chance to combine old and new skills and navigate new types of work environments. Each trial can reveal a surprising activity preference of your evolving creative self.

> ➢ You may become aware of an interest to *solve problems* related to the *functioning of manufactured objects* – computers, information systems, infrastructure – or the *preservation of things in nature* – such as plants, animals, oceans, etc.

An interest in any of these two aspects of reality can push you toward *Realistic environments* (R), where *technical skills* are required to solve concrete rather than abstract situations. You turn into a Fix-it Felix, one of the Disney protagonists in the Wreck-it Ralph movie. With his magic hammer, Felix can fix any damage in the Niceland building. Your technical skills are your hammer. The Niceland building is the space where you find the problems to solve with your hammer.[3]

---

[3] https://disney.fandom.com/wiki/Fix-It_Felix_Jr.

As a Fix-it-Felix type of expert, you rely on analytical thinking. Moreover, you'll face problems you haven't dealt with before and where deep-rooted thinking and methods do not suffice.[4] So, in addition to the technical skills, you can choose to develop *creative problem-solving skills,* as sales engineer Oscar Santolalla describes.

"One skill that comes from my studies, because I studied engineering in the beginning, is problem-solving. That helped me to become more proficient in technical aspects, learn new things, get interested in new things and be able to serve in different companies both in Peru and here in Finland. Until today, problem-solving is a big part of my day job."

Oscar is the person to go to if you want to learn more about Digital Identity, that is, the traces you leave online. Therefore, to test your creativity in solving maintenance problems in realistic environments, identify the first Niceland building and its people for whom you become the go-to expert.

> ➤ A renewed preference for abstract thinking and conceptual problems will direct your focus on *problem-finding,* which takes you to *Investigative environments* (I). Creators, such as professors Vincenzo Cerullo and Helder Santos, who take the challenge of scientific breakthroughs, are found in such environments. Their jobs are not only to solve health care problems but also to discover the problems that are worth the time and money to dig into. Herein, the development of *innovative research skills* is essential.

At the same time, creative minds in investigative environments have a penchant for *philosophical thinking,* parsing arguments for fundamental

---

[4] Puccio, G. and Cabra J., (2009), Creative problem solving: past, present and future, The Routledge Companion to Creativity, pp. 327–336.
Puccio, G., (1999) Creative Problem Solving Preferences: Their Identification and Implications, Creativity and Innovation Management, Vol. 8, Issue 3, pp. 171–178.

truths based on metaphysics, epistemology, or axiology. What is reality? Do we have free will? How are personal values formed and influenced? This type of thinking will turn you into a trendsetter and take you to innovative contexts.

To get started with direct experiences in an investigative environment, in the same way as some people go to the gym, you can join discussion groups in the area where you intuit there is so much more to discover.

> ➢ When you give in to your self-expression tendency, you engage in the exercise of a specific artistic skill (A). You perform in your first acting role. You compose a tune. You edit your first conceptual photo. The choice of audience is equally important as the skill to practice.

"Now, art is very closely connected with marketing, as well," says surrealism artist Dasha Pears. *"Business is an art form in itself, so in order to be successful and influential as an artist, in order to move people with your art and make an impact, a person often has to be a clever and inventive entrepreneur."*

Engaging in an artistic skill enables the option to mingle the artistic interest with enterprising, realistic, or investigative environments. The primary environment is the space where you create. The complementary milieu is the space of sharing what you create. The former provides freedom of expression, and the latter comes with constraints. The interaction between these two environments is the viable space for testing a new identity as an artist.

> ➢ You may discover *an interest in people,* which takes you to *social environments* (S). As a result, you turn into a people fixer. This tendency requires the ability to make others feel psychologically safe around you. Besides, it inspires you to improve your *communication skills* to cure, develop, or educate people.

Most often, the interest in promoting others' well-being is complemented by self-expression, as mirrored in Pamela Thompson and Harriet Fagerholm's entrepreneurial activities.

"...I help changemakers to embrace change through coaching and experiential workshops on what I call, 'The Art of Change,'" says Pamela.

"I use movement, painting, writing, singing, and sound," says Harriet. *"All these are expressions of that so you can get to know the creative impulse. Now, my latest projects have been to unleash creativity in individuals, which has been quite an amazing journey to see a person, after the age of 50, starting to bloom with art, for example."*

Creators who are a good fit here are the kind of folks who shape the world around them through their ability of connection, empathy, and compassion. Does this sound like you?

> ➢ To the extent that you get *tempted to take the lead,* you may become interested in problems pertaining to *enterprising environments* (E). Here, we find resourceful doers such as John Bates, Tulia Lopes, and Peter Ivanov, who support others in their missions. *Niche skills* in the form of soft skills (emotional intelligence competencies) or hard skills (machine learning, data visualization, TypeScript or Kotlin programming, etc.) will be the product you sell. In addition, *persuasion skills* will come in handy to guide others toward your personal goals. Step by step, each entrepreneurial project strengthens your inclination to look at the world through the lenses of responsibility, status, and power.

> ➢ We add *the spiritual environment(s)* to the five dimensions mentioned earlier. Here, we have creative people who rely on their self-expression and are motivated to strengthen the connection with a higher and invisible force – God or the Universe. These creators

can be spiritual gurus, meditation teachers, priests, or life coaches with *deeper awareness and wisdom*. Harriet Fagerholm's activities hinge on this dimension.

All in all, the adapted Holland's model helps us evaluate the compatibility between a dominant creative tendency and new types of work environments where it can be tested (see Figure 6-1).

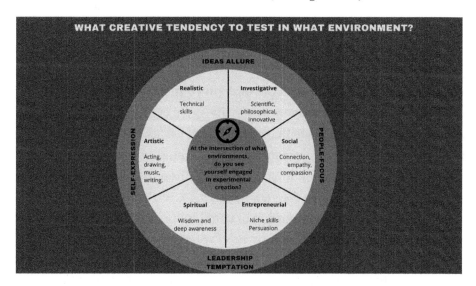

Figure 6-1. *Intersections of environments to create*

What are the RIASEs environments that you have directly experienced so far? It's imperative to dare to craft experiments in less familiar settings. Before committing to a specific creative interest, you are like the director of a theater play, artfully choosing the stage and planning the details of the scenes for the utmost impact on the crowd. Furthermore, you may benefit from orchestrating a couple of plays on the same or different stages before settling on the genre that makes your best potential shine through. Along the way, you'll learn to identify the environments where you can balance what is personally meaningful and feasible to create.

The second part discusses self-disruption habits for developing a creative identity.

Summary of Part 1

This part of the book helps you reflect on why you understand your creativity the way you do and what exploration habits you can form to develop your creative potential. Self-perceived creativity is the awareness of creative skills, interests and physical/virtual spaces that enable you to create new or original products. Underneath your current understanding of personal creativity, there are two fundamental levels of creative awareness. You can see your creativity as a strength or central part of your identity.

When you see your creativity as a generator of ideas, you can choose to speak out about your ideas more often in your current role or some side projects. When you see your creativity at the center of your being, you become motivated to engage in more disruptive activities that position you as an aspiring creator in a domain of interest. Yet, should creativity define you but you have not yet found your passion, observing your impulses to create could help you close the gap.

Your potential can be grounded in your ability to sense and express intense emotions – yours or others – or in your prowess to notice exciting problems to solve in the external environment. To gain clarity, you can develop new habits of exploration of the dormant creative impulses, as follows:

- Recognize what emotions, such as frustration, boredom, or despair, can indicate an experimental creation.

- Discover new patterns of curiosities.

- Establish external and internal success criteria to decide if an experimental project suits the kind of creator you are willing to become.

These new habits of self-exploration pave the way to a deeper level of creative awareness.

For astronomer Cecilia Payne, the new stage as a researcher was marked when she decided to make a list of research problems that she wanted to investigate. What might be the event that triggers a new cycle for your evolving creative self?

- The course that teaches you stage presence

- The start-up idea that needs to be pitched

- The journal that opens the call for papers

- The professional community that welcomes new members

- The colleague who asks for your support to solve a dilemma

Any of these opportunities can be your chance to tap into a new creative drive. And they can be right under your nose.

Self-Exploration Exercises: Orienting Yourself to the Next Stage of Creative Self-Development

Exercise 1: Map the Experiences That Give You a Sense of Meaning

What activities would you be ready to try in your free time even if, for the time being, you may not be highly competent to perform the respective activity? Kindly assign a number to each activity in the order of personal meaning:

- Playing a musical instrument

- Acting

- Painting

- Writing poems

- Writing short stories

- Writing a factual article about
    - History
    - Economy
    - Society
    - A field of science _____
    - Something else _____
- Inventing something _____
- Programming a website from scratch
- Designing your own clothes
- Having a speech in front of an audience about _____
- Preserving local traditions and rituals _____
- Initiating improvement in a small community of _____
- Working alone on a new project about _____
- Working in a new group of experts on _____

Exercise 2: New Possible Roles

At this stage of my career, I'm daydreaming about new experiences related to one of the following roles:

- Artist
- Activist
- Coach
- Entrepreneur
- Environmentalist
- Leader

- Manager

- Psychologist

- Researcher

- Scientist

- Something else _____

Exercise 3: Creative Career Aspirations

Considering the role you chose in Exercise 2, how does it match the activities selected in Exercise 1? To which of the following three career strategies does the fit belong?

- Career change to the role as a creative expert

  _____

- Career development to a higher position of _____

- Professional change to freelancers _____ or entrepreneurship _____

Food for Thought

What could be the next step to match the experiences that give you a sense of meaning and the new possible role in your creative career path?

Disclaimer: These exercises are meant to be an eye-opener of your work orientation toward emotional creativity or practical creativity. Yet, they should be taken with a grain of salt. The best way to develop a harmonious sense of personal and work creativity is to keep experimenting with your impulses to create.

PART II

Learn to Live Like a Creator

CHAPTER 7

Allow Your Tiny Genius to Roam Outside Your Comfort Zone

What is genius? Most often, genius makes us think of people of superior intelligence who radically transformed the domains where they contributed and, as a result, enabled technological, economic, and societal advancements. But it hasn't always been this understanding. In ancient Roman mythology, every man and woman was born with a unique genius, which, for men, took the form of a guardian angel following him from birth to death. The genius of women had the form of Juno, an ancient Roman goddess.[1] After the Renaissance, the meaning of genius became more exclusive, with only a few people showing genius in their original and exclusive work.

---

[1] `www.britannica.com/topic/Juno-Roman-goddess`
Simonton, D.K., (2012), The Science of Genius, Scientific American Mind, November/December Special Issue, pp. 35–41.
Simonton, D.K., (2021). Giftedness, Talent, and Genius: Untangling Conceptual Confusions. In: Sternberg, R.J., Ambrose, D. (eds) Conceptions of Giftedness and Talent. Palgrave Macmillan, Cham, pp. 393-406. `https://doi.org/10.1007/978-3-030-56869-6_22`

© Oana Velcu-Laitinen 2022
O. Velcu-Laitinen, *How to Develop Your Creative Identity at Work*,
https://doi.org/10.1007/978-1-4842-8680-7_7

Here, we'll adapt the ancient Roman thinking to consider **the tiny genius as the source of possible creative thinking inclinations with which you are born.** I was a teenager when my mother bought this trinket and placed it on the bookshelf in our living room.

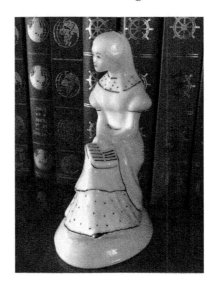

I identified with it as soon as I laid my eyes on it. The book in the girl's lap became the objectification of my tiny genius. If you look around you, what are the objects or symbols that express your tiny genius? The problem is that your tiny genius may be hiding in plain sight, which brings us to the next two questions. What is luck, and what does it have to do with your genius?

On a scale of 1 (not at all) to 5 (born under a lucky star), how lucky do you think you are? Do you believe luck is a random coincidence in some people's lives and brings positive, desired, or unexpected consequences? Or can luck be encouraged through personal initiative, exploration, and careful observation? In the first case, there is an implied laissez-faire attitude. You manage your day-to-day, diligently following your routine. And one day, luck will step in your way – if it's meant to step in. Yet, that's not how Harriet Fagerholm got to engage in her entrepreneurial activities.

Since young adulthood, she has had the curiosity to go to places that tested her sense of familiarity.

Harriet, a woman in her late 40s, has been an entrepreneur for the last ten years, exploring co-creation and supporting people in releasing their creative capacity. She does a kind of work that calls for her and is appreciated for. How about the previous times when she was doing something different as a senior lecturer at a university of applied sciences? Was she blessed with auspicious events at that career stage? To increase the odds of being fortunate to meet your genius, you may want to **step outside the comfort zone**, as Harriet did a few times in her adulthood.

"The most profound experience that has made me who I am today is through the international organization called AIESEC," says Harriet. *"I spent half of a year in Indonesia. I lived with two Indonesian families. I worked with students at university and I had a traineeship in a department store where they barely spoke English.*

I had this immense cultural experience of seeing a completely different world view. Seeing a society that was so spiritual and working with themselves from a spiritual perspective and with those close collective family ties. So, it kind of shook my existence in a way that I'm still reflecting on."

Harriet's fascination with Indonesian family culture resulted in her decision to write a Master's Thesis on cultural differences when she returned to Finland.

"And there I got the understanding of how we are actually creating the invisible environment around us," continued Harriet. *"So, it's through our underlying belief systems and values. They are the ones deciding why our educational or religious system or social system looks the way they look. Or why does the economy look the way it looks? What are those values? So, I mapped it up."*

The first time I saw Harriet, she was on a stage addressing an audience of about 200 people. She was barefoot. It felt as if everyone were sitting around her kitchen table, having a morning coffee. She told how at one step during her reinvention, she organized independent shows where she performed dialogues with the shadow, the parts of ourselves that we feel ashamed of. She's not a trained actress, clinical psychologist, or script writer. Yet, she works with herself to take the liberty to implement the creative ideas that she fancies.

It can be that you have not yet been in the right time and place where you meet your genius, your affinity towards domains of creation. It can be that you got the chance to discover it but are struggling to develop it. Either way, show your luck that you are ready to catch it by **opening up to new people and communities.** You can invite meaningful coincidences in your life by **frequently learning skills,** which are a **compromise between functional and appealing interests** under your existing life circumstances.

What have you learned in the last six months that your leading role does not require it, but you freely chose to learn? From one competence to the next, you'll come across the following happy coincidence, which will mobilize the genius in you. There can be three spaces outside the comfort zone where you could meet your luck: (1) when you meet people from different professions, (2) when you meet experts from the same profession but who work in other institutions, and (3) when you meet folks from cultural backgrounds that are not so close to your culture. When was the last time you met a new person and asked yourself, *"What is there for me to learn from this person?"* instead of, *"I'll show this person what I know"*? Provided you're willing to let yourself be influenced, direct and frequent contacts with individuals from other cultural and professional backgrounds can change your perspective on what you know and inspire creative action.

Of course, serendipity is undeniable when you are at the right time and place to discover an unexpectedly strong interest. In fact, serendipity reveals to you what you've been missing all the time, your area of creation. For me, it happened when I read a blog post about the habits of highly creative people, which then led me to the book Wired to Create.[2] Like a kid in a toy store, I thought creativity was the most interesting topic I had ever encountered. However, luck needs to be backed by purposeful action if you are to nurture your tiny genius[3]. As a creator, you must try out different creative interests before settling on the one for which you want others' validation. Consequently, there can be three psychological milestones in transitioning from a prospective to an established creator:

1) When a chance encounter **awakens your tiny genius**

2) The decision to **implement your first call to create**

3) The **commitment to your creative focus** and the role for which you desire recognition

The girl with the book on her lap continues to be on the bookshelf in my parents' living room. Yet, the part of it that became alive in me has roamed outside the borders of my hometown and country. Are you also prepared to search for and recognize the surprising things you didn't know you were looking for?

The world needs the sparkles of all genius minds, big and small, yours certainly. Einstein once said, *"If we knew what we were doing, we wouldn't call it research."* If we knew what our tiny geniuses could do, we would have already lived our lives. Meanwhile, all we can do is develop a lifestyle that empowers our geniuses to reach the three milestones of becoming a creator. Let's have a detailed look.

---

[2] www.huffpost.com/entry/highly-creative-people_n_56313441e4b063 179910bd4e
www.amazon.com/gp/product/0399174109/ref=as_li_tl?ie=UTF8&camp=1789&c reative=390957&creativeASIN=0399174109&linkCode=as2&tag=gregooscicen-20&linkId=ABBVJTCOH3PI75MX

[3] Johansen, M.K., and Osman, M., (2015), Coincidences: A Fundamental Consequence of Rational Cognition, New Ideas in Psychology, Vol. 39, pp. 34–44. DOI: https://doi.org/10.1016/j.newideapsych.2015.07.001

Exercise 1: *Practice the skill of taking the initiative outside the comfort zone*

1. Think of a person who is known for the impact they make in their field and who is at the edges of your professional network. How about reaching out to them and interviewing them about their work habits? What do their work days look like? How do they decide what is essential to focus on and what do they let go of? How about their years before gaining public recognition? What were the habits that they found conducive to their present success?

2. If you could organize an event in your company on a topic of your choice, what would that event be about?

    •   A community event. What is the goal of the community? What kind of people, in what expert roles would you hope to attract?

    •   Teach a particular skill set you think is currently missing in your organization but essential to developing. What would those skills be?

    •   If something else, what _____?

3. Imagine you had only one job: attending conference sessions and raising questions. What are the top three themes you'd choose to comment upon?

4. Which of the preceding three situations is scarier?

5. Which of the preceding three situations would you be ready for?

Exercise 2: *Upskilling or reskilling in search of new areas of interest*

Step 1: Please go through the following list of topics and choose ten that resonate with you:

`www.ted.com/topics`

Step 2: Out of the ten topics, what are the three themes you feel you could contribute to with your current knowledge?

Step 3: Out of the ten topics, what are the three issues about which you know hardly anything but are curious to learn more? When would be a good time for you to start acquiring more knowledge?

Step 4: If one of the three topics is related to your current role, you would prefer to strengthen your current competence. If at least one of the three topics is unrelated to your current position, then you choose to reskill. Which of these two choices appeals to you most?

CHAPTER 8

Crossing Paths with a New Curiosity

It took a long journey to realize that surreal fine art photography was the way I could express myself.

—Artist photographer Dasha Pears

Let's consider a contemporary parable written by writer David Foster Wallace: *"There are these two young fish swimming along, and they happen to meet an older fish swimming the other way, who nods at them and says,* 'Morning, boys. How's the water today?' *And the two young fish swim on for a bit, and then eventually one of them looks over at the other two and goes,* 'What on earth is water?'"[1]

In a similar way, we may ask ourselves, *"What on earth is the Self? Let alone, the Creative Self!?"* Your personality, life circumstances, and the surroundings are in a constant dance of influence over what you can create. **Serendipity has the power to awaken your creative self. You decide what to do about it.** As I was reading the book *Wired to Create*, I had an impulsive thought, *"I'll craft a creativity course."* I felt compelled to understand deeper the psychology of creativity. And what better way to learn a topic than teaching about it?

---

[1] www.newyorker.com/books/page-turner/this-is-water

© Oana Velcu-Laitinen 2022
O. Velcu-Laitinen, *How to Develop Your Creative Identity at Work*,
https://doi.org/10.1007/978-1-4842-8680-7_8

The discovery of a strong interest in a topic – intellectual, philosophical, artistic, entrepreneurial, environmental, spiritual – is a life-changing moment. It triggers the creator's journey underpinning the work identity reconstruction.[2] Making a parallel with Jonah's story from the Bible, the first project in a new role as a creator would be the equivalent of the initial part of Jonah's **journey** when he began to hear **God's voice**. Your creative role identity starts to form as you engage with new activities that make you think and act creatively.

"What on earth is water?", wondered the two young fish. Similarly with the young fish for whom water is unconsciously part of their identity, the more time we spend with some people – co-workers, relatives, friends – and engaged in particular activities – work, hobbies – the more likely that our sense of self is formed around the characteristics of the respective people, activities, and even physical environments. If you ever travelled to a conference and went to work out at the gym in the hotel, did you find yourself longing after your local gym? This is what it's like to have the surroundings part of your identity.

People and activities in our close proximity become unnoticeably and unquestionably part of who "I" is. Who is "I"? My body? My mind? My work? The volunteering activities? The person who has a hard time appreciating themselves? The personal "I" is thus built around distinctive physical traits, feelings, mental abilities, personal values, and interests, which make you unique – with all the good and bad sides – in your usual environment.

---

[2] Glaveanu, V., (2017), The Creative Self in Dialogue, The Creative Self, Effect of Beliefs, Self-Efficacy, Mindset, and Identity, Explorations in Creativity Research, pp. 117–135, https://doi.org/10.1016/B978-0-12-809790-8.00007-8
Glaveanu, V., and Tanggaard., L., (2014), Creativity, identity, and representation: Towards a socio-cultural theory of creative identity, New Ideas in Psychology, Vol. 34, pp. 12–21. https://doi.org/10.1016/j.newideapsych.2014.02.002
Markus, H. and Nurius, P., (1986), Possible Selves, American Psychologist, Vol. 41, No. 9, pp. 954–969. DOI: 10.1037/0003-066X.41.9.954

Who is "I"? My family? My community? The love/hatred I have for such and such people? The social "I" forms and develops around interpersonal relationships – *"Who are the people I consider part of my close circle?"* – and group affiliations – *"What is the country, institution, and ethnicity I belong to?"*

In a nutshell, you know who you are when you feel comfortable around certain people and when you are captivated by certain activities. However, **at times, it can happen that the very activities and people in the group where we are active may be a striking reminder of who "I" is not.** For instance, Dasha Pears wanted to be a visual artist, but peer comparison made her think she had too big shoes to fill.

"I was always interested in visual arts and I was trying to find my medium. When I was little I was drawing a lot, and then I went to an art school for kids and I was doing everything from sculpture to oil painting there. When I graduated from this school, I got an idea that I'm not at all talented, I'm so much worse than all the rest there."

The great thing for Dasha and all of us is that we are more capable in other ways, which we fail to see in the present. There are three possible selves associated with the personal "I" and who can shape the becoming creator:

- **The actual self** is based on the skills you possess at the moment and help you perform in the current role.

- **The ought self** is based on the expectations of influential people, like parents. These are the abilities that we exercise out of a sense of duty or obligation. Your parents believe that you should be above average in a particular domain. Later in life, your boss may have expectations about what kind of work you should engage in.

- **The ideal self,** based on the qualities and competences we'd like to have. Here, we find our hopes and aspirations. This possible self is an important driver for future creative action.[3]

These three selves negotiate their priority in directing our actions and decisions. To move from *"I am the person who gave up on being an artist"* to *"I am the person who hopes to be an artist,"* the ideal creative self needs to take the lead when coincidence or serendipity gives a helping hand.

Like the young fish, we may end up in a life circumstance where an object or a person can awaken a new curiosity about creative skills or intellectual interests. For example, the old fish brought up the issue of the environment to the two young fish. Will they investigate further how they can orient themselves in water? To the extent that this curiosity awakes their ideal selves, the young fish can choose to **explore what water is**.

Unlike Dasha's painstaking reinvention as an artist, for other artists, committing to a new interest happens smoother and faster, as witnessed by Matias Kupiainen, composer for the Finnish power metal band Stratovarius.[4]

"15 years ago, I was just a guitar player, and didn't consider myself as a producer or composer. But this kind of work like composing started 10 years ago when I stepped into this band and quickly realized that other people in

[3] Grant Halvorson, H. and Higgins, E.T., (2014), Focus, A Plume Book.

Higgins, E. T., 1989, Continuities and discontinuities in self-regulatory and self-evaluative processes: A developmental theory relating self and affect. Journal of Personality, 57 (2), pp. 407–444. https://doi.org/10.1111/j.1467-6494.1989.tb00488.x

Higgins, E.T., (1987), Self-discrepancy: a theory relating self and affect, Psychological Review, 94 (3), pp. 319–340.
https://doi.org/10.1037/0033-295X.94.3.319

[4] www.velcu.fi/matias-kupiainen-on-the-creative-process-originality-flow-and-intuition-in-composing-music/
http://stratovarius.com/?fbclid=IwAR2yIfze_bTUbO6DXi9-tJWh1GcxaVMMGCcscYrJoYq2Ouptq2pjl4EAkQU

the band were not motivated that much into composing. Since then, most of the material is coming from my pen. There was a demand and I answered the demand. When you have a collective, artistic call, there is a demand for something and somebody takes the role. In my case, it was exactly like that." (sic)

When solo entrepreneur Peter Ivanov, born in Bulgaria and living in Germany, was thinking of doing something different after 20 years in multinational management, he met a person who recommended a book to him. *"I read the* Strengths Finder 2.0 *by Gallup,"* the respective person said to Peter. *"I did the action plan and I changed my job."*

To many others, the Strengths Finder may mean nothing, but this book triggered Peter's curiosity. *"Oh, that's interesting, let's do that,"* he reflected. *"So, I did it and my top number one strength was, to my surprise, input. They call it input but what they mean is creativity. It is about coming up with new ideas. You never run out of ideas. Sometimes it's too much out of the box, it's crap, it's not productive at all but you generate lots of ideas and that's me."*

Once Peter became aware of his strength as an idea generator, he was empowered to take the first steps towards professional change by developing a methodology for managing remote teams.

The random encounter with a camera rekindled Dasha's interest in becoming a visual artist. *"So I gave up on this idea to become an artist until maybe 10 or even more years, when I found a camera,"* says Dasha. *"It wasn't even my camera, I borrowed it from a friend. I felt that yes, this is what I need to do, just to capture things how they look and show other people, 'Hey, there is so much beauty in the world.'"*

When the ideal creative self has outgrown the actual self, the first milestone on the creator's journey is reached. We may fancy and fear, at the same time, the idea of becoming a new person and **starting from a**

blank page in a new domain of interest.[5] A new creative curiosity comes along with a self-trust challenge. On a scale of 1 *(I feel like I always need someone's permission to live my life)* to 5 *(What others think of my actions is not my business)*, how easy is it for you to trust the creator in you before anybody else is validating your choice?

The teacher who teaches a new grammar rule, by playing a ball game with the pupils. The parents who want to have a manual for kids to follow during the class. Millennials who buy online whatever they need, be it groceries or a new home. Baby boomers who prefer physical visits to the store, touch the product, and look into the seller's eyes.

The world has always been in hegemony between the old way and new way of doing things. Moreover, these kinds of conflicts are internalized within each one of us and come out the day we encounter a new interest. As you implement an idea about a new business, an innovative product, a speech, a book, a video, etc., the pull between the current you and the possible you, causes unease.

On the one hand, there is comfort in the certainty of doing familiar things and being with the people you know. You are attached to the version of yourself who did everything you've done so far – competencies, achievements, and relationships. This is the part of you who has already gained others' acceptance.

On the other hand, you start to suspect there's some potential in you triggered by the serendipitous curiosity, which breaks the chain of external validations. So in the first experimental creation, you find yourself in an unknown territory where you build new skills and relationships. Where you yourself don't know what you are capable of. Not yet.

---

[5] Ashforth, B.E., and Schinoff, B.S., (2016), Identity Under Construction: How Individuals Come to Define Themselves in Organizations, Annual Review of Organizational Psychology and Organizational Behavior, 3(1), pp. 111–137. DOI: 10.1146/annurev-orgpsych-041015-062322

Who will win the inner conflict between the one you used to be and the one you could be? The sense of familiarity with previous experiences or the intuitive sense that gently informs you of an interest where your potential is yet to be proved? It depends on whom you decide to trust more in the present. Some creators may experience the **Jonah complex**: the fear of taking concrete actions toward the role that promises to express our creative potential.

In every aspiring creator, the voices of the **current self** and **the creative self** establish a **new relationship, a new "I."** The trust will form and consolidate as you experience yourself in each creative process. Each new activity is a farewell to our current self, how we knew it before the random encounter, and a humble welcome to the new creative self engaged in new activities. *"Could this be the new me?"* you might be thinking. Dasha got involved in family photography first, followed by wedding photography. *"It was like a process of development,"* says Dasha. *"I don't think it's ever one thing. So I started to become interested in objective reality, in documenting things that I see around myself and capturing the moment."*

Once started, the progressive exploration of your creative self will take you from one act of creation to another till you understand what and where your Nineveh is.

Exercise 3: *Who are you?*

1. Imagine you are at a networking event. Please describe in one sentence what you would tell others about what you do professionally.

2. What if you are in a space shuttle travelling to another galaxy? You are surrounded by people you have not met before. What would you tell them about yourself so they can understand what you value?

3. You are sitting at your desk. You stare at a blank page. Please write ten sentences answering the question, *"Who am I?"*

4. What are the similarities you notice in your answers in the preceding scenarios?

5. What are the differences you notice in your answers in the preceding scenarios?

6. What do these answers tell you about your personal and work identity?

Exercise 4: *What is your area of creation?*

1. What topic, if any, would you like to bring your perspective on?

2. What do you hope to get from engaging in this particular curiosity?

3. Who are the people who benefit from you becoming an expert on this topic?

A New Creative Curiosity, a New Set of Skills to Master

When luck strikes and you discover a new interest, the ideal self takes over and gets busy exercising a distinct set of technical competencies required by the new role. The core skills may require secondary competencies that strengthen your position as a creator in the domain of interest. What might these secondary skills be?

"Really, how to nurture your creativity? How to be good to yourself, if you have it, to take the best advantage with it?" asks Peter Ivanov. First, to help your genius evolve, you might want to focus on cultivating the creative thinking skillset, which will bring a certain *"je ne sais quoi"* to your products.

One way to stimulate your creative thinking is to take time for exercises that support a particular creative thought process.[6] For example, to boost your imaginative thinking, you might want to ask yourself "**What if" questions.** Thinking through the consequences disturbs the order of procedures in methods you've always followed in a particular situation. Assuming you are bored with the chocolate roll you've been baking lately, you can ask yourself, *"What if I made a chocolate roll with the cream on the outside? What kind of cream would be suitable?"*

Assuming you are an aspiring entrepreneur who wants to brainstorm solutions to the revenue model, you can ask yourself, *"What if I had three clients instead of 30? What would change in my business model?"* Asking "What if" questions bring to mind alternative future scenarios that diverge from habitual thinking.

Moreover, depending on the domain of creation, you may want to consider the following **three sets of discretionary skills that would support communicating the value of what you create**: (1) social adroitness, like empathy, generosity, and networking skills, so you'd learn how to connect at an individual level with others; (2) entrepreneurial artfulness, such as sales competence and a business mindset; (3) public speaking deftness to address larger audiences and share your worldview as a creator (see Figure 8-1).

---

[6] Carson, S., (2010), Your Creative Brain, Harvard Health Publications.

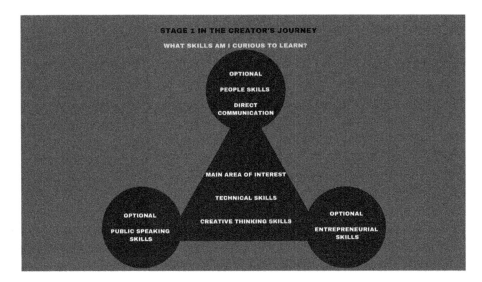

Figure 8-1. *Creator's optional skills*

In knowledge entrepreneurship, any of these secondary skill sets can become the core skills of a creator. For instance, considering Peter Ivanov's interest in managing remote teams, interpersonal skills became his master expertise. In addition, in the first years as an executive coach and speaker, he learned to master new business competencies, such as sales, which initially were a bit of a stretch for him.

"For example, as a senior manager, I never had to do sales. I had to sell concepts to the stakeholders but never had to close a deal with financials and so on. It was difficult for me. But believing in the value, you step in, you learn, you get patient and that's how it all developed."

Irrespective of your creator role, you may also want to develop some entrepreneurial skills. It means getting used to pitching the value of what you create to others. As we can see from Peter, unless you can delegate, skills in the entrepreneurial areas may not be your cup of tea, but they are necessary if you want to make it as a creator. If you can't convince possible clients to buy your products, then who?

For me, the preferred way to persuade clients is through speaking gigs. Being on a stage and talking about the key topics of your expertise is a transparent process which makes it easier for members of the audience to make up their minds if they want to work with you.

What are the master skills that help you turn the first curiosities into a concrete and new product? What are the secondary skills that you see as a necessary evil? At this point, the first part of the creator's journey ends, and the second part starts.

CHAPTER 9

Allow Yourself to Create for Different Audiences

What are the waters where I can create? This stage would correspond to the part of **Jonah's journey** when he ends up spending three days and nights in the belly of the big fish. Jonah's inner struggle over accepting God's mission is the time of poignant intensity of negotiations between the ideal creative self and the old self.

When your products address a concrete need that end users are aware of, it can be a smoother psychological transition to your new identity as a creator. For example, as Peter collected experiential evidence that virtual team management is an actionable pain point for companies, he wrote the first book on *Virtual Power Teams*. Yet, for other creators, like Dasha Pears, who deal with intangible needs that audiences may not even be aware of, the fight for hegemony between the future creative self and the expectations and familiarity of the past continues. Therefore, Dasha had a hard time trusting her choice in surreal fine art photography, where the images provoke unconscious activity in the viewers' minds.

© Oana Velcu-Laitinen 2022
O. Velcu-Laitinen, *How to Develop Your Creative Identity at Work*,
https://doi.org/10.1007/978-1-4842-8680-7_9

"So, when I got interested in creating this surreal world, I concentrated on that very much. At some point I also had a struggle of 'people won't need this,' when you show true emotions, when you document real feelings, the real moments of life. War photographer for example, that's important, and whatever I do, it's not important at all. Who wants to see them? Baking bread is important, doing this kind of stuff is not."

When there is ambiguity about the viability of your innovative products, self-doubts creep into the creator's inner dialogue to ensure that you are not wasting precious time on a wild-goose chase. Why do I want to create this? OK, it seems important to me, but why would it be necessary to others?

This is a crucial stage of the creator's inner dialogue when honesty is needed. If it's important to you to create, go ahead and enjoy the free manifestations of your tiny genius. If you couldn't care less about why engaging with your final products benefits others, you are more of a leisure creator. You do what you do because that's your way of having fun, dealing with your emotions, or managing the existential crisis. So keep enjoying your creative moments.

But suppose you care to share your creative work with others because you have a sense of involvement in the world. In that case, it's essential to keep looking for a balance between the meaning of your experimental creations for yourself and the value that others can derive. You need to actively test why others would be interested in what you create. As you persevere in new acts of creation, the creative self can be distracted by the ought social self or the collective self.

The Social Part of "I" Is in Unrest

What is the impact of your creation? For any other creator, not only Dasha, when you start engaging in new creative activities, self-doubt can be fueled by voices in your head coming from the expectations of the people in your close circle or your own expectations rooted in previous work experiences.[1]

Here are some examples of how the **conversations between the becoming creative and the social self** might go:

"I used to be an expert in this area – say, marketing. I've seen how advertising increases sales. How can I measure the impact of what I create now?" The progress is measured in emotional and financial rewards, and you'll have to settle for the former, for a while.

"I am the child of my parents who raised a daughter to have a steady job. So why am I working on a freelance project?" You'll have to learn to be more of an independent thinker.

"Men are the breadwinners in the family. How could I take a break from work to sort out my career?" Societies around the globe reached a developmental stage where, in couples of college and highly educated people, both members take turns in being the economic staple while the other is taking time for exploration and reinvention.[2]

While some societies are more accommodating for personal reinvention, the individual who takes it on may still experience it like going through a mangler. *"How do you, the creative self, dare take on an*

---

[1] Glăveanu, V. P., (2017), The Creative Self in Dialogue. In M. Karwowski and J. C. Kaufman (Eds.), *The creative self: Effect of beliefs, self-efficacy, mindset, and identity*. Explorations in Creativity Research, pp. 117–135. https://doi.org/10.1016/B978-0-12-809790-8.00007-8
Simon, B., (2004), Identity in Modern Society: A Social Psychological Perspective. Oxford:Blackwell.

[2] https://hbr.org/2019/09/how-dual-career-couples-make-it-work
Ronald Inglehart and Wayne E. Baker, (2000), Modernization, Cultural Change, and the Persistence of Traditional Values, American Sociological Review, Vol. 65, No. 1, pp. 19–51. https://doi.org/10.2307/2657288

active role?" admonishes the conforming side in you, which reflects the voices of some important people you unconsciously relate to. These **inner dialogues** between the voices of others in your head and the voice of your creative-self may distract you from what you can accomplish, as a creator.

After borrowing the camera from her friend, the years of inner debate ended fortunately for Dasha and those who follow her work, *"No, I'm gonna still do this."* She committed to surreal fine art photography, taking the risk that there would be considerably less demand for it than for family and wedding photography.

---

[3] One of Dasha's photos, My Way

A Part of the "I" Is Collective

For other creators, there may be an internal dialogue between the creative "I" and the "I" who needs to belong to an institution. With each experimental creation, this sense of belonging is being remodeled. When working on new projects, you're interacting with new people and work cultures that may or may not give you a sense of affiliation or membership. You may be convinced that there's usefulness in your work. And yet, you may feel you don't belong to the same group as others who do similar work.

Some years ago, I was contacted by Vio, a woman in her late 20s. "Effervescent" is the adjective that best captures her personality. Vio was settling into a new professional role as a service designer. She asked for my help to answer the question, *"Where is my place?"*

Years earlier, Vio had moved to Finland to work as a programmer. The more time passed, the stronger she felt about finding a better way to communicate with individuals in managerial roles. She heard a friend talk about the learning experiences in a master's program and immediately recognized that the respective program was what she'd been looking for. When she reached out to me, she had acquired the new degree and, for a few months already, had been working as a service designer. Yet, she felt like a misfit in the team.

In the first years of experimentation in different roles, the **collective part of the "I" is ruffled**. In the lowest moments of vulnerability, Vio oscillated between the emotional attachment to the activities she was doing before, the discomfort of her current status and the curiosity to explore other work environments.

The thought that brought her comfort through the highs and lows was that she is a creative individual eager to work in a team. But the question, *"Where is my place?"* would not give her peace of mind. Vio's journey of discovery continues. *"Why is the service design my cup of tea?" "In what ways is my creativity reflected in this role?"*

Assuming you did find your niche and a particular creative role fits you like a glove, you are yet to discover the fit with the work environment where you can create. *"To be a service designer is a satisfying role to express my creativity. But what is the organizational culture where I feel at home? Who are the like-minded people I can team up with?"* These are the questions Vio still reflects on as she changed jobs in another company.

Self-deception causes us to look through either the fearful lenses or the wishful thinking lenses. Either way, we are unable to see the places that best fit the creative potential. Accurate perception of the calls to create requires **internal work** based on carefully observing external actions and the associated thoughts, emotions, and behaviors (see Figure 9-1).

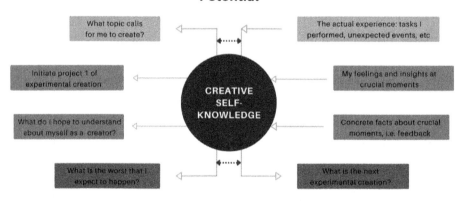

The Magic of Accurate Perception on Your Creative Potential

Figure 9-1.   *Creative self-knowledge*

Differently, the initial expectations formed when choosing a particular project may be in the way of seeing the direct experiences that follow. When you start to internalize your creative self-knowledge, you may realize that you fooled yourself over having found your focus as a creator. In reality, you have yet to discover the creative competences you want to be acknowledged by.

At this phase, feel free to experiment with your core skills as a creator in diverse projects. Say yes to others' invitations to create. Say yes to the spontaneous curiosities that arise in your mind. Curiosities are rare, so do not waste any of them. They will lead you to your niche. Reflection combined with active experimentation brings clarity and creative self-acceptance. *"What did I learn from this creative project?" "Are these the challenges I am willing to identify myself with?"*

Your creative self-knowledge grows slower than the number of experimental creations. *"I became more interested in creating my own world and my own reality,"* says Dasha after trying wedding and family photography. Nowadays, she is proud to call herself a surreal fine art photographer. As for Peter Ivanov, he wrote his second book as a virtual power teams expert.

"That's it! This is who I am, and that's what I will share with the world." To make it to the end of the second stage as a creator when you feel genuine content with your choice to create, you'll have to learn when to be stubborn to complete a particular project and when to search for something else that is a more accurate reflection of your creative potential.

Exercise 5: *The sense of belonging as a creator*

At this stage of development as a creator, I have work experiences which make me relate to creators who are

- Activists

- Artists

- Entrepreneurs

- Environmentalists

- Leaders

- Performers

- Philosophers

- Researchers

- Scientists

- If something else, then who _____

Be Like a Genius; Know When to Be Flexible and When to Persevere

There is no joy more intense than that of coming upon a fact that cannot be understood in terms of currently accepted ideas.

—Cecilia Payne

The joy Cecilia Payne refers to in the preceding quote is the reward, a fugitive moment of triumph you get after an extended period of cognitive effort, targeted at figuring out a sticky problem. As we can see, even for super smart people, turning their curiosities into competencies is anything but a walk in the park.

What is one thing that you usually wonder about? Have you ever wondered what the stars are made of? Cecilia did and got to a revolutionary finding for the mid-1920s when the scientific community was surprised to hear that the stars and the Sun are made up of a high proportion of hydrogen and helium, the two lightest chemical elements.[4]

Have you ever tried to divide a plane into small geometric patterns? The Dutch graphic artist Maurits Cornelis Escher did it. As a result, his illustrations defy our expectations about certainty and truth when, for instance, we look at a floor, only to realize in the next second that it could be a ceiling too.

---

[4] https://now.northropgrumman.com/cecilia-payne-gaposchkin-discovered-what-stars-are-made-of/ www.amnh.org/learn-teach/curriculum-collections/cosmic-horizons-book/cecilia-payne-profile

We tend to feel awe in front of creative achievements. But what do we know about how creative geniuses live their everyday lives? Cecilia Payne had a husband and two children. Both Cecilia and her husband, Sergei Gaposchkin, were scientists. They used to get into marital conflicts, where a regular source of arguments was a limited family income. Other times, they couldn't agree on who should go where and when for professional reasons. So when she attended a scientific event, he got to stay at home to babysit.[5]

As for Escher, he was grappling with a feeling of loneliness. *"Life is a school in which we exercise ourselves in loneliness,"* he wrote in 1955. He had to isolate himself from his family. He was so absorbed that he would not want to see people around him. At times he would feel guilty about it. And then, when the meticulous mental process was over, and the new idea was visible in print, people would not understand his language of symbols. Thus, he felt that *"I'm walking around all by myself here,"* "Why doesn't *anybody find beauty in what touches me so deeply?"*[6]

What are the commonalities with your life? Payne's and Escher's mundane experiences provide a formative message as remarkable as their work. We thus understand their ability to rise above life's imperfections so they could focus on the problems that piqued their curiosities.

If you wait for the perfect moment, you may never create anything. Instead, you need the flexibility of taking up new interests and the perseverance to practice the required skills.

---

[5] Cecilia Payne-Gaposchkin, (1996), An autobiography and other recollections, edited by Katherine Haramundanic, Cambridge University Press; 2nd edition, pp. 64.

[6] Escher, M.C., et al, (1989), Escher on Escher, Exploring the Infinite, Harry N. Abrams, pp. 140–144.

The Flexibility to Make Room for New Curiosities

In 1919, Cecilia was officially a student in natural sciences at Newnham College in London. A celebrated professor at the time, professor Eddington was going to lecture about his research on the solar eclipse. Four students at Newnham College had tickets, but Cecilia was not one of them.

At the last minute, one of the students who had a ticket couldn't go. That student happened to be Cecilia's friend. So, in the end, Cecilia got to attend Eddington's lecture, which was a transformative experience. Back in her room, she could write down the speech from memory. For the following three nights, she could not sleep.

The lecture gave her a nervous breakdown and made her realize she was not interested in biology anymore. Physics was her new passion. Yet, it was too late to change her course of study to astronomy, which was under the branch of mathematics. Thus, she completed the study track in natural sciences in two years instead of three. In parallel, she studied, on her own, physics and astronomy.

When she attended the advanced course in physics, she was the only woman in the room. As the tradition would have it, women had to sit in the front row. So, she would sit alone in the front row, listening to all the male students stamping their feet and applauding loudly in response to the professor's greetings as he entered the room.

"...at every lecture I wished I could sink into the earth. To this day I instinctively take my place as far back as possible in a lecture room," writes Cecilia.[7]

To date, Cecilia is one of the most eminent women astronomers. Her strong affinity for astronomy pushed her to cross gender boundaries and, years later, to leave her natal England for the USA.

---

[7] Cecilia Payne-Gaposchkin, (1996), An autobiography and other recollections, edited by Katherine Haramundanic, Cambridge University Press; 2nd edition, pp. 118.

A few years ago, I attended a sales workshop for the first time. Since I wanted to sell my own courses and I sucked at selling, I wanted to learn more about how to improve the efficiency of my sales process. The event took place in a part of the town where I don't usually go. So, it happened that I got lost and I arrived a bit later. When I opened the door, the speaker was on stage. But my jaw dropped when I saw an audience consisting entirely of men. Some of them, the speaker included, turned their eyes to me. I wanted to spin on my heels and run as fast as possible. Yet, with my last strength, I gently nodded and started pacing to the last row, imagining I was a mouse.

When was the last time you showed flexibility in last-minute changes about what to learn next? What was the obstacle you had to deal with? And what was the outcome of that experience? After the sales seminar, I introduced myself to the speaker and agreed on a meeting to explore the possibility of hiring him as my sales coach.

After all, I decided to spend my time on extended research on the creative identity rather than honing my sales competence. The decision was not the result of intimidation coming from the male participants. On the contrary, some of them were quite friendly and invited me to join them for a beer. It wasn't either that I was not convinced of the value of working with the sales coach. Rather, it was the outcome of seeing more accurately the next step I am willing to take in my journey. I preferred to spend more time writing than facilitating training.

The Perseverance to Create

The second skill that comes in handy in the second phase as a creator is the **discipline to keep creating even when the financial rewards are not encouraging**. When Escher found his love for the game of portioning the plane in recurring animal figures, he would spend sleepless nights wrestling with a new idea, searching for ordering principles. In the first three decades of his independent artistic career, critics considered his works too dull, too intellectual and not emotional enough. And still, he would not hesitate to start a new creative process each time he got a new idea that made him doubt his abilities to turn it into an original symbolic message.

"You produce wallpaper," his father reportedly said, although he did continue to financially support Escher for thirty years when his works brought a modest income.[8] His success would come around 1951, when American journals, such as *Time, Life,* and *Scientific American Journal,* started to publish articles about his work.[9] For the last twenty years, he enjoyed positive evaluations from the majority of critics and buyers from all over the world.

When you get a new idea for an act of creation, how long will you keep honing it before you are ready to share it with possible audiences? I mentioned it to a close friend when I started writing this book. She was excited and supportive of reading the first chapters. Two years later, when I told her I was rewriting the manuscript, she began to question if I would ever write the book.

When your patience to plough through the creative process outlasts your friends' motivation to champion your project, it's a sign that you are a creator working on a suitable experimental creation.

The first two stages of becoming a creator are primarily about inner struggles to bring **harmony between your creative self, your social self, and collective self.** It's about frequent experimentation to test viable interests as a creator. How could you know when to stop and when to persevere in a particular creative project that is meaningful to you and useful for your audience?

---

[8] Escher, M.C., et al, (1989), Escher on Escher, Exploring the Infinite, Harry N. Abrams, pp. 145.

[9] https://mcescher.com/about/eschers-route-to-fame/

Four Personal Needs to Create

In phase 2 in the creator's journey, you may have two competing interests, which bring along a new dilemma. Which curiosity to follow? This conundrum delays the moment of committing to your creative focus.

In my first stage, I had made a career change from academic life to knowledge solopreneurship driven by my curiosity about emotional intelligence. My first project in the new role as a coach consisted in designing and facilitating the course, *The Choice of Happiness.* The goal was to support participants develop human interaction skills for quality relationships – empathy, gratitude, and generosity. The experiment was considered a success. The participants appreciated the informative and experiential workshops. Meanwhile, I had tapped into my curiosity about the psychology of creativity.

To my surprise, creativity had a stronger hold on me. I thus wholeheartedly moved to design the second course, *Choose your Creative Potential.* It guided participants to identify the areas of their lives where they'd benefit from more creativity. This second time, despite all my marketing efforts, the course had an attendance of five enthusiasts.

What to do next? To continue with a course that proved popular but on a topic you like second best. Or to continue with a course that raises less interest for end users but is the top number one interest for yourself?

Should you find yourself dealing with similar dilemmas and making a choice rests upon your shoulders only, it may help to ground yourself in your need to create.[10] The need to create is a core human need. Engaging in acts of creation gives meaning, which can come from the sense of healing or improving some aspects of reality that you relate with – material, emotional, or spiritual elements.

Helder Santos, a professor in biomedical engineering at the University of Groningen, The Netherlands, focuses on alleviating people's illnesses.

"I think if you believe you are doing something that is meaningful – so, in our case, we are trying to somehow impact the society [by] solving problems, like in this case it is health problems – this actually gives you the motivation to actually wake up every morning and go to your job, and do it."

For some other creators, like Dasha Pears, their creations are grounded firstly in a manifestation of self-love, and secondly, in care for functioning societies.

"Before I started photography, I had lots of struggles. I wasn't a very happy person," says Dasha. *"The first reason I create art is that yes, I'm a better human being and therefore am more pleasant to be around. I'm a better mom, daughter, and friend.*

Second, my art inspires people to create something of their own. It may not be a photo or a painting, it can be a cake, a garden, a building, or cure for cancer.

Third, my art also helps people to find peace and gain mental control over their (sometimes hectic) emotions. So in this sense, if they are

---

[10] Kaufman, J.C., and Glăveanu V.P., (2018), A Review of Creativity Theories, The Cambridge Handbook of Creativity, edited by Kaufman J.C. and Sternberg R.J., pp. 27–43.
Luria, S.R., and Kaufman, J.C., (2017), The Dynamic Force Before Intrinsic Motivation: Exploring Creative Needs, The Creative Self: Effect of Beliefs, Self-Efficacy, Mindset, and Identity. Explorations in Creativity Research, pp. 317–325.
Ryan, R.M., and Deci, E.L., (2017), Self-determination theory: Basic psychological needs in motivation, development and wellness. New York: Guilford Press.
Singer J.A., (2004), Narrative Identity and Meaning Making Across the Adult Span: An Introduction. *Journal of Personality*, 72:3, pp. 437–459.

empowered by a positive desire to create, they have less negative incentives to destroy anything around them. And if more people want to create and not destroy, we'll hopefully have less hatred, pain, and anger in the world. It's idealistic, but it helps me on my artistic path."

When it comes to explaining the intrinsic motivation to create, creativity researchers use models of personal values and interests to investigate what drives creators to engage in creative activities.[11] For instance, one of the most recent studies on needs to create interviewed 24 professional creators on how they experienced the creative process.[12] They identified six themes to account for what drives us to create in environments focused on traditions and conventions – beauty, power, discovery, communication, individuality, and pleasure. A key implication from this study is that synergies between a core personal value and a strong interest determine creators' choices.

Since a creator is an individual who is willing to bring something new and original to society, in this book, we take a neuroscience perspective on how the brain navigates the social interactions in the habitual environment.[13] As a result, there can be **four possible needs** that feed your creative life force in completing acts of creation: the love of autonomy, the desire for fairness, the need for relatedness, and the intention to leave a legacy of personal values. Which one might define you?

---

[11] Kaufman, J.C., and Glaveanu, V.P., (2019), A Review of Creativity Theories: What Questions Are We Trying to Answer, in Cambridge Handbook of Creativity, 2nd Ed, Edited by Kaufman, J.C., and Sternberg, R.J., pp. 27–43.

[12] Luria S.R., and Kaufman J.C., (2017), The Dynamic Force Before Instrinsic Motivation: Exploring Creative Needs, in The Creative Self Effect of Beliefs, Self-Efficacy, Mindset, and Identity Explorations in Creativity Research, Edited by Karwowski M. and Kaufman J.C., pp. 317–325.

[13] https://schoolguide.casel.org/uploads/sites/2/2018/12/SCARF-NeuroleadershipArticle.pdf

The Love of Autonomy

You may realize that you must have a sense of psychological freedom and ownership in your work.[14] As Peter Ivanov says, you engage in creative projects because they are meaningful, challenging and interesting to yourself.

"Now as an entrepreneur, as a speaker of my own topic, as a book author, I have the creativity fully unleashed. So I can do anything I can imagine and I think it would deliver the best value for the audience."

Autonomy also means you are free to make the important decisions during the creative process. *"Who decides if a new song is a failure?"* I asked Matias Kupiainen, the guitar player, composer and producer in Stratovarius, the Finnish power metal band.

"I'm the first moderator," replied Matias. *"If I'm thinking this is an ok song, then I present it to the rest of the band members. But usually this means that I need to make the 10 songs first before I present."*

The desire to be solitary during the creative process doesn't mean that you are entirely independent mentally. After all, you want the product – a song, a gadget, a book – to be interesting for a particular audience. And you choose one representative of the audience to have in mind as you create.

"... we actually have this kind of saying in our work collective, 'What would Carlos like?'" continues Matias. *"Carlos is a typical Mexican, maybe 26 years old, coming from a bad background but loves metal music. And Carlos is the dude who is in the front row. Carlos likes really simple stuff. You have to remember he doesn't speak that much English. So, we are all thinking, 'Does Carlos approve?' We call it the Carlos factor. But of course, Carlos is the fourth moderator."*

Dasha preferred surreal fine art photography over family photography out of the need for an emotional outlet. Her autonomous creative process

---

[14] Kaufman, J.C., (2018), Finding meaning with creativity in the past, present, and future. *Perspectives on Psychological Science*, 13, pp. 734–749.

results in photos that speak to people that resonate with a particular concept of beauty – the beauty of the imaginary world, of seeing more than the eye can see.

From an external observer's point of view, the creator appears isolated from the world, but you don't experience it as such. You can have autotelic mental states when you experience a decreased sense of self and increased feelings of connectedness with something bigger than yourself, which is the subject of your creation.[15] The moments when you are not worried about what others think of your work, also known as flow, increase your self-determination to be an independent creator.

As for my dilemma about which course to develop further, I opted to redesign the course *Choose Your Creative Potential* into three new courses for three distinct audiences: leaders of organizational change, doctoral students in life sciences, and individuals who struggle with cultural adaptation. A marketing strategist might argue that these three different needs position you as a creator in three different markets. And that's correct.

Yet, from the psychological point of view, brand awareness is less critical at stage two in the creator's journey. Instead, the priority is to experiment with different projects until you have a clue about the creator identity that you are willing to embrace. As for myself, the more creativity courses I facilitated, the more I started flirting with the idea of writing this book. It marked the end of stage two on my path as a creator.

As a fun fact, some months after the first course, Choose Your Creative Potential, I was pleasantly surprised to hear that one of the attendants started writing a book when she attended the course. It reminds that you need to think twice about what you interpret as wins and losses in each experimental creation.

---

[15] Yaden et al., (2017), The Varieties of Self-Transcendent Experience, Review of General Psychology, pp. 1–18. https://journals.sagepub.com/doi/10.1037/gpr0000102

In conclusion, the sense of autonomy drives you toward activities that you find inherently meaningful. Also, it's human to create with an audience in mind, so choose the right representative. However, whenever you receive the clients' feedback, think of Matias. You are the first to decide what input parts to incorporate in your creation.

The Desire for Fairness

You have a strong sense of what is right and wrong. A study by Matt Lieberman shows that the experience of fairness activates the same brain regions as when eating chocolate.[16] Milk, dark, or raw chocolate. Which one do you like best? As chocolate comes in different flavors for different taste buds, so is fairness perceived individually by each person who looks at a specific situation.

Imagine you're looking at a horse pulling a carriage. Do you feel sorry for the horse? Or, are you relieved for the passengers that they have a vehicle to carry them from one place to another?

Some of us care that a group of people get the rewards they deserve, while others care that animals or elements of nature are treated respectfully. Whatever we create is a dedication to what or who we mostly care about to bring a touch of justice.

"Our world would be a better place if we had more women in leadership positions," writes Tulia Lopes in her book, Leading in High Heels.[17] *"As the maxim goes, if you help a woman, you are helping a community because whatever she gains she usually shares – with her family and community."*

After 20 years of working with women in managerial positions, Tulia observed mindsets that disempower and mislead women. Her message for

---

[16] Lieberman, M.D., (2015), Social: Why Our Brains Are Wired to Connect, Crown.
[17] www.amazon.co.uk/Leading-High-Heels-Professional-Excellence/ dp/3952428345/ref=sr_1_1?crid=P5WTV1ASWJZ3&keywords=leading+in+high+h eels&qid=1652360267&sprefix=leading+in+high+heels%2Caps%2C78&sr=8-1

restoring gender equality in leadership is, *"Your voice – as a woman – has more power than you can imagine."* Her latest project is to raise awareness about workplace biases that stunt women's careers.

Which of the following topics tempt you to roll up your sleeves and get involved?

- Inclusivity and diversity in the workplace
- Educational opportunities for kids from disadvantaged backgrounds
- Management innovation
- Recycling systems
- Something else _____

What other topic of equity puts you on fire, and you want to paint the town in red or graffiti with it?

The Need for Relatedness

You like people in general, but who are the people you resonate with and feel compelled to help? They will be the folks with whom you will develop a sense of connection through co-creation – you, as the initiator and they, as the developers, at the other end of the continuum.

"At this phase in my life, I'm called to reach out to and support driven women who have made work a priority over their own health, their relationships, and their well-being," writes Pamela Thompson in her book *Learning to Dance with Life: A Guide for High Achieving Women.*[18]

Pamela herself used to work day in, day out before and after she started her consulting and coaching businesses. She believes that becoming a

---

[18] www.amazon.co.uk/Learning-Dance-Life-Guide-Achieving/dp/0986290130/ ref=sr_1_1?crid=S3A8464Y5M66&keywords=pamela+thompson+dance&qi d=1652426257&sprefix=pamela+thompson+dance%2Caps%2C73&sr=8-1

mother saved her. She could take more distance from her work and notice the unhealthy toll on her body. Also, through her children, she learned the experience of being fully present at the moment.

These personal experiences motivated her to prevent other high-achieving women from burning out. So, she set out to write about creative living practices, like body wisdom, artistic expression and alignment with core values that enable more balance and clarity in life.

"*Creative Living Community*" is the takeaway of Pamela's book. It's about building a community of women around the globe who share a similar commitment: to live a life where we can find peace within ourselves, our families, workplaces, and beyond.

As for Dasha, as she comes up with new projects of self-expression, she becomes interested in inspiring the youth so that they can create what they love in their lives.

"*... I also show other people that you don't have to be unhappy with what you do now. If you want to create something, however crazy it might seem, you can still do it, it is possible. And that's also how I see my role. Now I also teach and that's a big big thing in my life.*"

In short, when you pursue a particular creative interest, you do it for the activities you are intrinsically motivated in and for growing a community where you feel a sense of belonging and appreciation. With each project, you plant the seeds of social transformation.

The Intention to Leave a Legacy of Personal Values

You need to form close connections and guidance for the next generation. Consequently, you challenge yourself to create a positive change in your family, ethnic milieu, or company culture by instilling a system of leading beliefs.

This need to create stems from your love for the family and culture you were born into, as we can see from Harriet Fagerholm's testimony on her evolving sense of self.

"I'm part of the Swedish speaking minority in Finland and recently I have explored my identity. Especially this Summer when I went back to my home area in Ostrobotnia where I was born, in the rough archipelago, rough conditions, where people struggled and had to collaborate to survive. So my roots are in that community, a very strong community and kind of a strong cultural identity, with some paradoxical elements in it. And I have realized now that there is where creativity is nourished where you have these elements involved and there is the close connection to nature."

In addition, Harriet realized that the relationships with her children and husband are at the core of her identity.

"I'm very happy to see how I've been able as a mother to transform the culture in our family, to become more open, to allow more emotions, to share ... So that's a kind of a sense of pride for me, that I have managed to do this inner transformation that I also do in my professional work, I've been able to do it in my own family."

One of her latest projects is the *Joy of Being* podcast on self-love and self-awareness. If you were to create your own podcast where you promote a core personal value as a heritage, what would the title be?

I would create a podcast entitled *Spontaneity and Continuity*. The goal would be to discuss how creativity can be modelled in daily interactions between adults and children, thus shaping the kids' sense of belonging to a community.

One day, I was watching my sons play with their friends when I started chasing them in an attempt to give a kiss to whoever got caught. The kids loved it and wanted to call the game the Thief of Kisses. Then, they would ask to play it again for a few days in a row. I got encouraged by their reaction, so we tried improvised storytelling as another way of spending quality time together. We took turns creating stories about Paul, a 10-year-old boy, who likes playing the guitar and touring around the neighboring streets. Paul's problem is his younger brother, Pavel, a 5-year-old, eager to show his dance moves in every show.

All in all, these kinds of spontaneous interactions are a bridge between the present and future generations. It's a legacy that, at best, will be captured in new social behaviors perpetuated among family and friends. At the very least, it is a fleeting moment of joy stored as a childhood memory.

Personal values – emotional awareness, connection, creativity, etc. – that are deemed necessary are embodied both in interpersonal interactions and in the cultural systems, usually through myths, music, folk stories, literature, and social media.

If a podcast is not attractive to you, what would you want to create that serves as a link between you and the generation to come? In some African cultures, braiding hair is a creative form of connection and expressing love between generations. What would your heritage be?

"We were the creators who lived before you. We were empowered by (your values)

- Emotional availability

- Compassion

- Competence

- Independence

- Equality for people

- Faith

- Forgiveness

- Knowledge

- Power and authority

- Taking risks

- Wealth, etc.

We hope you enjoy the world as we left it."

At this point in your development as a creative expert, which of these four psychological needs are driving you to create?

- The love of autonomy

- The sense of fairness

- The need for relatedness

- The intention to leave a reminder of guiding values in life

In between experimental creations, you may want to take one step back and look at the messages reflected in your work. What do you want to create next, and why? To succeed in discovering new drugs, professor Helder Santos believes in never giving up. Never giving up implies that you can find another way when you don't get the expected results, but you see the meaning of your actions. When one door closes, if you don't see a window opening, invent it. Welcome to the world of creators!

CHAPTER 10

Committing to Your Creative Focus

This third stage in developing the creative identity is about proving to others why your creations are valuable to them and maintaining your role status. It corresponds to Jonah's journey when the big fish spits him out on dry land, and he **starts his trip to Nineveh.**

The work of established creators needs constant validation from clients, bosses, critics, fans, etc. To this view, creators can benefit from breaking their routines and procedures now and then, as Dasha emphasizes when asked whether she is satisfied with the current stage in her career as a surreal fine art photographer.

"I wouldn't say I'm satisfied still because I, as I grow, as a professional, as an artist, I see a lot and lots of things that I still have to learn. And it's not that I can actually reach some point in my career and say 'okay, now I am finally done'.

I probably had this moment like maybe a year ago or two years ago, when I was feeling kind of relaxed but I very quickly realized that if I stay there with that kind of mindset – it wasn't anything to do with the really valuable and quality work that I was doing – it was just that if I stayed there I would totally stagnate and it means death for an artist and for any person, I think."

© Oana Velcu-Laitinen 2022
O. Velcu-Laitinen, *How to Develop Your Creative Identity at Work*,
https://doi.org/10.1007/978-1-4842-8680-7_10

When you are open to learning and discovering new ways to express your occupational creativity, you surprise the audiences that followed you throughout the years. Moreover, despite the popularity, there may be a need to attract new audiences. It requires exploring your radical creativity.

"I'm starting to feel a little bit that I don't know how to think outside the box in terms of how I deliver that stuff," says John Bates, Leadership Communication expert. *"Do I do a 'train the trainer' program and let people get licenses for different countries? Do I do a 'train the trainer' program, internal in the corporations and train their people who are already doing the communications there? Do I just focus on online trainings? But how can I make the biggest difference?*

And all these things that I said right now are typical things that people are doing. What's the outside of the box thing that I can do? How can I bring something that is new and different to this space?"

Established creators need to allow themselves to identify problems worth their focus that others in their field do not pay attention to. Being problem-driven means establishing yourself as an expert at the intersection between disciplines, which enables you to look at the problems tackled in a domain through disciplinary thinking and methodologies from another realm. This is what Escher did.

Escher took delight in the laws of symmetry in geometry to create aesthetic images although as he wrote to his son in 1959, he didn't feel at home either in the world of math or arts.

"I'm starting to speak a language which is understood by very few people. It makes me feel increasingly lonely. Mathematicians may be friendly and interested and give me a fatherly pat on the back, but in the end I am only a bungler to them. 'Artistic' people mainly become irritated."[1]

---

[1] Ornes S., September (2020), The Symmetry Pair, Scientific American, Celebrating 175 years, pp. 63. www.scientificamerican.com/article/when-scientific-american-made-m-c-escher-famous/

Escher did share two qualities with the artists and mathematicians: the attraction to solving puzzles and the perseverance in doing so. *"What can I do?"* he wrote to his son, *"when this sort of problem fascinates me so much that I cannot leave it alone? ... I cannot help mocking all our unwavering certainties. Are you sure that a floor cannot be a ceiling?"*

Some creators like Dasha Pears do find a group of like-minded fellows to work with, relatively early in her career as a surreal fine art photographer. *"Finding people who I can create with, that is always very inspirational. What I can learn from someone while collaborating, integrating."*

For creators like Escher, the lack of a sense of belonging to a group of people equally passionate with the problems that fascinate you can be the ultimate test for your commitment to the interests and skills that form your identity as an established creator. As we know, Escher passed the test.

Figure 10-1 summarizes the journey of the inner self as a creator. It starts with the meaningful coincidence of discovering a curiosity. Then, you start creating something you have never done before, like me making a course on creativity, Dasha engaging in wedding photography, and Peter deciding to transform his managerial experience into consulting expertise. At the outset, you're lucky if your fan club has two founding members, your mom and her cat. This stage is a test of self-doubt. Do you believe in yourself enough to develop mastery skills in the new role?

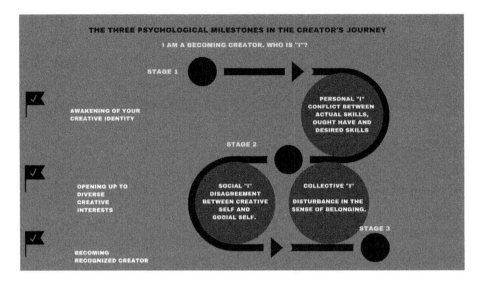

Figure 10-1. *The inner journey*

The shift from stage 1 to stage 2 happens as you actively experiment with different creative interests and audiences. Family members will judge your choices. Others, that is, colleagues, possible clients, and competitors, will evaluate the results of your work. However, the most blistering fight is within yourself, between the voices of your creative self, ought social self, and collective self. Each creative process is a test of choosing one of the possible creative selves that you may become. You can be a great performer in a particular role as a creator, but is the respective role satisfying you?

Evolving toward stage 3 happens when the creator commits to a specific creative focus. The dominant presence of the creative self lures you into accepting a new work-life style and new ways to relate to the people around you, both in personal and professional contexts. At each step, external evaluations will be a complementary gauge of the growing confidence in your choices as a creator.

And They Lived Happily Through the Loops of Feedback

"I don't take myself seriously," a friend in a writers' meeting once said. Nowadays, he is the author and editor of several works on language. In 2017, he was shortlisted for the Hammond House international literary prize.[2] Back then, as we were focusing on giving feedback on each other's drafts, I didn't ask what he meant. However, his comment stayed with me for years. What does it mean not to take your role as a creator seriously?

When you treat someone or something seriously, you show they are worthy of your respect. So how can you ignore the chest pain that wakes you up in the night as soon as your unconscious brings to your attention that there is a detail that you didn't implement right?

Receiving feedback is a necessary step when you implement a new idea. Yet, until others get to criticize your finished work, you yourself have an opinion about your progress or lack of it. The most vulnerable moments are when you find yourself immersed in yet another puzzle to solve. You're not even close to completing the final product; as usually happens, the deadline looms ahead. How can you navigate these moments without getting involved and consumed with figuring out the most delicate details?

The answer is that you cannot. You need to dig deeper until you find a satisfying solution. The trick is to be mindful about what happens to the underlying feeling of self-worth. The involuntary like or dislike of your abilities and actions as you wrestle with the new puzzle will influence your psychological functioning, overall productivity, and creative thinking

---

[2] https://sentinelquarterly.com/monday-writer/bruce-marsland/

over time.[3] When you struggle with an elusive solution, you may end up thinking, *"And I'm not even good-looking!"*

Being a creator means putting a great deal of thought and emotions into transforming an idea into a finished product. If we could only have a magic wand when we need it to turn ideas into reality! For instance, for the Finnish composer Matias Kupiainen, the ratio of failing to succeed at composing one minute of a song is 70/30 roughly.

"If I succeed in making one really good song, I have to fail on 10 before that. But the material that comes from the failed 10, I can use it later or modify it so the material never goes to waste. I recycle it. I would say it's a long process. Sometimes, just to make a three-and-a-half minute song might take me a month. Or sometimes, to make a ten-minute song, it takes me two weeks. It depends also on what kind of inspiration I have or if I have a clear vision of what I'm doing. Usually I have no clue of what I'm doing."

---

[3] Tierney, P., and Farmer, S.M., (2011), Creative Self-Efficacy Development and Creative Performance Over Time, Journal of Applied Psychology, Vol. 96, No. 2, pp. 277–293.

Pretz, J.E. and Nelson, D., (2017), Creativity Is Influenced by Domain, Creative Self-Efficacy, Mindset, Self-Efficacy, and Self-Esteem, Editor(s): Karwowski, M., and Kaufman, J.C., In Explorations in Creativity Research,

The Creative Self, pp. 155–170, https://doi.org/10.1016/B978-0-12-809790-8.00009-1.

Zeigler-Hill, V., and Wallace, M.T., (2012), Self-esteem Instability and Psychological Adjustment, Self and Identity, 11:3, pp. 317–342.

Baumeister, R.F., Campbell, J.D., Krueger, J.I., and Vohs K.D., (2003). Does high self-esteem cause better performance, interpersonal success, happiness, or healthier lifestyles? *Psychological Science in the Public Interest*, 4, pp. 1–44.

Deci, E.L., and Ryan, R.M., (1995). Human anatomy: The basis for true self-esteem. M.H. Kernis (Ed.) *Efficacy, agency, and self-esteem* (pp. 31–49). New York: Plenum Press.

Tafarodi, R.W., and Swann, W.B., (1995). Self-liking and self-competence as dimensions of global self-esteem: Initial validation of a measure. *Journal of Personality Assessment*, 65, pp. 322–342.

Especially when you see the material you work on as an extension of yourself, each creative process fiddles with the sense of self-worth, the thoughts and feelings about your abilities as a creator. On a scale of 1 (*this isn't me*) to 5(*it is so me*), please rate the following statements:

"For me, the sense of a job well done is as important as receiving validation."

"In general, I am satisfied with my creative performance."

"To me, receiving feedback is a chance to improve my skills."

The higher the average score, the more balanced the sense of self-worth, which helps to stay more focused, optimistic, and persist in finding a solution.[4] What would you say is your level of self-esteem: high, low, average? Does it stay constant for days? Or does the sense of self-worth fluctuate within the same day depending on the context?

A too high sense of self-esteem – *"I can be anything I choose to be," "I'm unaffected by failure," "I have a lot to be proud of," "I don't make mistakes"* – may result in ignoring some of the subtle nudges from the unconscious mind. Consequently, you may miss out on the opportunities to improve the product. On the contrary, a low sense of self-esteem – *"When I start a project that I care about, I frequently worry if I can complete it," "I usually feel bad about my performance," "I sometimes believe that my ideas are not important," "I sometimes believe I'm not good enough to be a creator"* – can make you more vulnerable to self-doubt, anxiety, and depression, which can kill your creative thinking and resourcefulness in carrying out an original idea.

Patience to labor away till you get the results that you yourself can accept is a virtue as a creator, as professor Vincenzo Cerullo noticed.

---

[4] Kernis, M.H., (2005), Measuring self-esteem in context: The importance of stability of self-esteem in psychological functioning. Journal of Personality, 73, pp. 1–37.

Kernis, M.H., (2003), Toward a Conceptualization of Optimal Self-Esteem, Psychological Inquiry, Vol. 14, No. 1, pp. 1–26.

Jordan, C.H., Spencer, S.J., Zanna, M.P., Hoshino-Browne, E., and Correll, J., (2003), Secure and defensive high self-esteem. Journal of Personality and Social Psychology, 85, pp. 969–978.

"I'm a very patient person. Science is a long journey with a lot of failure. So what I've noticed when I compare myself to other scientists or colleagues, is that I am quite patient and I can take failure very well, which I think is the key to success in science. As I always say to my students, 'this is a great job one day per year and the rest of 364 you are very frustrated."

In a way, creators across domains of expertise are like flowers. At their level of consciousness, flowers do their best to respect their natural cycles, despite confusing signals caused by climate change.[5] They may blossom a few days earlier each year, but they do wake up from the Winter slumber. They open their petals at sunrise and close them at sunset.

Similarly, the signals coming from the unconscious and pointing at a temporary problem in your creative process are there for a reason. They deserve respect, attention, and action. The frustration, panic, and the roller-coaster of self-esteem that come along need patience and a pat on the shoulder.

The higher the sense of connection with the subject of your creation, the more prone you are to deprecate your self-worth. Behind the monstrously crashing sense that you could do more and better, there is a sense of care and involvement with something bigger than yourself. This is the nature of the creative process: at times getting stuck and at times back on track. Each time, keep your self-esteem in check.

To date, I can only make suppositions about what my friend might have implied when he said he was not taking himself seriously. However, I take the liberty to interpret the comment as a reminder about the importance of listening to ongoing feedback – your own and others' – and trusting yourself to be able to act on it. It is a personal goal that serves well when you deal with a sense of dissatisfaction and failure during the creative process. It takes away the focus from yourself and places it on the next task to perform.

---

[5] www.hcn.org/articles/climate-change-is-disrupting-the-wests-spring-phenology

In brief, your job is to create, be patient when hitting the wall, and aim at a healthy dose of self-esteem. High enough to see in every failure a beginning to use your creator's skills and low enough to avoid an exaggerated self-appreciation of abilities and results. *"You only have to let the soft animal of your body love what it loves,"* writes poet Mary Oliver. So let the love for your work be more significant than the pride derived from receiving constant validation.

Part 2 Summary – Learn to Live Like a Creator

A creator is a person who discovers an intense curiosity toward a domain of knowledge or experience and chooses to get involved in acts of creation. Whether a scientist, entrepreneur, artist, or niche expert, you get motivated by the anticipation of presenting a surprising and valuable product to an audience.

There are three crucial milestones in developing a creator's internal sense of self:

1. When **serendipity** opens your eyes toward a **creative curiosity**, such as my interest in the book *Wired to Create*, Dasha's interest in a photo camera and Peter's decision to do a personal strengths test. At that crucial moment of coincidence, you can take the curiosity further or turn a blind eye to it.

2. When you **accept your calling as a creator** but experiment with different projects for different audiences in search of a role you are ready to embrace. The courses I created for different users and Dasha's exploration of wedding and family photography are illustrative of this stage.

3. When you **commit to a domain of creation** where
   you want to be recognized. For Dasha, this stage
   started when she found a way to come to peace with
   her preference for surreal fine art photography.

What is the stage you found yourself at?

Despite the individuality as a creative person and the peculiarities of the domain of choice, adopting the following five habits is particularly important for evolving to the recognition phase:

- The discovery of a strong interest requires ***secondary skills*** that strengthen the creator's image in the domain of interest. For example, the deliberate exercise of creative thinking, entrepreneurial, people, or public speaking skills can help the creator connect with and learn from possible audiences.

- ***Flexibility in following new curiosities.*** The willingness and courage to make time to develop new competencies that disrupt the ongoing projects.

- ***Perseverance in experimental creations.*** With each project, the determination to see your idea implemented must surpass external validation's scarcity.

- ***Identification of the psychological needs to create,*** which helps the creator make peace with the creative choice.

- ***A bit more patience*** *with the creative process* ***than pride*** *in receiving validation.*

What among the preceding habits do you find important, even if not urgent, to adopt in your current work context?

In the next part, we'll look into inner observation habits to increase the likelihood of "Aha!" moments for experimental creations in the first stage when the identity as a creator is formed.

PART III

Priming Your Mind for Creative Insight

CHAPTER 11

Why Habits of Inner Observation Strengthen the Identity As a Creator

I got to a point when I felt there was something missing. But I didn't know what it would have been.

—Tulia Lopes, Founder of Speak Up and Lead Academy

In the first part of this book, we discussed how schooling and work experiences influence your beliefs about your creativity and what role it has in your life. Creative mortification and frustration can deter you from actively developing a professional path as a creator. In the second part, we mapped out the inner dialogue between the creative self, the ought self, and the current self, which results in self-disruption habits that strengthen your creative identity.

This third part aims to understand how to open up to new information in a new domain of interest, which can gradually lead to your first insights into experimental creations.

© Oana Velcu-Laitinen 2022
O. Velcu-Laitinen, *How to Develop Your Creative Identity at Work*,
https://doi.org/10.1007/978-1-4842-8680-7_11

Insight, also known as the Aha or Eureka moment, is an unexpected shift in consciousness when you understand your creative purpose. *"Insights are like gifts from the unconscious minds."*[1] They may feel sudden but they are the result of mental activity, rambling on in the depths of the unconscious, for years.

The initial insight toward embracing a new role as a creator is the moment when you recognize that your cup of tea is a new domain of creation – in the arts, engineering, science, technology, entrepreneurship, leadership, etc. It can be a domain very closely related to the one you're currently active in. Or, it can be a domain at a similar distance as the Earth is from the Moon. As you get acquainted with the new domain, your creative potential becomes more decisive in guiding your choices of activities to get involved in.

To gain new insight into the kind of creator you are, you may want to pay attention to what you see, in a different way, from the inside out. Activating your inner awareness can boost your ability to notice opportunities to create. The creative process is set in motion when subtle cues enter your perception and trigger the urge to make sense of it all.

In between the discovery of a word, sound, idea, or event that captivates you and the moment when you find your place as a creator, there are many episodes of experimental creations (see Figure 11-1). When you start creating products for which the creator in you wants to get recognized for, you can congratulate yourself. You identified your zing as a creator. Until then, with each experimental creation, you refine your creative focus.

---

[1] Kaufman, S.B., and Gregoire, C., (2015), Wired to Create, Tarcher Perigree, pp. 69.

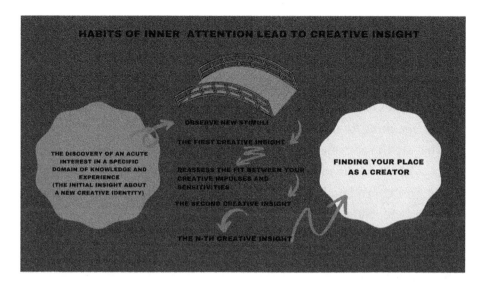

Figure 11-1. *The N-th creative insight*

At the N-th creative insight, you'll access the alignment zone as a creator, where there's harmony between your creative impulse, the domain of interest, medium of expression, and environment. Becoming a creator is a process of self-discovery, one act of creation at a time.

The Attraction Toward a Particular Domain

Whatever the domain where you'd like to bring your contribution, it will not be enough for you to acquire all the relevant information and know what to do with it. To increase the likelihood of becoming a recognized creator, you need to feel a highly acute interest – which psychologist Mihaly Csikszentmihalyi calls psychic energy[2] – in a particular aspect of the knowledge domain or practice. You have to feel a connection with the ideas and practices in the respective domain. But not the regular unity

---

[2] Csikszentmihalyi, M., (2008), Flow: The Psychology of Optimal Experience, Harper Perennial Modern Classics.

with the elements of the environment, which makes you feel part of it, like *"Observing flowers is a way to relax."*

You'll need to do more than that. You'll need to give in to your sensitivity, the perception of subtleties that compel you to add something to it that makes it your creation, like *"Flowers are my players in creating stories of meaning for others."*[3]

What are the activities you want to engage in because they are relaxing? What are the topics of interest that tease your mind, make you want to get involved and create for an audience? Your creative potential lies in the latter category of interests.

Escher is known for his love for the "game" of dividing a plane into small recognizable figures that repeat themselves. How did he come to embrace this love?

"My first intuitive step in that direction had already been taken as a student at the School for Architecture and Decorative Arts in Haarlem. This was before I got to know the Moorish majolica mosaics in the Alhambra, which made a profound impression on me."[4]

Intuitive choices precede the discovery of acute interests. For Escher, this part ended in 1936 when he took his second trip to Spain, when the Moors' use of mathematical-abstract motifs on their walls and floors intrigued him even more.

The second part of the development of an acute interest starts when you use deliberate strategies to acquire new learning and nurture your affinity. When Escher returned from the second trip to Alhambra, someone in the mathematicians' community informed him that the regular division of planes in congruent figures is part of the study of

---

[3] Konrad, S. and Herzberg, P., (2017), Psychometric Properties and Validation of a German High Sensitive Person Scale (HSPS-G), European Journal of Psychological Assessment. pp. 1–15. 10.1027/1015-5759/a000411.

[4] Escher M.C., Ford K., and Vermeulen J.W., (1989), Escher on Escher, Exploring the Infinite, Abrams, pp.83.

geometric crystallography.[5] Therefore, he got interested in reading topical articles. In the end he *"dared, that is, to work on the problem of expressing unboundedness in an enclosed plane that is bound by specific dimensions."*[6]

To turn a strong interest into acts of creation takes years of stubborn commitment to learn, question existing knowledge and practices, and train your skills. The acceptance of your natural sensitivity provides the inner drive to create again and again.

"Any schoolboy with a little aptitude can perhaps draw better than I," wrote Escher to his son Arthur, on November 2, 1955, *"but what he lacks in most cases is that tenacious desire to make it a reality, that obstinate gnashing of teeth and saying, 'Although I know it can't be done, I want to do it anyway.'"*

This surrender to sensitivity will change the way you interact with the people and resources in your surroundings.

Take the Creator in You for a Couple of Dates to Observe New Sensitivities

In 1924, two years after Escher first saw the geometric patterns of the mosaics in the Alhambra palace, he engaged in the first experimental creation involving the regular division of planes. It consisted of an imprint on a piece of cloth with one single animal theme. He exhibited it among his other works. It wasn't successful.

---

[5] Donnay, V.J. (2003). Chaotic Geodesic Motion: An Extension of M.C. Escher's Circle Limit Designs. In: Schattschneider, D., Emmer, M. (eds) M.C. Escher's Legacy. Springer, Berlin, Heidelberg. https://doi.org/10.1007/3-540-28849-X_31

[6] Escher M.C., Ford K., and Vermeulen J.W., (1989), Escher on Escher, Exploring the Infinite, Abrams, pp. 84.

When we want to enact a role as a creator, in line with new creative sensitivities, it feels like we're taking a considerable risk. Risk causes fear. Fear leads to ambiguity. Feeling uncertain or doubtful kills creative thinking.

Despite understanding the benefits of the new role, gaining the trust to create something you have not made before won't happen overnight. You must have fallen in love at least once, haven't you? Did you marry the person the next day? Assuming the other person felt the same, you must have gone through a period dating, of discovering the layers of sensitivity between each other. In the same way, you can develop your new interest through many creative acts.

As in a love relationship, the vulnerability enables trust. We need the willingness to open ourselves up to the creative side. Only then can we become intimate with our sensitivities, which softly move us toward new experiences and competencies as a creator.

It was in 1936, after Escher's second trip to Alhambra, that he resumed experimenting with animal shapes. By 1939, he had collected a significant number of trials on animal motifs, which became his inspiration for one of his first successful compositions, *Symmetry Work 25*.

Escher himself considered his design, *Watercolor Maquette for Leiden Town Hall*, to be the most accurate embodiment of his interest in the regular division of planes. It was created in 1941 and the artist benefited from *"the greatest amount of freedom by the people who commissioned the work."* After that, the study of the regular fitting of planes led him to designs that express a development, a circuit or a transformation.

When a romantic relationship transforms into a marriage, you assume the risk of a new life where the loved one occupies the central place. In the same way, when you allow your creative side to take the lead, you'll look at the world through the creator's eyes, through new habits of observation which pave the way to the alignment zone.

Composing music is Matias Kupiainen's area of creation.

Surreal fine art photography is Dasha Pears's fit zone.

Designing new vaccines is Vincenzo Cerullo's playground.

Cultural transformation is Harriet Fagerholm's playground.

Nano-biomaterials are Helder Santos's playground.

Leadership communication is John Bates's playground.

Public speaking is Oscar Santollala's playground.

Leading through uncertainty is Pamela Thompson's playground.

Virtual teams management is Peter Ivanov's playground.

Bringing women's voices on the stage is Tulia Lopes's playground.

What is your playground of knowledge or experience where you are ready to take your chances and practice your skills as a creator?

CHAPTER 12

Follow Your Sense of Beauty

All our knowledge begins with the senses, proceeds then to understanding, and ends with reason.

—Immanuel Kant

In the Romanian culture where I was born, there is a tradition when a baby turns one year old. The mother prepares a tray on which she selects objects, like a book, a pen, money, car keys, mobile phone, toothbrush, hair brush, mirror, scissors, etc. Faced with the tray, the baby chooses one object. The adults interpret the choice. It becomes the prophecy for the chosen profession of the adult to be.

Behind this ritual that has a primary purpose of creating a festive atmosphere, there is the realization that human beings are born with a range of sensitivities toward specific objects in the environment. It takes years to understand and act upon our sensitivities for some of us.

© Oana Velcu-Laitinen 2022
O. Velcu-Laitinen, *How to Develop Your Creative Identity at Work*,
https://doi.org/10.1007/978-1-4842-8680-7_12

Sensitivity is the perceptual engagement with some stimuli that arouse somatic reactions in a particular situation.[1] High levels of sensitivity are correlated with creativity. Highly sensitive people seem to be more open to sensory input and more aware of what's going on in their internal and external environment. To be a creator means that you become the kind of person who prefers to spend your time making sense of the sensitivities in a domain of interest. Discovering the meaning of your sensitivities is the new habit of the mind that prepares newbie creators for their first acts of creation.

Once you make peace with your psychic energy toward a domain, perception and attention to sensitivities are two important brain functions for funneling the creative energy.[2] The brain constantly digests pieces of information, out of which some are important for your ongoing tasks, and some are not. However, the brain filters some information which is less relevant for the immediate goals but is recognized as necessary for your creative intentions. Through a flexible processing system of attention, this information is nonetheless transferred to the short-term memory, where

---

[1] Berleant, A., (2015), Aesthetic Sensibility, Ambiances; DOI: https://doi.org/10.4000/ambiances.526.
Aron, E.N., Aron, A., and Jagiellowicz, J., (2012), Sensory Processing Sensitivity: A Review in the Light of the Evolution of Biological Responsivity, Personality and Social Psychology Review 16(3):262-82, DOI: https://doi.org/10.1177/1088868311434213

[2] Friedman, R.S, Fishbach, A., Förster, J., and Werth, L., (2003), Attentional Priming Effects on Creativity, Creativity Research Journal 15(2):277–286. DOI: https://doi.org/10.1207/S15326934CRJ152&3_18.
Sisi Liu, (2016), Broaden the mind before ideation: The effect of conceptual attention scope on creativity, Thinking Skills and Creativity, Vol. 22, pp. 190–200. www.sciencedirect.com/science/article/abs/pii/S1871187116301389.
Banerjee, S., Grover, S., Sridharan, D., (2017), Unraveling Causal Mechanisms of Top-Down and Bottom-Up Visuospatial Attention with Non-invasive Brain Stimulation Journal of the Indian Institute of Science, Volume 97, pp 451–475. https://link.springer.com/article/10.1007/s41745-017-0046-0.

it waits for a physiological response.[3] Especially in the first stages of the creative process – problem exploration and identification – the creator's ability to instantly recognize an unexpected pattern of sensitivities triggers the path of creative insight.

What might be your creative sensitivities that shed light on the information that matters for your creative endeavors? Beauty is in the eye of the beholder, they say. The perception of what is beautiful, novel, and captivating is unique to each creator, based on six types of sensitivities[4]:

1. **The human connection,** which John Bates, Leadership Communication Expert, describes as follows.

    "... it's interesting because sensitivity made a difference for me in the work environment. Sensitivity helped me a lot in business, in reading people. I think that some of the soft skills that made a big difference for me in my success are things like empathy and really, really listening. I could listen to people say things and I could say that again but make it much more succinct and more memorable."

    If you're anything like John, it's easy to tune into others' emotions and motives. This enables you to form deep and meaningful relationships. This is why the quality of conversations is as important for you as gourmet food is for others. You see beauty in human interactions.

---

[3] Carruthers, L., (2016), Creativity and Attention: A Multi-Method Investigation. Doctoral thesis; www.napier.ac.uk/~/media/worktribe/output-1052411/ creativity-and-attention-a-multi-method-investigation.pdf.

[4] Kaufman, S.B. and Gregoire, C., (2015), Wired to Create, Tarcher Perigree.

2. When you look into the eyes of a dog or a cat, do you feel that they get you? Do you find yourself talking to your plants when you water them? Closely related to human connection, another source of creative sensitivity can be the **sense of extended connection** with animals, other elements of nature, or a higher intelligence beyond life and death.

3. The third type of sensitivity to beauty is the **subtlety of** the **physical senses.** You enjoy the fine distinctions of tastes, scents, sounds, movement, or visuals of the objects you see around. For instance, refined taste buds can be the source of talent in cooking, perfumes creation, or winemaking. Likewise, a heightened visual sense can be the secret behind the gifted performers in any of the visual art forms, such as painting, sculpture, photography, design, etc.

4. What is the latest movie that made you cry while others remained as hard as nails? The **ease of being moved** is the fourth source of beauty. You are in tune with your emotions and are deeply touched by someone's gesture, a dance performance, a song, a theatre play, etc., where life's meaning is explored and expressed.

5. The **intellect sensitivity** – You may be one of the folks for whom abstract concepts and systems, such as models and theories, have an exceptional beauty, so much more when they explain an aspect of reality that has a special meaning for you.

6. The **awareness of needs in the environment** –
   you observe unfulfilled but relevant needs in
   your surroundings – others' life circumstances,
   a particular community, workplace, etc. – which
   others may be ignorant of. As a result, you want to
   get involved to work on a new business idea, social
   entrepreneurship, or a project of raising awareness,
   like Greta Thunberg's environmental activism.

Which of these six sensitivities defines the creator in you? One way to discover your creative sensitivities is to ask yourself, *"What are the acts of creation that I notice in my surroundings and I want to imitate?"*

Author and neurologist Oliver Sacks writes in his book, The River of Consciousness. *"All of us, to some extent, borrow from others, from the culture around us. Ideas are in the air, and we may appropriate, often without realizing, the phrases and language of the times. What is at issue is not the fact of 'borrowing' or 'imitating', of being 'derivative', being 'influenced', but what one does with what is borrowed or imitated or derived; how deeply one assimilates it, takes it into oneself, compounds it with one's own experiences and thoughts and feelings, places it in relation to oneself, and expresses it in a new way, one's own."* [5]

The depth to which you can assimilate others' ideas to your own experiences depends on your sensitivities. You then become more and more attentive to pieces of information that you may have previously ignored. Therefore, you discover new meanings of creative living, embodied in the match between your inner and external awareness, that call upon you to create (see Figure 12-1).

---

[5] www.oliversacks.com/oliver-sacks-books/the-river-of-consciousness/
Oliver Sacks, (2017), The River of Consciousness, Picador, pp. 120.

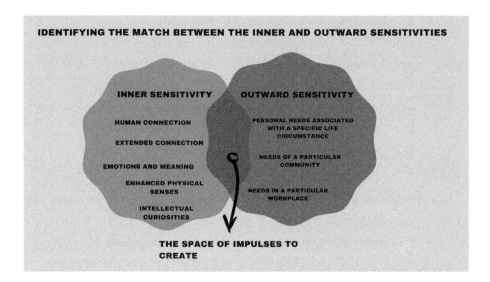

Figure 12-1. *Match inner–outward sensitivity*

Moorish artists inspired Escher's work. Who are the creators, and what are their projects that tempt you to adapt to your environment? Try it out without overthinking the pros and cons of these actions.

Some people count their blessings. You can count the sensitivities which result in an experimental creation.

Habit 1: The Discipline of Observing Your Sensitivities

In time, the interchange between your inner and outward sensitivities refines your creative focus, as photographer Dasha Pears witnesses. She considered taking on artistic projects dictated by a sense of social responsibility for a while.

"I think my professional interest would be to go and become a more conscious and responsible artist. Not to just express myself and my personal feelings and emotions and my images. But also to make people think

about some problems of their society which can be changed and draw their attention to them, that would be great. I'm not at that point yet and I thought that it should come naturally to people, but with my example, it does not."

Eventually, the emotional sensitivity triumphed.

"Over the years I've developed a style, which I now call psychorealism. With my art I make emotions and different psychological states tangible and bring them into the real world. With this, I try to help people accept all of their sides, both light and dark, and make peace with them, not fight them or try to hide, but also not let them run wild. This is my philosophy and my goal is to touch as many people as possible with it in a visual art form."

For a more effective transition from one project to another which is truthfully grounded in your creative sensitivities, you can choose to keep a personal record, like a journal, of the stimuli – words, images, ideas, sounds – which cause increased emotional reactivity while you are engaged in a specific task.

Environmental cues can help to reinforce the habit of jotting down your creative sensitivities. Cues are information that signals the brain that it's time to behave differently in a certain situation. First, choose signals that have a meaning for you, put you in the right mood, and speak to you, *"Now it's time to listen and see differently."* Second, you can select the activities you prefer to experience through the eyes of the creator. Here are three examples of cues and activities:

1. What are your sources of information? Assuming you have a favorite podcast you listen to, how about keeping a pen and paper close by? Then, as you listen, be ready to write down possible new concepts and ideas.

2. What do you normally do after hours of intense focus on knowledge acquisition, for instance? How about setting a reminder clock to go for a walk? Pay

attention to what is going on around you. Do you notice any possible associations between the street stimuli and the previously absorbed information?

3. When you join a public event, who are the people you socialize with? How about looking for at least a new person that appears interesting to talk with? Frame the conversation as a game of discovery of a new reality. Imagine there's a planet hovering above the head of the person you're conversing with. The deeper the discussion, the better chances to map onto their universe of experiences, beliefs, and values. What do you learn from this person that can be used for your creative aspirations?

With such a structure, you can observe and capture your thoughts that spontaneously arise during your engagement in any learning experience. When **there's a click between what you see or hear and what you feel**, you'll have one of the **"Aha" experiences**. *"This is what I'll create next"* kind of thought.

Out of self-curiosity – Optional Exercise 1:

What would be one activity that is meaningful to you in which you engage weekly and where you'd like to follow the recurring creative sensitivities?

At your earliest convenience, choose three weeks to keep track of words, images, ideas, and sounds that arouse your sensitivities as you engage in the respective activities.

Write down the following sentence:

"During the next 3 weeks, (enter dates), as I engage in this activity (name it), I will pay attention to words, images, and ideas that excite me or intrigue me."

Keep this sentence somewhere in sight in your home or office.

Right after the activity, choose a physical place that inspires you and the necessary resources – pen, paper, and glue – so you can add them to a collage. "On date _____, I started thinking about _____."

At the end of the three weeks, take a one-week break. After, you get back to the composition. What kind of pattern do you see in the pieces of information collected there?

Habit 2: Question Your Interpretations

It's not what you look at that matters, it's what you see.

—Henry David Thoreau

If we zoom in the process of looking at something, this is how it unfolds. When you look at something – an object, a landscape, a chart, etc. – your eyes fall on one element, considered most relevant, unusual, captivating, or intriguing compared with the rest. This focus on outstanding detail triggers a stream of thoughts. In the creative process, the trigger is as important as what follows: the interpretation of what you see. In turn, the interpretation is based on factual knowledge and personal memories that come to mind.

Briefly, perceptions lead to automatic interpretations. Let's do a thought experiment, shall we? What is the first thing that catches your eye when you look at the following photo? Kindly take a few seconds to note down what comes to your mind.

Let's imagine there's a third observer for whom the flower with a striped pattern is the first striking thing. The interpretation is accompanied by meaning-making, *"What does it mean to me?"*

"Ah! I don't like artificial flowers." This person can be thinking. Then, the subsequent thoughts, *"None of the flowers are real," "I like natural flowers," "Maybe I should buy some," "But, I feel sad when they wither," "How can I enjoy natural flowers in my flat, without feeling sorry when they go to the rubbish?", "How can you recycle dried flowers?"*

The third observer's stream of thoughts may end in the form of a question, *"What can we make out of withered flowers?"*

Getting back to the sequence of thoughts you wrote down, it's certainly different from the third observer's hypothetical thoughts. This thought experiment illustrates how the human brain makes stories out of anything we look at.

The brain is a storyteller, a chatterbox that constantly engages in interpretations of the words, sounds, and physical sensations that are deemed essential in a particular situation. Especially when we are in a new situation, the storyteller is even more alert in making sense of what's going on and suggesting ways to cope.

When we are intrigued by a new situation, when the storyteller concocts a juicy interpretation, questions arise and trigger the desire to find answers. All this can happen within seconds of perceiving a stimulus that catches the attention. The storyteller awakens the inquirer, who disrupts anything we might have been doing before. Consequently, the inquirer steps in to sort out the meaning of the attraction.

Let's return to the perception of flowers as a universal embodiment of beauty and how each human mind is unique in making interpretations. For instance, this is how a flower's beauty can inspire curiosity and wonder in a poet, who has a special eye for the details in the surrounding and how they impact the emotions:

"Do you have some secret message for me?

You can talk; I am discreet.

Is your greenery a secret?

Is your perfume a language?"

From To a Flower by Alfred de Musset.

This is how the beauty of a flower can be interpreted by a person in whom an intellectual sensitivity, visual sensitivity and the capacity to be moved mingle:

"I can appreciate the beauty of a flower," says physicist Richard Feynman. *"The fact that the colors in the flower evolved in order to attract insects to pollinate it is interesting; it means that insects can see the color. It adds a question: does this aesthetic sense also exist in the lower forms? Why is it aesthetic? All kinds of interesting questions which science only adds to the excitement, the mystery and the awe of a flower."*[6]

Which of the preceding two interpretations on the beauty of a flower do you relate to – the poet's or the scientist's? Could it be that both views speak to different sides of your creative self?

---

[6] https://vimeo.com/55874553?ref=fb-share&fbclid=IwAR3SB9CVpXiHl-5 CZn-mryWK2cqjEDWe6KIshWz7wfZLM61nX8wqWGhMGdo

The focus on the external elements of a flower leads to a poetic expression. The focus on the microscopic elements of a flower form a scientific inquiry. This collaboration between the two voices in the creator's mind, **the interpreter** and **the inquirer**, decides the role and activities to engage in the preparation stage of the creative process.

"What can we make out of withered flowers?" The third observer, in whom there is an assumed sensitivity to nature, may ask themselves.

This thought experiment points to the importance of paying attention to the questions stemming from a newly discovered pattern of sensitivities. The more meaningful some questions feel, the stronger the impulse to acquire new knowledge and experiences. New learning experiences lead to a snowball of questions, further information acquisition, and eventually, to the first insight to create something.

Summing up, when you discover an acute interest in an aspect of reality, you can choose to be diligent about observing your sensitivities in the respective area. Mind your interpretations. What questions of wonder might arise?

Optional Exercise 2: Looking back at the patterns in creative sensitivities you collected in the previous exercise, what inquiry questions come to mind?

Habit 3: Cultivate Your Intuition About What Questions to Focus On

Our inner world of awareness, sensitivity, and attention is wrapped in questions of curiosity which, whenever vetted by creative intuition, will nudge us toward experimental creations.

Let's assume that the question *"What can we make out of withered flowers?"* is loaded with meaning for the third-party observer in our thought experiment. In addition, if there's an intuitive nudge to follow up on this question, the creator would start engaging with the environment in a novel way, gathering new information and asking new questions. *"What initiatives of recycling flowers are out there?"*

It's one thing to be curious to get an answer to this question because you get satisfaction from discovering new information about the floral industry. However, it's a different kettle of fish to feel the eagerness to start an entrepreneurial project of recycling flowers for new uses.

To make the mental leap from *"I'm curious to know more about* _____*"* to *"I'm curious to create* _____*,"* we need to have the *gut feeling* that pushes us to take a specific creative action, such as the first steps to build an art initiative, a handicraft group, or any other entrepreneurial idea stemming from the interest in transforming withered flowers.

During the research of existing initiatives, the intuitive nudge about creating a world of dry flowers would awaken other creative sensitivities, like the sense of human connection. Together with the sense of extended connection with nature, these two sensitivities would lead to new questions, like *"What can I do differently?"* and *"What if flowers can connect people?"* This would generate an insight like, *"I'll kick-start the flowers club!"*

Insight is the glue between the exploration and implementation stages of the creative process. The flowers club would be similar to a book club except that it would connect people through stories of empathy and geography. Instead of a specific book, the discussions would be built around the withered bouquets brought by the participants.

"What was special about the day you bought these flowers?"

"If the flowers could see the color of your consciousness, what would that color be?"

"If flowers could smell your feelings the day you bought them, what would the smell be like?"

"What kind of climate do these flowers like?"

"Who were the people who picked them up?"

"What does a day of their lives look like?"

"Who were the people involved in the logistics?", etc.

The discussions around such questions would become the invisible bond between people who engage their hands in making decorative objects out of the dying flowers.

The gap between a question – *"What can we make out of withered flowers?"* – and an insight for experimental creation – *"I'll start the initiative of the flowers' club."* – is filled with creative intuition. Without it, there would be no initiative. (See Figure 12-2.)

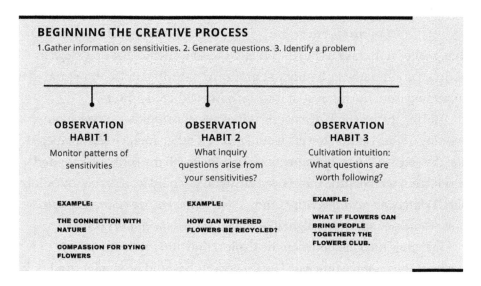

BEGINNING THE CREATIVE PROCESS
1.Gather information on sensitivities. 2. Generate questions. 3. Identify a problem

OBSERVATION HABIT 1	OBSERVATION HABIT 2	OBSERVATION HABIT 3
Monitor patterns of sensitivities	What inquiry questions arise from your sensitivities?	Cultivation intuition: What questions are worth following?
EXAMPLE:	EXAMPLE:	EXAMPLE:
THE CONNECTION WITH NATURE	HOW CAN WITHERED FLOWERS BE RECYCLED?	WHAT IF FLOWERS CAN BRING PEOPLE TOGETHER? THE FLOWERS CLUB.
COMPASSION FOR DYING FLOWERS		

Figure 12-2. *Summary of inner observation habits that lead to creative insight for experimental creation*

What Is Intuition and Why Is It Important?

Intuition is your inner guide, the feeling of knowing without evidence that will inform you about which creative sensitivities and questions to follow up. For instance, my intuition informs me of my curiosity about the psychology of creativity. It guides me as I'm writing this book.

"What is intuition to you?", I asked Helder Santos, professor in Biomedical Engineering.

"I think it's something that, down there, you know 'I should go in this direction, I should do it this way.' So, if you want to put it in simple terms: A small voice inside that tells you when you have some kind of doubts... 'Am I doing it the right way? Should I go in this right direction or not?' So I think intuition is exactly that, your own self telling you that if you're thinking like this, and if you think that is the way to go, just go and do it.

I could even say: Don't be so rational, but be more intuitive... I don't know if that makes sense, because sometimes if you think too much, you can start to block things. But intuition is a different thing, it comes from your inner [self]. Because if I'm going to be too rational, I might actually lose intuition," Helder concluded.

This is how John Bates, Leadership Communication Expert, describes his understanding of Intuition.

"It's a good question. The first place that my mind goes to because of the work I do is that your intuition is your paleomammalian ancient brain and it really dialed into reality. It sees things. It notices patterns that you never consciously notice. But it can communicate with you but it doesn't have language. But it has to communicate with you with a gut feeling.

So I think part of intuition is that piece of my brain that is so ancient and wired so animalistically deeply that it can pick up signals from the environment that I won't get consciously. I'm pretty sure that some of the things that I have developed have come about because my ancient brain noticed people's reactions to things and helped me formulate something that would work with that, or deal with that, or answer that, whatever. And I do think there is a collaboration between the logical brain and the completely non-logical, no reason, no language, ancient part of the brain like that. And it will toss those ideas up to my conscious brain through enough feelings and intuition."

Therefore, for some of us, intuition is the intelligence of the unconscious and it is rooted in the evolved capacities of the brain to react to the environment.[7] Another way to describe intuition is as the communication between our bowels and the brain. In the book, *The Developing Mind*, Daniel Siegel defines the brain as the brain in the skull, *"head brain,"* integrated with the intestinal input, the *"gut brain"* and the heart's input, the *"heart brain."*[8] The right hemisphere of the head brain is influenced by the data that comes from the gut and heart brain. These inputs form the wisdom of the body and shape our emotional state.

Hence, the right hemisphere of the head brain processes our emotional states and the gist of a context we find ourselves in. But it doesn't have the linguistic function. It's the left hemisphere that has the capacity to assign words to what we experience. Therefore, the collaboration between the left and right sides of the brain can help us make sense of who we are and how we relate to the environment, in a particular context.

When we find ourselves in new situations, when we don't have sufficient information nor previous experiences to compare with and we have to decide quickly how to react, this kind of hemispheric communication helps us make a fast evaluation of what we see, what is true and what action to take to successfully manage the situation. Let's call this **"instinctive intuition,"** shall we?

The higher the uncertainty avoidance in a person, the less willingness to take the risk of listening to their intuitive voices.[9] Listening to your intuition is like a dominoes game. Family culture and close social relationships matter for imitating intuitive based-judgements. In turn, macro-cultural forces, such as culture, political system, and history, can influence the extent to which parents and caretakers use their intuition and pass it on to children. For example, in most Western societies,

---

[7] Gigerenzer, G., (2007), Gut Feelings, Penguin Books.
[8] Siegel, D.J., (2020), The Developing Mind, The Guilford Press, pp. 465.
[9] Hofstede, G. (2001), Culture's consequences, 2nd edn, Thousand Oaks, CA: Sage.

economic changes shifted the importance away from obeying authority figures to reliance on personal judgement, initiative, and responsibility.[10]

"For me it is a very tricky question and topic because I think that I grew up with basically having no intuition and never paying attention to it," said Dasha Pears. *"And now I'm trying to develop this thing. I don't know how it relates to my art. I'm just trying to sort of feel something about things in the life around me, when making any decision in my life, not just artistic. When it comes to my art, I just do what I feel, and I don't, I never call it intuition. I didn't call it anything, just this is how I create, that was my process."*

When you are raised with strong authoritative parental figures, you are used to following someone else's voice. Why does it matter to believe in your instinctive intuition? As we can see from the neurological integration of the brain, we are wired with intuition. It brings relevant information for decision-making, ever since childhood. However, without the ability to understand the instinctive intuition in action, we cannot develop our unique identity as an individual. If we disregard the inner voice, we get confused about our potential and sabotage our ability to deeply feel life.

"But I think intuition comes into play more when you have to decide between several things," continues Dasha. *"There are two choices that might be obvious to other people, but you take the third one. And people ask, 'Why?' But you still do it because you feel like it.*

I still don't have it, I think."

When we decide what creative idea to engage in and during the implementation, it's intuition which directs our attention toward the beneficial actions. Hence, we benefit from understanding our intuition. Admittedly, gut feelings do not always signal the most accurate

---

[10] Esteban-Guitart, M. and Ratner, C., (2011), A Macro Cultural Psychological Theory of Identity, Journal of Social Distress and the Homeless, 20(1-2), pp. 1–22. www.researchgate.net/publication/272309885_A_Macro_Cultural_Psychological_Theory_of_Identity

information to pay attention to.[11] But they are our best performance tools under uncertainty. The challenge is to take the risk and stay open to it.

Because intuition involves a feeling that cannot be explained logically, it requires courage to follow it until further evidence. For instance, scientific work may be one of the environments where you may be thinking that there's no place for intuition. Helder Santos believes the opposite to be the case:

"Because we are scientists, sometimes we think – and that was my thinking many years ago – that intuition should not be part of the scientist's thinking. Which I think is totally wrong, at the moment. But I have to say, if I'm going to discuss with some of my colleagues or professors, they will tell me that I am not thinking correctly. Because they think that no, in science you cannot use intuition. But that's not true. You can, and in some cases it's actually a better way to do things.

My wife has helped me quite a lot to do that, and through the years I also learned more, because sometimes you come to these, as you said, you have these kinds of contradictions, and then what shall you do? And if you are not firm… You also have to be a bit confident.

But I think people have a bit of a lack of self-confidence sometimes. So they're afraid to take the risk, so they go more to the rational side."

When was the last time you thought, *"I'll go with my gut"* or *"I'll sleep on it"*? These idioms point to the relevance of bodily experiences for making decisions. If human thought is the outcome of a dynamic

---

[11] Daniel Kahneman, (2013), Thinking Fast and Slow, Farrar, Straus and Giroux.

interaction between the mind, body and the environment, then creative thought does not form solely in the head either.[12]

The body contributes to the formation of cognition by affecting the perception of information through its sensorimotor capabilities. Thus, to stay open to your intuition, you can start by learning to be in touch with your body's signals.

On your own, you could practice observing the sensations of your body by frequently noticing the physical reactions to words that have a meaning to you, such as *"mother," "childhood," "success,"* etc. Moreover, if you want to have someone holding you accountable, you could seek an expert trained in personal guidance, like Pamela Thompson.

"I studied body-centered coaching a number of years ago…," says Pamela. *"A lot of my clients are successful people and very intelligent people. They tend to have relied on their logical left brain and so I help them reconnect with their bodies through learning mindfulness, body scanning, and mindless walking meditation … Your body, I believe, always knows the truth."*

The folk wisdom, *"Follow your intuition"* is a cliche but it does remind us to interact, in a respectful way, with our bodies. Rather than considering the body as a carrier from point A to point B, we can pay attention to it as a source of wisdom and intuition. The more we learn to work with our intuition, which depending on the context can be felt as a sense of certainty or fear, the more we trust in ourselves and take responsibility for our actions.

---

[12] Gallagher, S., (2015), How embodied cognition is being disembodied. The Philosophers' Magazine. 68, pp. 96–102.www.researchgate.net/publication/276474146_How_embodied_cognition_is_being_disembodied
Glăveanu, V. P., (2014), The psychology of creativity: a critical reading. Creativity 1, pp. 10–32.www.researchgate.net/publication/275607027_The_Psychology_of_Creativity_A_Critical_Reading
Malinin, L.H., (2019), How Radical Is Embodied Creativity? Implications of 4E Approaches for Creativity Research and Teaching. Front. Psychol. 10:2372. doi: 10.3389/fpsyg.2019.02372.

Optional Exercise 3: The Before and After Trust

*When you participate in a public event, choose a stranger to talk with,
in line with the thinking, "This person looks trustworthy." At the end of
the discussion, revisit your initial thought. Is the person still trustworthy?
What is the information that makes them reliable in your eyes? What is the
evidence, if any, that contradicts your initial intuition? Would you want to
stay in touch with them?*

You may decide to ignore the evidence collected during the talk
and continue to rely on your intuition. You may resolve to pretend that
you never spoke with that individual. Or, you may have a couple more
meetings before making up your mind. What strategy would you go for?

If you repeat this exercise many times, you will understand what drives
you to talk with a stranger. Is it that you unconsciously feel comfortable
around that person because they share some characteristics of your
ingroup? Or is it because they are absorbing? Perceiving similarity in people
and situations does not mean that it is your instinctive intuition – a sense of
trust – guiding you. Quite the contrary, it can be that intuition is taking you
to a challenging conversation that makes you feel nervous and confident
that it will be a useful experience. When you follow your intuition, you'll
pass through the eye of the needle, get rid of ineffective biases and get on
the other side, more open to new people and information.

How to Discern Your Creative Intuition

When you follow a creative sensitivity, it can lead to another. And then
you'll have competing sensitivities that call for you to create. Continuing
with the hypothetical scenario of the flowers club, after some months, the
creator may realize that they have developed a liking for both withered
flowers photography and a growing interest in the memory of flowers. As a
result, they may be wondering, *"Should I engage in abstract photography or
the science of flowers?"*

As with any other creative dilemmas, without intuitive thinking, we can enumerate all the pros and cons of two potential courses of action and still be undecided about the most suitable alternative to follow. The benefit of intuition is that it helps make decisions that feel personally meaningful, with little effort and no conscious deliberation.[13]

A word of caution. We should be careful not to confuse intuition with insight. Insight means *"seeing into"* the amount of information available and providing the solution to a current problem or situation. Intuition enables you to filter which information is worth considering for insight into life problems. Then, there are analytical problems, such as programming, where insight is achieved through logic and reason.

Choosing one course of creative action over another, such as the choice between abstract photography or floriculture, belongs to the more complex problems of creative identity development. For these kinds of life problems, there can be more than one possible solution and there are no specific steps on how to decide. Working out our way toward a satisfying solution, which is to notice the next opportunity to create, can be left to intuition, creative intuition, more precisely.[14]

---

[13] Hogarth, R.M., (2010), Intuition: A Challenge for Psychological Research on Decision Making, Psychological Inquiry, 21, pp. 338–353.

[14] Carson, S., (2010), Your Creative Brain, Harvard Health Publications, Harvard Medical School.

Dijksterhuis, A., et al., (2006), On making the right choice: The deliberation-with-out-attention effect. Science, 311, pp. 1005–1007. www.researchgate.net/publication/7291642_On_Making_the_Right_Choice_The_Deliberation-Without-Attention_Effect

Dijksterhuis, A., and Nordgren, L.F., (2006), A theory of the unconscious thought. Perspectives on Psychological Science, 1, pp. 95–109. www.researchgate.net/publication/254124133_A_theory_of_unconscious_thougt

Hardman, T. J., (2021), Understanding Creative Intuition, Journal of Creativity, Vol. 31, pp. 1–6. https://doi.org/10.1016/j.yjoc.2021.100006

Creative intuition is the feeling of knowing that arises when knowledge and experiences are combined in novel ways. It is *"a vague anticipatory perception that orients creative work in a promising direction."*[15] This anticipatory perception of truth is a key input to insight formation, the "Aha!" moment of the creative process.

In a nutshell, creative intuition serves the progress of the creative process. Instinctive intuition serves to manage the everyday ambiguities. For instance, in traffic, instinctive intuition comes in handy when you anticipate that the driver from the next lane will overtake without signaling. It allows you to act upon unconscious cues and spontaneously react in a present situation. Creative intuition allows us to make new connections between what we see and already know to discern what pieces of information and courses of action are helpful in the creative process.

Alternatively, creative intuition is the unconscious intelligence at work, exploring future favorable outcomes. Instinctive intuition can be viewed as implicit memory at work, exploiting the present beneficial outcomes. From the point of view of the cognitive processes, creative intuition is associated with divergent thinking, whereas intuitive intuition is related to convergent thinking.

Finally, creative intuition requires a longer processing time between stimuli and reaction, whereas instinctive intuition arises immediately after perceiving the stimuli. Therefore, it can take a long time to absorb knowledge and experiences until our creative intuition starts guiding us in the preparation stage of the creative process.

Creative intuition is experienced as a reassuring sentiment as if coming from outside you, *"Trust this direction."* It feels as if someone is cheering for

---

[15] Policastro, E., (1995), Creative intuition: an integrative review. Creativity Research Journal, 8, pp. 99–113.
Dane and Pratt, (2009), Conceptualizing and Measuring Intuition: A Review of Recent Trends, International Review of Industrial and organisational Psychology, Vol. 24, pp. 1–40.

you, which makes a lasting memory. To gather further information about how the choice can be beneficial for your creative interests, you'll have to engage in the respective action.

The challenge is that we can confuse the voice of our creative intuition – even for the highly intuitive among us – with other emotions, such as fear or hope. Therefore, in real-life contexts you may want to deepen your awareness of how these emotions are sensed in your body. Learning to tell the difference can become your new way of listening to the world.

As an illustration of how you can tune into the subtle experiences of your body during creative intuition, instinctive intuition, fear, and wishful thinking, let's do the following exercise, shall we?

Repeat to yourself, "yes," seven times.

Repeat to yourself, "no," seven times.

Repeat to yourself, "truth," seven times.

Repeat to yourself, "dream," seven times.

What are the receptive body areas? By saying "yes," you may experience some sensations in the pit of the stomach, where intuitive intuition is felt. "No" resonates in the pelvis, where the lack of emotional support is felt. The word "truth" is sensed at the throat level. So whenever you have a creative intuition about a possible action, say it out loud to yourself. If the throat feels relaxed, it indicates the action is favorable. The word "dream" is a type of wishful thinking which can relax the chest area.

In everyday life, your feelings get entangled in the sympathetic (stimulating arousal) and parasympathetic (stimulating relaxation) nervous systems of the body. *"Should I engage in abstract photography or in horticulture?"* In this scenario of the dilemma of creative possibilities, the fictional creator could opt to spend some time engaging both in the study of photography and the biology of flowers. They will make mistakes, but also learn to observe their direct experiences of creative intuition, fear, and wishful thinking.

After exploring these two possible paths, should the fictional creator settle for abstract photography, they will become a newly minted artist in this niche or in the domain of emotions, such as art therapy. Should they commit to horticulture, they could become a content creator of botanical knowledge. Ultimately, their creative sensitivity toward flowers may not lead to any new role as a creator. Instead, they may settle for photography as a creative hobby that nurtures their everyday well-being. There can be as many creative outcomes starting from this dilemma as creators who are living it.

To conclude, we are born with a neural system of intuitive intelligence, which unfolds or is restricted in interrelational and microcultural contexts. As a creator, it is beneficial to develop both instinctive and creative intuition. Instinctive intuition comes as an immediate reaction to a stimulus. Creative intuition is an emotional knowing, the feeling of self-assurance that the choice of an action – specific new knowledge and skills – will bear fruits in the future, without knowing what the final outcome will be like. The challenge is to stay humble and learn your body's signals of creative intuition, fear of the unknown, or too much positive thinking about an expected outcome.

CHAPTER 13

Manage Your Mood to Follow Your Intuition

So far, we have argued that in order to increase the odds of coming up with an original idea for experimental creation, we want to look at the environment in a different way than we are used to. This means forming habits of observation of creative sensitivities, generating questions of inquiry and making intuitive choices. These new habits direct our attention to what is within our control to find our place as a recognized creator. Yet, it seems that we are not always in the mood to act upon our intuition.

Research shows that positive moods motivate us to be more confident in our creative intuition. A 2003 study investigated the effect of emotional states on the ability to make intuitive judgments about the consistency of the relationship between three given words, such as "goat, pass, green."[1] The findings show that a positive mood activates remote verbal associates in memory, which improve intuitive coherent opinions. By contrast, negative mood engenders close associates and dominant word meanings, thus impairing intuitive coherence judgments.

---

[1] Bolte, A., Goschke, T., and Kuhl, J., (2003), Emotion and Intuition: Effects of Positive and Negative Mood on Implicit Judgments of Semantic Coherence, Psychological Science, Vol. 14, Issue 5, pp. 416–421.
https://journals.sagepub.com/doi/abs/10.1111/1467-9280.01456

In another study, decision makers who are more aware of their emotions and experience certain moods – either highly positive or mildly negative – are more likely to use their intuition.[2] Therefore, in the exploration stage of the creative process, when you plunge yourself into new knowledge or experiences of interest, learning to increase self-awareness and regulate positive moods facilitate intuitive decisions.

There's this fable of a rabbit and tortoise. A tortoise invites the rabbit to a running contest, which the rabbit confidently accepts. To the rabbit's surprise, as it is about to reach the finish line, it sees that the turtle was already there.[3]

What had happened? The rabbit underestimated the qualities of the turtle who kept going, step by step, without taking a break. Instead, the rabbit didn't question for a second that it wouldn't arrive first. Therefore, when it felt tired, it didn't hesitate to take a short nap.

The turtle felt tired but kept advancing, slowly but surely, relying on its perseverance and ignoring the rabbit's laughter. So, we want to be like the turtle in the fable, walking the creator's path by betting on our creative intuition to filter the background noise and focus on what matters to complete acts of creation. What if your creative intuition becomes your strength?

In the remainder of this section, we will look into habits of emotions management to make more space around the intuitive voice guiding the creator's path. As a side effect, you'll experience a boost in your emotional well-being.

---

[2] Sinclair, M., Ashkanasy, N.M., and Chattopadhyay, P., (2010), Affective antecedents of intuitive decision making, Journal of Management & Organization, Vol. 16, Issue 3, pp. 382–398, DOI: https://doi.org/10.5172/jmo.16.3.382
[3] www.moralstories.org/the-rabbit-and-the-turtle/

Habit 4: Emotions, Moods, and Ensuing Stories

Emotions and moods are two levels of emotional experiences. Emotions are directly related to a specific stimulus – object, person, or event. For example, your reactions when looking at the following photo are examples of emotions.

Emotions are temporary interferences to the mood. They are like thunder, intense and short-lived. On the other hand, moods – optimism, boredom, depression – can be of longer duration, varying from days to months. Compared with emotions, moods are like a slow fire, less intense, but they occupy more of our information processing capacity. When you look at the preceding photo, the more positive your current mood is, the more details you may have observed. In addition, moods affect emotional reactions and how we interpret what we see in the photo. Let's test how this interrelation works. What might the person at the end of the pier be doing?

A person in a jovial mood may be thinking, *"The person at the end of the pier is waiting for a friend to pick her up by boat to go to a party."* A person in a sad mood may be thinking, *"The person at the end of the pier is lamenting her loneliness."* Someone who just came from a meditation class may be thinking, *"The person at the end of the pier is daydreaming."*

Every person looking at this photo is making their own unique interpretations. Based on this example, it's useful to further notice how your mood influences the spontaneous reactions to stimuli and the automatic stories that the mind concocts. Therefore, it's worth taking care of your mood, as much as is within your control.

The moods affect the quality of your life experiences and the visions you aspire for. For example, the hypothetical creator we got acquainted with in this book may be thinking, *"Should I spend my time creating my portfolio in abstract photography or taking my first course in plant varieties?"* If you're facing similar dilemmas, whatever path you take as a creator, make sure that the decision is based on inherently meaningful interests, not on the fear of not being good enough or some grandiose dreams rooted in egomania.

Optional Exercise 4: *At exercise 1, you were invited to choose an activity that has meaning for you – at work or in your free time – and jot down possible ideas, objects, sounds, etc., that are striking as you engage in the respective activity.*

This exercise aims to keep track of your mood at the outset of the respective activity for another three weeks.

"During the next 3 weeks, (enter dates), as I engage in this activity (name it), I will pay attention to words, images, and ideas that excite me or intrigue me."

"On date _____ , I had the following feelings _____, _____, _____. I started thinking about _____."

When you complete this task and look at your records, can you see any correlations between the feelings and the thoughts you logged? What are the moods that are more prolific for you? How can you get yourself into those moods before moments of knowledge acquisition?

Habit 5: Practice Gratitude – When Pleasantly and Unpleasantly Surprised

Negative events are stickier to mind and for a longer time than positive events. For instance, for how many hours or days are you ruminating about an unpleasant interaction with someone? How about the time when someone surprised you in a good way, how long did you indulge yourself in the joyful feeling? Moreover, ominous signals from the environment get priority in the brain's perceptual processing system, which require an immediate action. Studies show that the emotional content of words affect reading, by prioritizing the focus on the material that arouses intense emotions over reading the words with a neutral value.[4]

As you transition from aspiring to established creator, some of the individuals you interact with may speed-up the progress by providing useful information, resources and reinforcements. Others will be a test for your determination to succeed.[5] Some years ago, I was asked by the

---

[4] Citron, F.M.M., Gray, M.A., Critchley, H.D., Weekes, B.S., and Ferstl, E.C., (2014), Emotional valence and arousal affect reading in an interactive way: Neuroimaging evidence for an approach-withdrawal framework, Neuropsychologia, 56(100), pp. 79–89. www.ncbi.nlm.nih.gov/pmc/articles/PMC4098114/
Bradley, M.M. and Lang, P.J., (1999), Affective norms for English words (ANEW): Instruction manual and affective ratings. Technical Report C-1, The Center for Research in Psychophysiology, University of Florida, pp. 1–49. https://pdodds. w3.uvm.edu/teaching/courses/2009-08UVM-300/docs/others/everything/ bradley1999a.pdf.
Citron, F.M.M., Weekes, B.S., and Ferstl, E.C., (2012), How are affective word ratings related to lexico-semantic properties? Evidence from the Sussex Affective Word List (SAWL) Applied Psycholinguistics. pp. 1–19.

[5] Dimov, D., (2007), Beyond the Single-Person, Single-Insight Attribution in Understanding Entrepreneurial Opportunities, Entrepreneurship Theory and Practice, pp. 713–731.
http://citeseerx.ist.psu.edu/viewdoc/download?doi=10.1.1.452.2631&rep =rep1&type=pdf

project manager of an integration program financed by the city of Helsinki to facilitate a course for a group of foreign job seekers who had recently relocated to Finland.

At that time, I had a few months of experience under my belt as a creativity coach. Despite knowing that acculturation was not a top interest I wanted to focus on, I accepted the offer. I could not resist the temptation to test how personal strengths training would be received by people whose primary need was to make ends meet.

While it's beneficial to anticipate and prepare for difficulties in undertaking a new initiative,[6] the experiencing self finds a way to take the narrating self by surprise. I worked hard on adapting the course to the intended audience. However, during the second workshop, I felt some discordant vibes in the air. Right after, the program coordinator informed me that two participants complained about the course slides. It then dawned on me that I had designed the content as if I was going to work with individuals with a Master's Degree when 80% of my course participants did not have a Bachelor's degree.

Getting obsessed with the things that go wrong in a new project can result in mental paralysis and chronic stress. Hence, to maintain your health and the quality of your work, it's wise to think twice about the bad and the good that happens to you.

What does it mean to you to succeed in your creative initiatives? In a nutshell, to succeed refers to two kinds of outcomes. There's the external success reflected in the achievement of recognition, wealth, influence, etc. And there's the **internal success,** which we define in this book as the ability to **create a constructive internal dialogue** about what's important to focus on at crucial moments of the creative process. How much time do

---

[6] Kappes, H.B. and Oettingen, G., (2011), Positive fantasies about idealized futures sap energy, Journal of Experimental Social Psychology, Vol. 47, Issue 4, pp. 719–729. www.sciencedirect.com/science/article/abs/pii/S002210311100031X?via%3Dihub

you spend thinking about your measures of external success? How much time do you spend paying attention to the thoughts and emotions related to the progress being made or the lack of it?

"What, if anything, could I be thinking and doing differently when I feel stuck with this new project?" When you are committed to keeping an existing client, attracting a new one, or establishing a connection with an influential person, but you face obstacles, it helps to have the mindset, *"What is there for me to learn from this bottleneck?"*

As counterintuitive as it is for a mind designed to be lured by the negative, to advance on the chosen path as a creator, you'd benefit from learning to sink into the goodness existing already in your life. Hence, gratitude is a habit we need. Approaching each experience and person with gratitude is like a game of hidden gems. With every failed expectation, there is an important piece of information for you to decode, which will open your mind to the next action.

Gratitude is an emotion or thinking that can occur when a person, luck, or a divine intervention supports you to achieve your goals. The experience of gratitude comes with at least three psychological benefits. First, it **stimulates your creative thinking**. As a result, a wider range of possibilities comes to mind.[7] Second, it can rebuild your psychological and social resources, by helping you **reframe the expectations** with which you engage in social interactions. And third, it **prevents detrimental actions**, such as giving up or blaming ourselves or others. In short, gratitude empowers you to see an abundance of solutions.

There are two moments when you can choose to practice your grateful thinking – when you receive unexpected help and when things don't go as you planned. When you are the receiver of goodness, the favors that come your way can pass by unnoticed unless you allow your body to delight in

---

[7] Fredrickson, B. L., (2004), Gratitude, Like Other Positive Emotions, Broadens and Builds, The Psychology of Gratitude, pp. 145–166. http://perpus.univpancasila.ac.id/repository/EBUPT190074.pdf#page=162

them. What is one thing, one word, one gesture that has recently made a temporary positive impact on you? It doesn't have to be related to your creative pursuits. Even the tiniest gesture of mundane kindness, like someone's smile, is worth being mindful of.

As for bigger acts of generosity, when another person does spend their time doing something that helps you progress with your creative project, can you take a moment and contemplate what the status of your project would be like if it weren't for the benefactor's effort? The less you take for granted the help that others offer you, the more you open your eyes to the luck that accompanies you on the creator's path.

The capacity to feel appreciative when receiving help is genetically encoded in human nature, across cultures. So, to some degree, we all feel naturally grateful now and then; for instance, when watching the sunset or receiving an unexpected raise. However, the true test of gratitude is when things don't go as you think they would. When you expect applause, you receive rotten tomatoes in the face. In my case, I was hoping for appreciation for great course content; instead, I heard complaints.

When you anticipate benefits from an external source and don't receive them, disappointment, bitterness, and frustration can ensue naturally. Furthermore, because negative feelings are stickier and last longer, you may enter a tunnel vision that shows pitch black on the chosen path. Such moments are perfect timing to exercise gratitude for the status quo.

The personal strengths course delivered to the foreign job-seekers consumed much of my emotional energy. Quitting could have been a reasonable option. But I chose to look at the mismatch between the course material and the participants' experiences as an opportunity for me to practice my humility and empathy. I thus resolved to change the content for the remaining sessions. When you reframe an unwanted situation through gratitude, there is a hidden strength to discover about yourself. I thus discovered the ability to find some pockets of time to customize the materials based on the latest information about the audience. When the course ended, the coordinator offered me an unanticipated bonus, and the course participants wrote to me a *"We love you"* card.

"What is there for me to learn from this bottleneck?" Assuming you are interested in turning grateful thinking into a loyal habit of mind, there can be **four starting points to reframe a moment of impasse** and shed light on the goodness that is actually present in the respective situation.

1. The bigger picture. The current challenge belongs to **a project that you volunteered to take responsibility for**. Isn't it a privilege to wake up in the morning knowing you are free to choose the activities that benefit your personal growth?

2. The past successes. What are the **milestones** you have reached already? You must have gone through a series of small wins to get to the point where you feel stuck. What might be the personal qualities reflected in them? Can one of those strengths be used in the current situation?

For example, creative qualities, like **empathy** and **hypothetical thinking**, can help you bring refreshing angles to the present obstacle. Who is one key beneficiary in the current project? What if you asked them about the value they see in the project? These questions would enable you to change your perspective and see the project through other people's expectations.

When I decided to rework the course content, I asked the program coordinator what she would do if she were in my shoes. She recommended a book. I read it, and it gave me new ideas.

3. The **close people** who support you through thick and thin. The present difficulty is sweeter in others' company than alone. Talk about what bothers you. It is healing to let some steam off without worrying

that it's interpreted in a thousand negative ways. Who are the people in your life on whose shoulder you can cry? My kids are the most empathetic listeners to my conundrums.

4. Taking **a few days' break** from thinking about the entire project. Finally, the fourth way of reframing how you see your predicament is being thankful for **breathing**. Breath is a precious gift, a shelter from panic when you don't know which way to go. As long as you can walk on the earth's surface, there is hope for creative action. Sometimes, you need to disidentify from a project to be able to relate to it in a new way. So, how about taking a few days to pay special attention to your connection with your breath, as if this were the sole purpose of your life?

Which of the four ways to reframe your thinking in an impasse is most natural to you? Let's dwell on breathing as essential energy of life to be grateful for when things don't turn out as you want them to. Tempted to roll your eyes and gasp, *"Oh, please. Not another breathing exercise!"* How about sticking tiny cotton balls in your nostrils? How does it feel?

How many times during a day do you turn your attention inwards to check out the journey of your breath in your body? What are the situations when you would have the patience to take ten deep breaths to fill your stomach like you'd fill a balloon with hot air? Such activities connect your body and mind, allowing your unconscious mind to work smarter.

Summing up, in situations where you may perceive threats, there is a good amount of goodness lurking as well. When you intertwine grateful thinking through moments of disillusionment, you'll establish the foundation for positive mood and creative thinking. You'll notice more progress on your goals. You'll be better prepared to cope with the anxiety of unwanted events. You'll be more motivated to redeem your strategies toward creative pursuits.[8]

I was switching off the computer in the room where I delivered the course for immigrant job-seekers, when one participant approached me. *"Do you have one minute?"*, she asked.

I nodded and she continued. *"I have been wondering about something during the course but didn't dare to speak in front of others. Is cooking a talent? Can I consider myself talented at cooking?"*

Habit 6: The Ratio of Self-Judgement to Self-Compassion

Insight is the third stage in the creative process, following the problem exploration and incubation stages. The inner observation habits discussed so far are meant to increase the likelihood of the "Eureka!" moment when you discover an interesting problem to solve. After insight, there comes the moment of debate when you discuss with yourself whether the identified question is valuable and worth working on. Psychologist Mihaly Csikszentmihalyi considered this stage, the period of self-criticism and extreme insecurity whether to move on to implementing the new idea.[9]

In addition, when we take a microscopic view of the creative process after the initial Eureka, we realize that till the final product is materialized, the creator's mind undergoes a continuous assessment of the quality and

---

[8] Bono, G., Emmons, R. A., and McCullough, M. E., (2004), Gratitude in Practice and the Practice of Gratitude, published in Positive Psychology in Practice, Editors Linley, P.A., and Joseph, S., pp. 464–481, https://doi.org/10.1002/9780470939338.ch29 Emmons, R. A., and McCullough, M. E., 2004, The Psychology of Gratitude, Oxford University Press.

[9] Csiksxentmihalyi, M., (2013), Creativity, the Psychology of Discovery and Invention, Harper Perennial Modern Classics.

progress of their work, which is marked by tiny "refinement insights."[10] Hence, self-criticism continues to be a constituent theme of the creator's self-talk until the creator feels somewhat satisfied about the outcome, which will be shared with the audience. From the moment you become aware that there is something about the status quo of the work that doesn't satisfy you and until the moment of progressive insight, you'll experience emotional pain, irritation, and despair.

These moments are similar to the hours of labor before a mother gives birth to her newborn. A beautiful idea is about to be materialized. You're eager to receive it. But, just as the fetus takes its time inside the mother's uterus, the new solution evades you. This experience is tormenting. "What is wrong with me?", "Why am I being slow in thinking through this conundrum?", etc.

The judgmental voice is freaking out about you not being able to deliver the desired quality in time. At the same time, creative intuition tries to calm you down. It tells you to rest assured, a new action will soon be taken, but it doesn't tell you exactly what it is. We want to be like the turtle in the fable. We want to tame the inner critic and not the other way around. Self-compassion is the skill of being understanding toward yourself in moments of perceived failure rather than judging yourself harshly.[11]

Self-compassionate thoughts can be like a springboard toward renewed energy to initiate a new loop of a secondary creative process which is embedded in the larger process marked by the "big vision insight."

---

[10] Vlad Glaveanu, V., Lubart, T., Bonnardel, N., Botella, M., de Biaisi, P.-M., Desainte-Catherine, M., Georgsdottir, A., Guillou, K., Kurtag, G., Mouchiroud, C., Storme, M., Wojtczuk, A., and Zenasni, F., (2013), Creativity as action: findings from five creative domains, Frontiers in Psychology. https://doi.org/10.3389/fpsyg.2013.00176

[11] Neff, K.D., (2003), Development and validation of a scale to measure self-compassion. *Self and Identity*, 2, pp. 223–250.
Silberstein-Tirch, L., (2019), *The Everyday Guide to Self-Compassion. How to be nice to yourself,* Althea Press, Emeryville, California.

"May I be respectful with the painful experiences during experimental creations." It's not a way to find excuses and justifications for low levels of achievement but a way to avoid beating yourself up when you are dissatisfied with your performance.

You may not be used to being kind toward yourself – your emotions, thoughts, and actions – but you can learn to avoid burnout in a project by treating your highest expectations of yourself with gentleness. After the fear of dying before you complete your work, what is your utmost terror as a creator? The fear of feeling you're good for nothing. The dread of opening yourself up to an environment, which can result in embarrassing yourself, being judged and rejected. The shame of making wrong decisions. The risk of wasting time and money to arrive at a dead end.

You may be thinking, *"I'd rather be paralyzed by fear than lower my performance standards about myself with self-compassion."* Yet, research shows the opposite. A self-compassion intervention training showed that 158 students, of an average age of 25, experienced an increase in the desire to reach their full potential, at a six-month follow-up after the course.[12]

Self-compassionate people aim as high as less compassionate ones, and unlike the latter, they also recognize that sometimes goals are made to be modified. In other studies, people with high levels of self-compassion were found to have less motivation anxiety and procrastinate less than the participants with low levels of self-compassion.[13] Also, people who reflected from a self-compassionate perspective on a failed test spent more

---

[12] Dundas, I, Binder, P-E., Hansen, T.G.B., and Stige, S.H., (2017), Does a short self-compassion intervention for students increase healthy self-regulation? A randomized control trial, Scandinavian Journal of Psychology, 58, pp. 443–450. https://self-compassion.org/wp-content/uploads/2018/05/Dundas2017.pdf

[13] Breines, J.G., and Chen, S., (2012), Self-Compassion Increases Self-Improvement Motivation, Personality and Social Psychology Bulletin, XX(X), pp. 1–11, DOI:https://doi.org/10.1177/0146167212445599
Sirois, F.M., (2014), Procrastination and Stress: Exploring the Role of Self-compassion. Self and Identity, 13 (2). pp. 128–145. ISSN 1529-8868 https://doi.org/10.1080/15298868.2013.763404

time studying for the second test than the participants who were instructed to take a self-esteem approach to the first poor performance.

Moreover, individuals who are prone to self-criticism enjoy a boost of creative thinking under self-compassion.[14] You need self-compassion to keep self-criticism under control and let the creativity flow. Hence, sustaining a habit of self-compassion may come in handy. For instance, you can select what is the self-critical thought in need of relief. Next time when you have a low moment, treat it like a friend. Invite it for a beer and ask it, *"What's up?"*

Optional Exercise 5: Next time you feel at a creative impasse, you may find yourself fighting feelings of guilt, self-doubt, inadequacy, or shame. Take a short break of self-compassion for the experienced emotions.

What kind of information might the emotions be pointing at? Are there any useful facts that update the status quo of the project? What is the next step you would be ready to take?

Usually, feeling bad about the lack of progress is driven by a specific fear. Validate whatever fears you identify. Show them understanding. Thank them for being interested in keeping you alive. Some fears, like the fear of losing financial safety, can be addressed with practical measures, such as smarter time management and savings. Some other fears, like losing reputation, are there to live with if you are a creator. Then ask yourself, *"OK, what creative task to perform next?"*

What if you find yourself tempted to quit? Having low moments is part of the condition of being a creative person. A bit of sleep or some chocolate can help so the tough part of you gets going when the going gets tough.

Finally, remind yourself of your breath. Start by noticing its rhythm and play with it. Breathe gently, then fast, then gently again. Activated breath

---

[14]Zabelina, D.L., and Robinson, M.D., (2010), Don't be so hard on yourself: Self-compassion facilitates creative originality among self-judgemental individuals, Creativity Research Journal, Issue 3, Vol. 22., pp. 288–293. www.tandfonline.com/doi/abs/10.1080/10400419.2010.503538

is an inspiration. Inspiration is hope, possibility, and change. You're about to gain a new understanding of your predicament through your inner critic. Give yourself a big hug and say, *"May I trust my creative intuition to take the lead."* This kind of thinking boosts your psychic energy in coming up with the following insight, which advances the implementation of a new idea.

CHAPTER 14

What's Next? Reassess the Creative Sensitivities That Will Drive You Toward the Next Project

In this part, we discussed inner attention habits that bridge two crucial moments in the creator's journey: the awakening of an acute interest in a domain of expertise and the first insights to create something disruptive to anything you did before. After completing the first act of creation, you have a deeper awareness of your creative sensitivities and impulses, which you can reassess for the following creative vision (see Figure 14-1).

© Oana Velcu-Laitinen 2022
O. Velcu-Laitinen, *How to Develop Your Creative Identity at Work*,
https://doi.org/10.1007/978-1-4842-8680-7_14

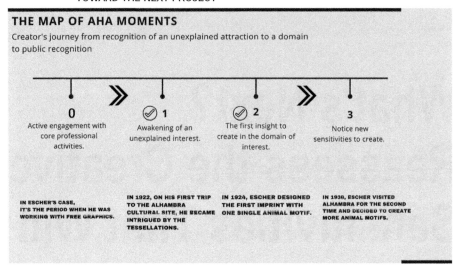

THE MAP OF AHA MOMENTS

Creator's journey from recognition of an unexplained attraction to a domain to public recognition

0	1	2	3
Active engagement with core professional activities.	Awakening of an unexplained interest.	The first insight to create in the domain of interest.	Notice new sensitivities to create.
IN ESCHER'S CASE, IT'S THE PERIOD WHEN HE WAS WORKING WITH FREE GRAPHICS.	IN 1922, ON HIS FIRST TRIP TO THE ALHAMBRA CULTURAL SITE, HE BECAME INTRIGUED BY THE TESSELLATIONS.	IN 1924, ESCHER DESIGNED THE FIRST IMPRINT WITH ONE SINGLE ANIMAL MOTIF.	IN 1936, ESCHER VISITED ALHAMBRA FOR THE SECOND TIME AND DECIDED TO CREATE MORE ANIMAL MOTIFS.

Figure 14-1. *Map of "Aha" moments*

"He who wonders discovers that this in itself is wonder," Escher said.[1] Escher's interest in the Moors' mosaics illustrates the importance of making time for wonders in the form of creative sensitivities that do not necessarily fit with existing projects. The bigger the misfit, the longer the transition to a new domain of creation. It took Escher 12 years – between 1924 and 1936 – to refine his fascination with the division of a plane into congruent figures and establish himself as a creator in this artistic niche, which is nowadays known as Escherism.[2] What would Escher have been interested in designing in a 3-D virtual space?

As a creator, wondering about your creative sensitivities and impulses increases the sense of intimacy with the subtleties of a domain of interest, which is a fundamental driver for future creative insights. The creative

---

[1] https://mcescher.com/about/quotes/

[2] www.pinterest.com/search/pins/?q=escherism&rs=typed&term_meta[]=escherism%7Ctyped

Schattschneider, D., and Emmer, M., (Editors), (2005), M.C. Escher's Legacy, Springer.

sensitivities show the beauty to which you resonate. The creative impulse
draws attention to the affordances in the environment where your pattern
of sensitivities can make a difference.

In each experimental creation, the ability to pay attention to what
matters is determined by two attentional mechanisms in the brain,
the top-down and the bottom-up.[3] The top-down attentional system,
represented by prior experiences, current creative goals, knowledge,
and skills, is in constant communication with the bottom-up attentional
system, represented by possible creative sensitivities and impulses.
In addition to spotting what is of interest for the current project, the
perceptual system of your brain can pick up something of interest for a
future act.

In the following figure, you can see the four types of creative impulses
on the outer circle. In the inside circle, you can see the five types of creative
sensitivities.

---

[3] Corbetta, M., and Shulman, G. L., (2002), Control of goal-directed and stimulus-
driven attention in the brain. Nature Reviews Neuroscience, 3, pp. 201–215.
DOI:https://doi.org/10.1038/nrn755

Posner, M., (1980), Orienting of attention. The Quarterly Journal of Experimental
Psychology, 32(1), pp. 3–25. DOI:
https://doi.org/10.1080/00335558008248231

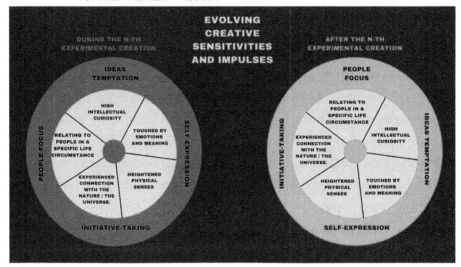

Think of the creative activities at the center of your most recent experimental creation. Please complete the following list of activities through the lens of your creative sensitivities.

Self-expression activities:

- *I joined a writers' workshop on the theme ------.*

- *I enrolled in a video editing workshop on the theme ------.*

- *I took part in a painting course, with a focus on ------.*

- *I started a blog/podcast/YouTube/Vimeo channel on the topic ------.*

- *I tried my hand at writing a screenplay with the title ------.*

- *I composed my first tune in the genre ------.*

Taking initiative:

- *I took part in an entrepreneurial program with a focus on ------.*

- *I took part in a leadership program with a focus on ------.*

- *I contributed to the planning of a new public event in town. My role was ------.*

- *I created a course on technical competencies related to -------.*

- *I initiated a community project outside the organization where I currently work on the theme ------.*

- *I formed a change management program in my organization in my role as ------.*

Problem-solving activities:

- *I read many books on a new topic ------.*

- *I took a product development course ------.*

- *I built something that can be considered an invention in this domain ------.*

- *I designed new experiments to bring more understanding to the problem of ------.*

- *I came up with a unique solution addressing the issue ------.*

Personal and professional growth activities:

- *I joined a coaching program focused on ------- .*

- *I facilitated a workshop on communication skills for individuals in the following roles ------, ------, ------, etc.*

- *I designed a mindfulness course with a particular focus
  on ------.*

- *I crafted a soft skills course ------ for individuals who face
  the following challenge ------.*

- *I volunteered to join a change management program in
  my company. My role was ------.*

What activities are not in any of the four categories, and which you
want to add?

If you think of your latest experimental creation, what felt right about
the activities that you performed? What didn't feel quite right?

What was a surprising and distinctive element that caught your
attention and you'd be curious to look into for the next experimental
creation?

Let's now return to the hypothetical scenario of the creator who sees
beauty in the withered flowers. Let's assume that this person develops a
high intellectual curiosity about how plants develop a memory of winter
and pick up cues from the environment to flower in the Spring. It leads to
their first experimental creation, say a blog post on the topic.

What if the two circles – the yellow (known impulses and sensitivities)
and the green one (possible impulses and sensitivities) – in the preceding
figure can spin randomly? This is a visual analogy of the creator's aleatory
interaction with the environment, which can result in the awakening of
disruptive sensitivities. The recalibration of the intensity of previous and
newly discovered sensitivities sparkles the impulse to take on new creative
activities. In the hypothetical scenario, let's imagine that after writing the
blog post, the creator experiences a more substantial intellectual curiosity
about the memory of plants. This can lead to a dominant impulse toward
the research realm, manifesting in acquiring scientific knowledge in
experiential botany.

What if the heightened scientific interest in the memory of cells awakens the empathy for people who deal with illnesses or traumas? The compatibility between these two sensitivities can result in the impulse to engage in creative activities to improve the emotional well-being of the respective group of people.

What if there is another creative sensitivity that awakens – like emotions and meaning or visual sensitivity – and feels more compelling than the exercised intellectual curiosity? This would orient the creator toward self-expression, which becomes the dominant creative impulse and is expressed through an artistic medium, like taking photos for photography contests.

Last, what if the imaginary creator experiences a series of direct experiences of connection with the plants that they studied? This sensitivity can push them in the initiative-taking direction toward environmental activism. Thanks to their intellectual curiosity, they can bring fact-based arguments to the general public about how climate change affects the flowers' life cycle.

This series of imaginative scenarios illustrate a relentless interplay between creative sensitivities, impulses, and activities, kept in motion by unpredictable events in the immediate environment and society.

This part of the book advocates the importance of thinking habits of inner attention that prime your mind for creative insight. *"My destination is no longer a place, rather a new way of seeing,"* once said the French writer Marcel Proust. Seeing new patterns of sensitivities, inquiring into your interpretations, understanding your creative intuition, and managing your emotions are the creator's way of carpe diem.

In the next and last part of the book, we discuss how to achieve high engagement in feedback conversations.

PART IV

Adopt a Creative Communication Style in Feedback Conversations

CHAPTER 15

The Three Principles of a Creative Communication Style

When and With Whom to Talk About Your Ideas

> *As an entrepreneur, you create your brand, you create your product, you create the value that you give. I say, 'You create' but it's not just you. It starts with me, because I'm a bit introverted, I need to start a channel of these ideas and energy, visualize it and then I get feedback and improve it. Particularly if it's about value, you need to bounce it with the customers, otherwise you may be completely wrong.*
>
> —Solopreneur and Book Author, Peter Ivanov

As Peter points out, in entrepreneurship, the development of new products starts with an initial insight. Still, there are stages of co-creation with potential customers to guarantee the idea's feasibility. New ideas don't live in a vacuum in any other professional field. They come from an external source through you to a particular audience.

© Oana Velcu-Laitinen 2022
O. Velcu-Laitinen, *How to Develop Your Creative Identity at Work,*
https://doi.org/10.1007/978-1-4842-8680-7_15

We don't come up with ideas for the sake of ideas but for the sake of entertainment, improvement, or innovation. And someone else, other than the person who generates the idea, must see its utility. An **entrepreneur's** product has value when the targeted customers are willing to pay for it. A **scientist** with a new research idea may want to have it validated by their team. An **expert** with a change initiative in mind may want to bounce it off their organizational superiors. The challenge consists of creating the conditions for constructive conversations – where there's both critical and positive thinking – to hone in on new ideas.

Especially in the first two stages of becoming a recognized creator, when you haven't completely internalized the subtleties of the field, you want to talk about your new ideas to ensure the likelihood of being useful. Like everyone else who comes up with new ideas, there's the tendency to fall in love with them. Hence you may be too attached to them to see their expected utility in their entirety.

In between the moment when you get the first insight about a product, a theory, or initiative and the moment when your audience interacts with it, there are **three opportunities for creative communication – creating engagement with your idea and possible epiphanies**. First, when you come up with a new idea and you're thinking, *"What will others think of my idea?"* You can fret about it and ruminate on it on your own. Or, you can share it with peers with whom you have a non-competitive relationship**.**

Second, there's an experimental phase when you develop a prototype. At this stage, you'd benefit from conversing with mentors or senior experts with the necessary knowledge to give their opinions.

Third, after the implementation phase, when customers interact with the final product, you can initiate dialogues related to the experiences of representative members of your audience.

How do you know who to choose to discuss your new ideas with? They can be the respected experts in your close network. Moreover, you may want to expand your social network. For that, you may want to initiate discussions with reliable, intelligent, and caring people you haven't talked to before but with whom you'd like to identify common ground.

The cherry-picked person is an expert who appreciates your competence. In turn, you value their competence and trust them to have the ability to listen. It's unlikely to have a quality conversation with someone who doesn't think much of you or has previously shown a lack of empathy or flexibility in thinking. Of course, in all truthfulness, you can be wrong about who the right person is. However, appreciation, trust, and connection are a safe bet.

In brief, the first principle of a creative communication style is to choose wisely the moments of feedback and the audience who provides it. When others' opinions are communicated with the intention to help you, they can open your eyes to what needs to be revised at crucial stages in the creative process and, even more, to unexpected new projects.

Become a Participative Storyteller

The rationale of feedback dialogues is to look at the feasibility of your idea through others' eyes. Every evaluation dialogue implies that you count on the reviewer to offer insightful perspectives. Unless you choose a tree to talk to, how can you prod the listener's interest in your ideas?

The second principle of a creative communication style is that you become the storyteller of your work, coming to feedback sessions prepared to deliver concise and catchy messages. What is the plot? Who are the main characters? What do they aim to accomplish? What are their obstacles?

Above all, what do storytellers excel at? They are good at spotting the moments when they can bring a surprising twist to the storyline, which keeps the audience hooked. Unlike the usual speakers who come with a previously crafted script for the listeners, in a conversation, you have to improvise when you sense a stale or tense discussion. And that's why your role as a participative storyteller gets a bit more challenging.

They say that hell is full of good meanings, but heaven is full of good works. As we speak and listen, new goals arise spontaneously in mind and can deviate from the established goal at the outset of the dialogue. Taking the social neuroscience perspective, during the dialogue, the brain can pick up instant threats, which may or may not be real, but they certainly put either you or your conversation partner in a defensive position. This state of mind obstructs the focus on finding solutions and makes you obsessed with the risks perceived in the dynamics of dialogue.

As a storyteller, you must constantly monitor the collocutor's interest level in the conversation. You facilitate the conditions for your brain and your conversation partner's brain to stay in a receptive state, characterized by curiosity, joy, and interest. The parties involved are then open to receiving and taking in new information.

In short, a participative storyteller ensures that the audience is stimulated with ideas. However, the extent to which you succeed in creating an engaged conversation depends on what kind of speaking and listening you are capable of.

We'll now turn to the third and last principle of a creative communication style, which involves adopting a mindset of creative integrity. It's about listening with **creative integrity** and speaking with **humor** (see Figure 15-1).

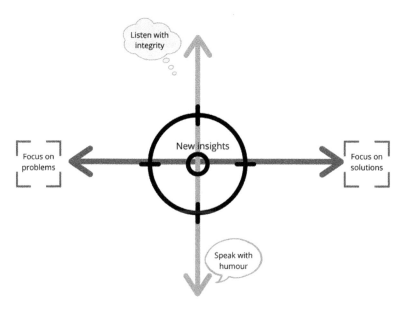

Figure 15-1. *Constructive conversation*

The Creative Integrity Mindset

Sit down before the facts as a little child, be prepared to give up every preconceived notion, follow humbly wherever and to whatever abyss nature leads you, or you shall learn nothing.

—Biologist Thomas Henry Huxley, on unbiased
understanding

The preceding quote stresses that preconceived ideas are an invisible barrier to learning. Although T.H. Huxley was referring to scientific thinking in conducting research, the same type of thinking is beneficial when leading a feedback conversation. When you start a dialogue with the intention to learn one thing you didn't know before, you may want to postpone jumping to conclusions about what you hear. In addition,

T.H. Huxley talks about a humble attitude as an enabler of learning. Knowing that we know less than we think we know, we can choose to get curious instead of anxious, especially in vulnerable moments of a conversation when we digest the critical bits of an argument.

In conducting research, the ability to observe beyond learned rules is a fundamental driver to discovery. In dialogue, listening is key to learning one thing you didn't know you needed to know. There's listening and listening. There's *"I'm pretending to listen but in fact all I want is to hear my voice."* And there's *"I'm here all ears and open to the unexpected."* The former type of listening comes easy to us. As for the second way of being present in a conversation, we need to rehearse it a few times before it becomes second nature. To this view, we can choose to anchor our thoughts in the present in two ways. First, there are the words, the body gestures, and the emotions of the person you converse with.[1] What do they say?

Secondly, you can listen to what you hear, to your emotions and to your reactions. In fact, good listening is an exercise of awareness of your inner dialogue. And when the internal dialogue gets clouded by the steam of dense emotions, that's when integrity can step in.

When the emotional arousal shows that you think you are under threat, it's time to remind yourself that you are committed to learning new things and not solely confirming what you believed at the outset of the conversation. Although, let's face it, getting a confirmation of your beliefs feels as good as a chocolate cake. It makes you feel good in the moment but not necessarily the next day when you step on the scale.

The social psychologist and humanistic philosopher Erich Fromm defined integrity as the ability to stay true to your values, so much more in situations when the values are challenged.[2] Integrity is thus about the coherence between your values and actions, through thick and thin.

---

[1] Rock, D., (2016), Quiet Leadership, Harper.
[2] Fromm, E., (2014), Man for Himself, An Inquiry Into the Psychology of Ethics, Routledge, 1st edition.

Is creativity one of your core values? If so, then creative integrity can save your conversations by appealing to your creative thinking to create a stimulating dialogue. When was the last time you were exposed to criticism or even worse, your ideas were dismissed? How did you react? In these pages, we elaborate on what it means to bring more of your creative thinking in expressing your thoughts and reframing what you hear. **This is the mindset of listening with integrity, your willingness to accept the uncomfortable moments of a conversation and initiate a change in perspective, starting with your perspective – the set of assumptions about possible implementation strategies related to your creative idea.**[3]

Therefore, the third principle of a creative communication style is to approach every feedback dialogue as a storyteller with a creative integrity mindset. It's about being a wizard listener before a charismatic speaker.

Listening with creative integrity means seeing the moments when you can brighten the atmosphere with a smile (see Figure 15-2). In addition, listening with creative integrity means taking the opportunity to clarify misunderstood concepts through the use of analogies. Last but not least, listening with creative integrity involves spotting the moments for hypothetical thinking about probable solutions. In the following chapters, we'll elaborate on the three core concepts in Figure 15-2: humor, analogies, and change in perspective.

---

[3] For further reading on perspective as a relation that you establish with the world in order to create possibilities of action, please check out Vladeanu, V.P., (2020), The Possible, A Sociocultural Theory, Oxford University Press https://global.oup.com/academic/product/the-possible-9780197520499?cc=ro&lang=en&#

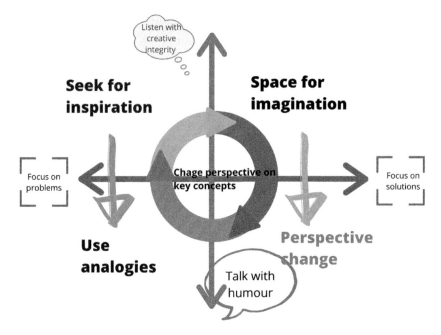

Figure 15-2. *Creative integrity*

CHAPTER 16

Talking With Humor

What Is Humor?

"What are the best qualities that you think helped you enjoy the success you currently have?", I asked the creators interviewed in this book.

Persistence, believing in yourself, and creativity were the most commonly referred to. Other skills, individually mentioned, were the ability to embrace change, continuous learning, curiosity, empathy, hard work, interest, motivation, patience, purpose, and self-inquiry. Nobody talked about humor.

When a group of preschoolers in Helsinki were encouraged to think about their strengths, out of thirteen kids, seven said that humor is one of their top qualities. How about you? Are you a below-average or above-average kind of funny person?

Researchers define humor as a "form of intellectual play; that is, play with ideas."[1] Humor is a social activity which connects two or more people, the person creating the humor and the person(s) receiving it. Creating humor is about noticing something you find amusing and feeling compelled to share with others. Understanding humor is about hearing or seeing something that makes you laugh involuntarily. It's easier to react

---

[1] McGhee, P.E., (1983). Humor Development: Toward a Life Span Approach. In: McGhee, P.E., Goldstein, J.H. (eds) Handbook of Humor Research. Springer, New York, NY. https://doi.org/10.1007/978-1-4612-5572-7_6, pp. 219.

© Oana Velcu-Laitinen 2022
O. Velcu-Laitinen, *How to Develop Your Creative Identity at Work*,
https://doi.org/10.1007/978-1-4842-8680-7_16

to humor than to create it. Are you the one who cracks jokes at work and at home? Or, are you the one who likes to be surrounded by others with a sense of humor?

On a scale of 1 (*never thought about it*) to 5 (*I live to make others laugh*), during a day, how important is it for you to be able to say something that amuses others? The starting point for bringing more humor in your conversations is the willingness to notice opportunities to lighten the mood. A sense of humor starts to shape early in life, around the age of two and it is quite important for the development of children's social and cognitive skills.[2] If you have the chance, can you ask your parents what kind of a toddler you were? Did you laugh like a drain? Were you the jester, making the adults laugh?

Humor is a form of creativity that involves two thinking abilities, insight and divergent thinking.[3] First, humor requires insight, the ability to quickly see the solution – the funny aspect – through the details of a situation. Insight happens when there's a mental restructuring in the information available about a problem, which results in a sudden understanding of the solution.

Let's consider Duncker's (1945) candle problem as an example of a humorous situation. The psychologist Karl Duncker invited participants to do an experiment and attach a candle to the wall. The subjects received a box of matches, a box of thumbtacks and a candle (see Figure 16-1).

---

[2] Martin, R.A., and Ford, T.E., (2018), The Psychology of Humour, An Integrative Approach, Second edition, Academic Press.

[3] Koestler, A., (2014), The Act of Creation, One 70 Press.
Murdock, M. C., and Ganim, R. M., (1993), Creativity and humor: Integration and incongruity. *The Journal of Creative Behavior, 27*(1), pp. 57-70. https://doi.org/10.1002/j.2162-6057.1993.tb01387.x
O'Quin K. and Derks P., (1997), Humor and creativity: A review of the empirical literature. In: Cresskill, NJ: Hampton Press; pp. 227–256. Runco M.A., ed. *Creativity research handbook.* Vol. 1.

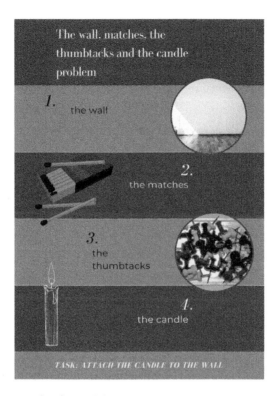

Figure 16-1. *Duncker's problem*

Now kindly take a few seconds to think about how you would solve this problem. Ready?

The solution consists in emptying the box of tacks, attaching it to the wall and using it as a support for the candle. Now, what if you wanted to make others laugh as you solved this riddle? You may be trying to attach the candle directly to the wall with the thumbtacks. Or you may be melting the candle and gluing it to the wall.

What is the insight that produces the humor? Those who may be watching you implement these alternative solutions may be amused as long as they see the correct answer in the first place.

Second, humor requires divergent thinking and the ability to see new affordances in new contexts, like using the emptied tacks box as a support for the candle. Preschoolers are the best at seeing multiple uses for objects.[4] The little humans have fun associating an object in their hand with an imaginary one and engaging in a specific play. For them, a stick can be a sword. Or, riding on a rod means riding a horse.

Bergen and Rousta (2018) argue that the ability to create humor evolved along with the development of playful and creative behaviors because it facilitated new perspectives when coping with everyday problems and crises.[5] Although the expression and appreciation of humor are unique for each living in a particular environment, the existence of humor appears to be a significant and universal human experience.

What Creates Humor?

When children begin to learn about their physical and social surroundings, they show their understanding by laughing in situations where they see stimuli incompatible with their present knowledge. At each stage of cognitive development, humor comes with insights into the change of perspective on what we see or hear. *"I can see X. I expect Y. Yet, I can see Z happening. Z is the opposite of Y. I laugh."* The mismatch between Y and Z is called incongruity.

Riding a stick is a healthy playful behavior in a four-year-old kid. An adult riding a stick must be a mother entertaining her kid. Or, a Monthy Python comedian.[6] **Incongruities** are thus differences between what we

---

[4] Gabora, L., (2018), The Neural Basis and Evolution of Divergent and Convergent Thought, The Cambridge Handbook of The Neuroscience of Creativity, pp. 58–70.

[5] Bergen, D., and Rousta, M.M., (2018), "Developing Creativity and Humor: The Role of the Playful Mind," in S. Luria, J. Baer, and J. Kaufman (Eds.) Creativity and Humour, Academic Press, Elsevier, pp. 144–175.

[6] www.montypython.com/

expect to see and what we actually see. The awareness of incongruities – understanding the punchline, which contradicts the initial assumptions – is key to producing laughter.[7]

The developing divergent abilities of children enable them to come up with new incongruities not only in the use of objects but also in the use of body movement, words, and sounds. For instance, putting a banana in front of their mouth and pretending it's a big smile is for their amusement and to make others laugh too.[8]

Although humor originates in physical play, as children grow self-aware and observe how others behave, the use of humor becomes more versatile and evolves simultaneously with other forms of play – physical, verbal, imaginary, socio-dramatic, etc.[9] According to McGhee, the fourth and last stage of incongruities development, known as the stage of word play or *"multiple meanings,"* develops around the age of 7 when children gain higher cognitive sophistication, such as the ability to play with ideas and figurative speech and the ability to notice cause and effect.[10]

A ten-year-old child can engage in pretend play by attaching some grass at the end of a stick. The decorated stick can impersonate the teacher to whom the child can tell all the things they don't dare to say straight

---

[7] Suls, J. M., (1972). "A two-stage model for the appreciation of jokes and cartoons: An information-processing analysis." In J. H. Goldstein and P. E. McGhee (Eds.). The psychology of humor: Theoretical perspectives and empirical issues, pp. 81–100. New York: Academic Press.
Suls, J.M., (1983). "Cognitive processes in humor appreciation." In P. E. McGhee and J. H. Goldstein (Eds.) Handbook of humor research, pp. 39–57. New York: Springer.

[8] Loizou, E., (2005) Humour: A different kind of play, European Early Childhood Education Research Journal, 13:2, pp. 97–109, DOI: 10.1080/13502930585209701

[9] Pellegrini, A. D., (2009). The role of play in human development. Oxford, UK: Oxford University Press.

[10] McGhee, P.E., (1983). Humor Development: Toward a Life Span Approach. In: McGhee, P.E., Goldstein, J.H. (eds) Handbook of Humor Research. Springer, New York, NY. https://doi.org/10.1007/978-1-4612-5572-7_6.
http://jim.shamlin.com/study/books/2564/08.html

to their face. The child may play alone, never revealing to anyone their imaginary dialogue, or they may share the play with friends.

A joke is followed by laughter, but not always. At the same time, children start to internalize other people's different perspectives. The ten-year-old kid is aware that their friends may be amused but not the teacher. The teacher may or may not be amused to find out that they were impersonated as a stick, although the humor does shine light on the lack of psychological safety in the classroom.

"I'm reading a book on Anti-Gravity. I can't put it down."[11] The "multiple meanings" stage continues throughout adolescence. We enter adulthood with a formed style of humor, drawing on two sources. First, on the personal tendencies toward perceived incongruities between body movements, words, sounds, and mental states – yours and others'.

Second, depending on the caretakers and the broader culture, by adolescence, we assimilate a combination of two dominant types of humor. Some teenagers may use humor daily, at times in a positive way, other times aggressively.[12]

"Let's place work on a high pedestal so it cannot be reached." "Working hard keeps you in shape, but being lazy doesn't kill you either." These are examples of satirical humor I grew up with. Whatever forms of humor we may have been raised with – physical, puns, irony, satire, observational,

---

[11] This joke is a reflection of the incongruity between the actual meaning of the word "gravity" and the figurative meaning of the expression "putting a book down." https://jokesquotesfactory.com/funny-nerdy-jokes-dorky-geeky-puns-oneliner/

[12] Chang, J.H., Chen, H.C., Hsu, C.C., Chan, Y.C., Chang, Y.L., (2015), Flexible humor styles and the creative mind: Using a typological approach to investigate the relationship between humor styles and creativity. Psychology of Aesthetics, Creativity, and the Arts. 9(3), pp. 306–312.

etc. – the sense of humor continues to develop throughout our lifespan and through influential social interactions.[13]

Summing up, humor stems from making non-obvious connections between two incongruous objects, thoughts, or word meanings. In verbal humor, the initial information sets the context, which activates the listener's knowledge and expectations about what comes next. The awareness of the incongruity between the initial expectations and the latest information provided in the punchline results in surprise and laughter.

"I had an argument with a 45° angle. It was a sharp one."[14]

Optional exercise 1: *Step 1 – What are your favorite sources for consuming humor?*

- *Stand-up comedy shows*

- *Humor websites*

- *Cartoons*

- *Comedy movies*

- *Something else _____*

For five days in a row, do not let a day pass without hearing/ reading a joke.

Step 2 – Adapt a joke per day.

For each of the jokes you liked, how could you adapt it to fit one of your daily experiences?

Step 3 – Joke-making diary – Create your own jokes.

---

[13] Nezlek, J.B. and Derks, P., (2001), Use of Humour as a coping mechanism, psychological adjustment and social interaction, *International Journal of Humour Research*, 14-4, pp. 395–413.

[14] This joke reflects incongruity in double meanings of a sharp argument and sharp angle.

After the five days of copying the jokes you like, choose a week to log the concepts or objects of the day at work. For instance, the 45° angle can be an everyday requirement in a programmer's life. For each concept/object, write down as many characteristics as possible. Also, jot down the goal for which you applied the respective concept/object.

What were the possible challenges toward the completion of the goal? For each challenge, try to come up with a metaphor. This will be the context of your joke. In the above-mentioned pun, the metaphor is "argument." Next, think about which of the characteristics of the concept or object of the day would be fitting the meaning of the metaphor?

"I argued with a 145° angle. It was a dull one; I won it fast."

Do not worry about producing roaring laughter. It's enough that you become accustomed to identifying the necessary ingredients for a nerdy joke.

When Do People Laugh Best?

Did you laugh at least once today? When are you more in the mood for a good laugh? At the crack of dawn or when the night falls? A 1999 study on 30 men and 50 women aged between 17 to 79 years old shows that people's appetite for humor increases as the day progresses, in the evenings mostly.[15] In particular, the younger participants reported laughing twice more than the older participants at the end of the day.

In considering the various sources of laughter – spontaneous reaction, the media, reproducing jokes, and remembering past funny experiences – approximately 88% of the laughter happened when participants were with other people rather than alone (12%). Compared with the men in the study, women showed a significantly higher frequency of spontaneous laughter with others.

---

[15] Martin, R. A. and Kuiper, N. A., (1999). Daily occurrence of laughter: Relationships with age, gender, and Type A personality. Humor: International Journal of Humor Reseach, 12 (4), pp. 355–384.

When considering the initiator of laughter, approximately 64% of the moments of laughter were a response to someone else's humor. The participants themselves initiated only 36% of the humorous moments.

An intriguing finding is that ageing seems to negatively affect the tendency to laugh, only for the women in the study. Women under the age of 24 reported a mean of 22.7 laughter moments per day, whereas women over 60 reported an average of half this number, namely, 11.7 daily laughter moments.

It can be that the older you get, the fewer reasons you see to laugh about. Another explanation for the significant decrease in the frequency of laughter for older women might be that there are fewer people to socialize with in retirement and fewer occasions to use or hear humor. On average, women outlive their husbands, although there's no recording of the participants' marital status in the study.

All in all, these findings reinforce the notion that laughter is a social phenomenon, with the majority of laughter happening as an impulse, in the company of other people. So what are the situations, and who are the people who inspire you to say something funny?

"What did a dot tell to a sphere when they both got drunk? I bet that now you cannot walk straight."

Optional exercise 2: *Step 4 – Joke-making diary – Test your humor among friends*

Assuming you spent five days in a row crafting a newbie joke per day, now you should have five jokes under your sleeve. Which one are you most proud of? Who are the three friends who can lend their ears to your winning joke? Be ready to share your humor next time you meet them.

Afterwards, note how you feel being the person cracking jokes in your diary. Also, record how your friends reacted.

You can repeat exercises 1 and 2 twice (this results in four additional weeks). What are the ensuing benefits, if any, that you notice in the interactions between you and your friends?

The Benefits of Positive Humor in Work Contexts

No animal laughs save Man.

—Aristotle, *On the Parts of the Animals* (pp. 29)

On a scale of 1 (*it's distracting*) to 5 (*music to my ears*), how much do you like to hear laughter at the workplace? Humor is human.

One of my glorious moments of humor production was during a workshop of business ideas generation. The workshop took place in an open space of a startup accelerator center. The combined laughter of the participants reached out to the neighboring offices and attracted to the workshop the people who hadn't initially planned to join.

The use of humor and listening to humor boost the creative thinking abilities. In a survey of the sense of humor among school teachers, the teachers' humor was significantly correlated with four creative thinking skills: imagination, flexibility, originality, and open-mindedness.[16] The use of appropriate humor seems to encourage the students to perform better on tasks that involve creative thinking – Torrence Test of Creative Thinking – students' internal motivation, the level of comprehension, and attention to the learning material in the class.[17, 18]

---

[16] Chen, C-H., Chen, H-C., and Roberts, A.M., (2019) Why Humor Enhances Creativity From Theoretical Explanations to an Empirical Humor Training Program, Effective "Ha-Ha" Helps People to "A-Ha," in *Creativity and Humour Handbook*. Editors Luria, S., Baer, J. and Kaufman, J, pp. 83–108.

Kerlinger, F.N., and Pedhazur, E.J., (1967). Attitudes and perceptions of desirable traits of teachers. Final report, project 5-0300. US Office of Education (269 pp.)

[17] Ziv, A., (1983), The influence of humorous atmosphere on divergent thinking, Contemporary Educational Psychology, Vol. 8, Issue 1, pp. 68–75.

[18] Powell, J.P., and Andresen, L.W., (1985). Humour and teaching in higher education. Studies in Higher Education.10(1), pp. 79–90.

Other experimental studies showed that when people experience positive emotions, as a result of watching a comedy or receiving a candy as a surprise, as compared to neutral or negative emotions, they show greater cognitive flexibility, which enables more creative problem-solving.[19] The experience of positive emotions leads to a more efficient organization and integration of memory and more effective thinking, planning, and judgment.[20]

The use of positive humor has considerable cognitive and emotional benefits in the ideation stage of the creative process as well. For instance, a study of the product design process found that improvisational comedians came up with 25% more creative product ideas than professional product designers in generating new product ideas. Why? The exercises used in improvisational training stimulate associative thinking, which is needed when you entertain ideas. In the same study, when a group of 11 designers received an improvisational comedy training prior to a brainstorming session, the number of ideas they produced increased on average by 37%.[21]

These findings provide support that the spontaneous joy that is associated with humor can prod a person to think more broadly and flexibly. In addition, there are social effects through which humor can

---

[19] Isen, A.M., (2003), Positive affect as a source of human strength. In: Aspinwall L.G., Staudinger U.M., eds. A psychology of human strengths: Fundamental questions and future directions for a positive psychology. Washington, DC: American Psychological Association; pp. 179–195.
Isen A.M., Daubman K.A., and Nowicki G.P., (1987), Positive affect facilitates creative problem solving. Journal of Personality and Social Psychology., Vol. 52, No. 6, 1122–1131.
[20] Isen AM, Johnson MMS, Mertz E, and Robinson GF., (1985), The influence of positive affect on the unusualness of word associations. Journal of Personality and Social Psychology. Vol. 48, pp. 1413–1426.
[21] Kudrowitz B.M., (2010), *"Haha and Aha, Creativity, Idea Generation, Humour and Product Design,"* Doctoral Thesis, Department of Mechanical Engineering at the Massachusetts Institute of Technology.

enhance creativity in organizations.[22] The expression of humor maintains psychological safety in a conversation, reduces the social distance between people, and is effective in managing potential conflicts.

The use of humor at work indicates that you care about your job and the people you work with. Also, it shows a sense of confidence and familiarity with the individuals you want to amuse. In a study on 279 Slovenian nurses, respondents were asked about their openness toward using humor – puns and other types of verbal language – in the dialogues with their patients.[23] The nurses who used humor reported an enhanced sense of belonging to the nursing profession and saw humor as an alternative tool to assist patients.

Humor has a social bonding function not only with people working in the same organization but with strangers too. Have you recently listened to a talk when the speaker charmed you with their wit in the first minute already? When people use humor, they disclose some of their values and perspectives on important matters. We thus form a quick impression about them. And, we tend to like outsiders who express a similar outlook on life through humor. Incidentally, shared values and similar experiences explain why you like listening to some comedians and not others.

---

[22] Eliav, E., Miron-Spektor, E., and Bear, J., (2017). Humor and creativity. In book: Humor in the Workplace: A psychological perspective. Publisher: *Psychology Press*. Editors: Robert, C.

Baas, M., De Dreu, C. K., and Nijstad, B. A. (2008). A meta-analysis of 25 years of mood-creativity research: Hedonic tone, activation, or regulatory focus? *Psychological Bulletin*, 134(6), 779–806.

[23] Goriup, J., Stričević, J., and Sruk, V., (2017), Is Education for Using Humour in Nursing Needed? (Slovenian Case Study on Sociological and Ergonomic Aspects of the Impact of Humour on Nursing Professionals), Acta Educationis Generalis volume 7, 2017, issue 3, pp. 45–62, DOI: 10.1515/atd-2017-0023.

When others sincerely like your humor, they likely find you more trustworthy, credible, and honest, even when the intention for using humor is to persuade. A lighthearted atmosphere makes people more receptive and reflective to counterarguments when making business decisions.[24]

At the end of the workshop on business ideas generation, one of the event organizers came to talk with me and said, *"I hope you'll come to work with us again."* A few weeks later, one of the participants wrote to me. He had come up with a business idea during the workshop. Nowadays, he's the founder of a business hub that brings together Extended Reality emerging companies and ecosystems in Europe.

In brief, humor adds the spice that makes people think out of the box. Also, the receivers of humor feel emotionally closer to the person who initiates it, provided that the values and experiences expressed through humor resonate with the receivers.

---

[24] Lyttle, J., (2001), The Effectiveness of Humour in Persuasion, The Case of Business Ethics Training, The Journal of General Psychology, 128(2), pp. 206–216.

CHAPTER 17

Leading Feedback Conversations With Improvised Humor

Becoming the Person With a Tinge of Humor

People holding power positions agree with the benefits of humor at work. In business settings, there's hope to hear jokes initiated by leaders, as we can see from a survey of 329 Fortune 500 CEOs performed by Fortune magazine, which found that 97% of CEOs agree with the importance of humor in business.[1] Leaders with a sense of humor can increase the

---

[1] Li, Z., Dai, L., Chin, T., and Rafiq, M., (2019), Understanding the Role of Psychological Capital in Humorous Leadership-Employee Creativity Relations, Frontiers in Psychology, Vol. 10, pp. 1–11, DOI=10.3389/fpsyg.2019.01636

© Oana Velcu-Laitinen 2022
O. Velcu-Laitinen, *How to Develop Your Creative Identity at Work*,
https://doi.org/10.1007/978-1-4842-8680-7_17

employees' engagement and creativity in the workplace.[2] In addition, a work culture that is open to wit inspires anyone to be as funny as they can be.

Work engagement determines how people perform at work. Professionals, who experience job satisfaction more frequently, are more likely to engage in "organizational spontaneity" to help coworkers and raise constructive viewpoints.[3] Moreover, when leaders make funny remarks about mistakes, they encourage the "we are in the same boat" thinking, employee retention, and innovative behaviors and attitudes.

The creative process is not only about the generation and implementation of novel and useful ideas but also about the way you talk about your ideas. During feedback conversations, the use of humor is an invitation to deeper understanding, opinion revision, and problem solving on both sides, – the creator and the evaluator.[4]

---

[2] Rosenberg, C., Walker, A., Leiter, M., and Graffam, J., (2021), Humor in Workplace Leadership: A Systematic Search Scoping Review, Frontiers in Psychology, Vol. 12, DOI=10.3389/fpsyg.2021.610795

Evans, T.R., and Steptoe-Warren, G., (2015), Humor Style Clusters: Exploring Managerial Humor, International Journal of Business Communication, pp. 1–12, DOI: 10.1177/2329488415612478.

Sobral, F., and Islam, G., (2015). He who laughs best, leaves last: the influence of humor on the attitudes and behavior of interns. Academy of Management Learning and Education, 14 (4), pp. 500–518. doi: 10.5465/amle.2013.0368

[3] Lyubomirsky, S., King, L., and Diener, E. (2005). The Benefits of Frequent Positive Affect: Does Happiness Lead to Success? Psychological Bulletin, 131(6), pp. 803–855. https://doi.org/10.1037/0033-2909.131.6.803.

Donovan, M. A. (2000). Cognitive, affective, and satisfaction variables as predictors of organizational behaviors: A structural equation modeling examination of alternative models. Dissertation Abstracts International: Section B: The Sciences and Engineering, 60(9-B), 4943.

George, J. M., and Brief, A. P. (1992). Feeling good-doing good: A conceptual analysis of the mood at work-organizational spontaneity relationship. Psychological Bulletin, 112(2), pp. 310–329. https://doi.org/10.1037/0033-2909.112.2.310.

[4] Wood, R. E., Beckmann, N., and Rossiter, J. R., (2011). Management humor: Asset or liability?, Organizational Psychology Review, 1(4), pp. 316–338. https://doi.org/10.1177/2041386611418393

You may be thinking, *"Am I or am I not a born comedian?"* Turning the reader into a celebrated humorist is not the intention of this book. The goal is to become a funnier person by understanding how to leverage your everyday experiences in relationships with superiors, peers, and subordinates. Becoming a funny creator is about the willingness to bring your sense of humor in conversations with people with whom you want to build trust.

Humor is not my strength but I do love to amuse those around me. So, I stubbornly and spontaneously invent funny statements to make my audiences smile. And there are moments when I make blunders. Like the time when I visited a prospect client who pointed a photo on the wall. In it, it was the current CEO as a five year old girl shaking hands with the CEO at that time. I heard myself saying, *"She looked cuter back then"*. Yet, I am addicted to the good feeling when I see that I do manage to make some people laugh. So I am willing to start all over again.

Similarly, it's enough that you are ready to take the lead in a feedback conversation by bringing up the humorous side of a situation. It creates an atmosphere of psychological safety, engaged creativity, and intellectual honesty. A joke per conversation may keep everyone's close-mindedness away.

Who are the funniest people around you? What can you learn from them?

"I just got damn well fed up with being formal all the time."

As we can see from the preceding New Yorker cartoon,[5] the experts in creating humor are apt at using the elements in a situation that can be combined for a humorous effect. It's a habit you can also practice in three steps: get playful, get ready, and be flexible. The first step is about getting yourself in the mood to create a lighter atmosphere. The second step is about training your spontaneity in delivering a funny comment. The third step is about trying different styles of humor that are likely to be appreciated by the interlocutor in a particular context.

A gentle reminder. Going through these three steps doesn't mean you will become a cannon of jokes. You will rather experience more moments when you surprise yourself by saying something that brings temporary cheerfulness and detachment from the seriousness of a dialogue.

To conclude, using humor in a conversation is like singing in a choir. Someone has to signal the right note. Can you be that someone? Let's build up amusing moments.

Step 1: Get into a Playful State of Mind

Have you noticed your usual states of mind when you involuntarily come up with funny remarks? Mood influences the tendency to observe the funny side of a situation and communicate it to others.[6] If you're like most people, when stressed, irritated, or anxious, using humor is the last thing to occur naturally.

---

[5] www.newyorker.com/cartoons/contest#winner

[6] Luria, S., Baer, J., and Kaufman, J., (2018), *Creativity and Humour*, Academic Press, Elsevier.

McGhee PE., (2010), Humor as survival training for a stressed-out world: The 7 humor habits program Bloomington, IN: AuthorHouse.

Feingold A. and Mazzella R., (1993) "Preliminary validation of a multidimensional model of wittiness", *Journal of Personality*, 61, pp. 439–456. https://doi.org/10.1111/j.1467-6494.1993.tb00288.x.

Playfulness or joyful spontaneity is an emotional state that enables you to reframe the situations in such a way that you and those who accompany you experience those situations as entertaining, intellectually stimulating and/or personally interesting.[7] A playful mind is a fertile soil on which to plant the seeds of humor. Also, your playful energy is the trigger that the interlocutor's unconscious mind tunes into before you get to say anything.

To develop an **elastic playfulness** of mind, keeping a joke-making diary described in Chapter 16 is an excellent start to deliberately getting into a frolicsome state of mind in a chosen situation. Alternatively, you can choose to practice reframing everyday situations with a funny twist. For example, what do you see that can be interpreted as funny when you go for a walk? Or when you are in a boring meeting? Or when you are standing in the queue at the supermarket?

One day, I went for a short walk to empty my mind after an intense workday. It didn't take many minutes to notice that more and more people passing by me were wearing sporty outfits. I was wearing jeans, which made me feel like an outlier. I imagined the title of the local newspaper writing, *"Shocking news! Amateur walker roaming in our forest paths."*

---

[7] Proyer, R. T., (2018), Playfulness and humor in psychology: An overview and update, *Humor*, vol. 31, no. 2, pp. 259-271. https://doi.org/10.1515/humor-2016-0080

Proyer, R.T., (2017), A multidisciplinary perspective on adult play and playfulness, International Journal of Play, 6:3, pp. 241-243, DOI: https://doi.org/10.1080/21594937.2017.1384307

Proyer RT., (2014), Perceived functions of playfulness in adults: Does it mobilize you at work, rest, and when being with others?. European Review of Applied Psychology. Vol. 64, pp. 241-250. https://doi.org/10.1016/j.erap.2014.06.001.

Bateson, P. (2014). Play, playfulness, creativity and innovation. *Animal Behavior and Cognition*, 1(2), pp. 99-112. doi: 10.12966/abc.05.02.2014.

Lieberman, N. J., and Edwards, A.J., (2014), *Playfulness: Its relationship to imagination and creativity*. Academic Press.

When you get used to noticing the comic discrepancies between what you experience and others' behaviors in informal contexts, you can move to the next level. You can start observing the funny perspective in work situations. In feedback dialogues, you can opt to tune into playful states at three decisive moments.

- When you introduce the idea of your project, your why. Why did you choose the particular challenge?

- When you describe the solutions you crafted – its strengths, weaknesses, and audience.

- When you invite the conversation partner to share their take on a particular issue, such as the pros and cons of the solutions you presented.

When the level of energy poured into the discussion drops, it's time to call for some playfulness. It signals a short break to reset everyone's thoughts with a smile.

Step 2: Get Ready to Make Room for a Witty Comment

This step is about getting used to spontaneously describing what is the funny aspect that you see in a situation. Earlier, we enumerated three pivotal moments in a feedback conversation. Each of those moments has three stages of development: (1) an entrance when you define the aim; (2) a middle part when you rephrase what's being said with the intention of going deeper in the discussion; and (3) an ending, when you summarize the discussed points for the sake of being on the same page with the interlocutor. Also, the summary concludes one part of the discussion and announces the transition to the next topic. (See Figure 17-1.)

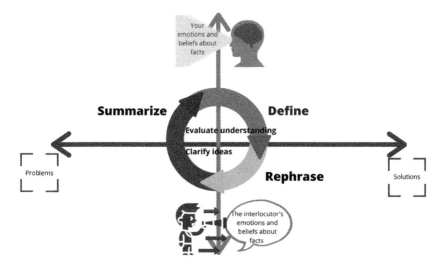

Figure 17-1. *Transition moments in a conversation*

When you define, rephrase, and summarize ideas, there are some embedded assumptions that most of the time, pass unnoticed. However, you can make some implicit assumptions explicit through humor. Here you can see **three strategies** to bring more awareness to your reality or the other person's reality.

- **Opening Up Smile** is about the ability to come up with an amusing introduction about yourself that opens up the topic. The goal is to help the listener relate to you.

For instance, you could start by talking about your work habits. *"This project made me work like a beaver at day and sleep like a log at night. I discovered a new favorite morning activity: to hit the snooze button."*

By emphasizing what is specific about your life as opposed to generally accepted productivity habits, you introduce the listener to your world and simultaneously set an amusing tone for a conversation. What might be your habits or experiences that you could mention as an entertaining contrast to stereotyped models of success?

Another way to start a conversation in a humorous tone is to laugh at the fear of being under scrutiny. *"We are expected to discover that other people's work has limitations. My work is flawless."* This sarcastic comment is an allusion to uncertainty, which is an integral part of the work-life of innovators, scientists, artists, entrepreneurs, etc. Playing with the contrast between the fear of the unknown and your attitude to it can make you more relatable in the eyes of the person you converse with.

What other elements of contrast between your personal experiences and what is accepted as true could you use at the outset of a dialogue?

- **Say it twice, please** refers to inviting the collocutor to rephrase their comment. The aim is to double-check the accuracy of your interpretations of crucial ideas.

Rephrasing is saying something again in a different way for a shared understanding of an essential point in the dialogue. When you rephrase, the assumption is that you understood the key message that was communicated to you. Sometimes, conversations reach a point of confusion when both parties think they are talking about the same thing when they actually don't. When you feel there's ambiguity in your discussion, you could be asking, *"What do you mean by (... mirror what was said ...)?"*

As a humorous alternative, you could add a silly, weird or witty comment, which is based on observed contradictions between what the interlocutor says and what you hear the interlocutor saying.[8] *"Are you saying what I heard you saying?" "To my ears, it sounded like 'Mayday',"* etc. As a backup plan, you can always have a ready-made cartoon to show when you sense that the conversation gets too confusing.

---

[8] Nusbaum, E.C., Silvia, P.J., and Beaty, R.E., (2017), Ha ha? Assessing individual differences in humor production ability. Psychology of Aesthetics, Creativity, and the Arts.;11(2):231–241 DOI: https://doi.org/10.1037/aca0000086

*"I know we didn't accomplish anything, but
that's what meetings are for."*   9

When you feel lost in a discussion, it's a good sign that many ideas have been bounced around. The humorous interventions help the interlocutor stay positive while they clarify what they are thinking.

- **Agreement smile** – *"So, what we covered so far is...", "So far, I feel that we are looking at the same book cover."* Summary sentences notify the interlocutor that there's time to move on to another topic or to conclude the discussion. How can you summarize the progress made in a dialogue in a way that infuses such transition moments with refreshed energy?

You may witness disparities between initial expectations and the themes that came up during the dialogue. *"During this discussion, you made me realize I need to hold my horses and extend the deadline."* Or *"At the beginning of this talk, I was nervous you'd tell me I put the cart before the horse when I worked so much on this new idea without testing it."*

---

9 www.boredpanda.com/the-new-yorker-cartoons/?utm_source=google&utm_medium=organic&utm_campaign=organic

Also, you may have had moments when you were aware of the differences between your emotions and beliefs and those of the interlocutor. *"I had to bite the bullet and admit you had a point when you said ..."* These funny reviews celebrate the highlights of the exchange of information. As you can see, in some previous examples, idioms were used. The use of idioms in the right context can also have amusing effects.

The American essayist and humorist E.B. White noticed a significant truth about jokes, *"Explaining a joke is like dissecting a frog. You understand it better but the frog dies in the process."* It is true that when you don't instantly get a joke, looking into the logical elaboration of the punchline will not make you laugh. Quite the contrary, you may feel more and more stupid for not getting the joke in the first place. There's an exception. When you want to develop your funny side, understanding the mechanisms of a particular joke is an investment in your potential to create laughter.

Some bits of humor in the introduction, middle part, and conclusions of a feedback conversation draw the boundaries of lightheartedness around a sensitive and serious topic for the creator: what is the next move in the creative process?

Step 3: Get Flexible to Adapt to an Appropriate Style of Humor

If you like telling sex jokes to friends, what makes you think it is a good idea to use them in a professional setting? Jokes are a matter of personal taste and values. Usually, there is a difference between the appropriateness of the jokes you tell in your free time and the jokes you tell in work contexts. Even in a long-term professional relationship, like mentor-mentee, humor can backfire. How can you crack a joke that will be well received in a feedback conversation?

First, maintain the evaluator's sense of psychological status. To this view, identify the core beliefs and knowledge you have in common with your interlocutor. Second, develop a style of humor that connects people. Third, be mindful of the emotional state of the interlocutor. Fourth, be ready to accept the moments when your humor is not appreciated.

Maintain the Interlocutor's Sense of Status by Carefully Curating the Content of the Jokes

Here, status refers to the subjective feeling of being valued by another person and not to the status that comes along with the professional role. In a discourse, the brain is unconsciously monitoring how others value you. When you feel appreciated, you experience positive emotions. When you feel criticized or ridiculed, your brain releases cortisol, a stress hormone, which will hamper your creative thinking. When making a joke, in order for the laughter to be produced, the listener needs to feel that their status is going up. Differently, the jokes make them feel good.

Sometimes, the official status can skew people's perception of what an effective use of humor is. For instance, when the listener sees themselves in a work relationship with someone in a power position, like leader–follower, professor–student, or mentor–mentee, it can be difficult for the initiator of humor to anticipate the emotional impact of a joke on the receiver.[10]

In a 2001 study, students and professors showed disagreement in their perceptions about the degree to which professors use humor to motivate students, provoke thinking, and reinforce knowledge.[11] Eighty percent of

---

[10] Levine, J., and Redlich, F.C., (1960), Intellectual and Emotional Factors in the Appreciation of Humor, The Journal of General Psychology, 62:1, pp. 25–35, DOI: https://doi.org/10.1080/00221309.1960.9710271

[11] White, G. W., (2001), Teachers' report of how they used humor with students' perceived use of such humor, *Education*, Vol. 122, Issue 2, pp. 337, Accessed 22 Apr. 2021.

professors reported that they use humor to accomplish these educational goals. However, only 55% of the students shared the same understanding.

Who would you want to invite to an exchange of opinions on your creative work: a peer, a mentor, a new acquaintance, or a representative of the users' group? Irrespective of their professional status, it's most beneficial for you as a creator to perceive and position yourself as an equal. One way to overcome possible biases of superiority or inferiority in the use of humor is to ask yourself, *"Why would this statement lift people up?"*, *"Why would this comment amuse or de-stress them?"*

Coming up with funny remarks boils down to being committed to telling the truth and caring about making the interlocutor feel valued. And it happens that behind every joke, there is a commonly agreed belief. For example, let's consider the following New Yorker cartoon with God as the main character.[12]

GOD FINDS ALL THE PRAYERS OF MANKIND IN HIS SPAM FOLDER.

---

[12] https://www.pinterest.com/pin/521854675550382975/?mt=login

Do both you and the interlocutor believe in the same God's existence? What if the interlocutor is agnostic or atheist? Then, assuming you and the interlocutor have lax religious beliefs, why would the joke be relevant at a particular moment in the dialogue? A joke is thus appropriate when it brings to awareness common beliefs, values, and knowledge related to the present situation.

A 2006 study interviewed undergraduate college students about instances of appropriate and inappropriate humor in the classroom.[13] The students identified 1315 humorous moments created by teachers during the class, out of which 774 moments fit the context. Funny remarks and behaviors related to the course material were considered the most appropriate humor (47%). Insulting students or other people with whom the students identified based on gender, race, religion, sexual orientation, or political affinity was considered inappropriate humor.

These findings can apply in work contexts as well. Therefore, to maintain the sense of the interlocutor's status, it may be a safe bet to stick to jokes relevant to the discussion themes and familiar facts within a domain of expertise, as illustrated in the following xkcd comic, *Interstellar Memes*.

---

[13] Wanzer, M.B., Frymier, A.B., Wojtaszczyk, A.M., and Smith, T., (2006), Appropriate and Inappropriate Uses of Humor by Teachers, Communication Education, 55:2, pp. 178–196, DOI: https://doi.org/10.1080/03634520600566132

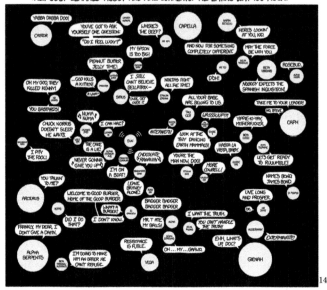

The punchline is, *"The strongest incentive we have to develop faster-than-light travel is that it would let us apologize in advance."* Folks with basic knowledge in stellar systems and the last three decades of pop culture will find this comic amusing.

In brief, to make sure that both you and the listener get amused, look for funny comments and stories based on shared beliefs and knowledge with the listener. What do you know about the reality of your possible evaluators?

Optional exercise 3: *Mapping the common areas with your interlocutors*

---

[14] https://xkcd.com/1212/
https://imgs.xkcd.com/comics/interstellar_memes.png

Since jokes require shared implicit knowledge and beliefs, a helpful exercise before important conversations is to sit with yourself for a few minutes and revise what you know about the person you are about to meet.

Personal values _____ , _____ , _____ , etc.

Life circumstances _____ , _____ , _____ , etc.

Knowledge _____ , _____ , _____ , etc.

Hobbies _____ , _____ , _____ , etc.

The content for humor has to draw on one of the above-noted five areas.

Practice the Sense of Humor That Fuels People's Creativity

Using humor requires confidence. What is the style of humor you use habitually? The tendency to use humor in everyday situations is triggered by two goals: to improve your value or to improve the value of your relationship with others.[15] And there are two styles in achieving these goals: a harmless way and a mischievous way (see Figure 17-2).

---

[15] Martin, R. A., Puhlik-Doris, P., Larsen, G., Gray, J., and Weir, K., (2003), Individual differences in uses of humor and their relation to psychological well-being: Development of the Humor Styles Questionnaire, Journal of Research in Personality, Volume 37, Issue 1, pp. 48–75, https://doi.org/10.1016/S0092-6566(02)00534-2.

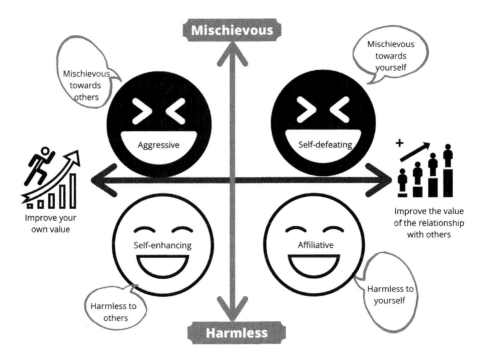

Figure 17-2. *Humor Styles*

Each individual disposes of four humor styles, to varying degrees, directly related to personality traits and moods.

You have the self-enhancing style when you want to reaffirm yourself and express your perspective with graciousness toward others. Most often, it is used when being alone. It's about reframing your perspectives through funny narratives to cope with difficulties and negative states of mind or to boost your playfulness.

When you want to bring the value of a particular relationship into the spotlight while establishing your position favorably, you have the affiliative style. This style is shown when you are around people in a work context.

The self-enhancing and affiliative styles are correlated with the innocuous tendency to laugh and be amused. Unfortunately, the following two types are more harmful.

When you are tempted to speak highly about yourself and express it in a hurtful way toward others, you have an aggressive style. It shows a lack of respect for the feelings of others, and it has a mocking, ridiculing, and humiliating tone. Within social groups, the use of hostile types of joking, like teasing or sarcasm, can exclude individuals from another group, establish power and status differences, and have a compelling appeal to accepted social norms. It thus fosters social divisiveness, the kind of *"the better us"* versus *"the losers them."* Blonde jokes, religious and political affiliation jokes are examples of this style.

And the fourth style, the self-defeating manner, results in situations when you speak highly about others while undermining yourself. It entails the willingness to make fun of yourself more than one would feel comfortable with, to be the butt of jokes.

Which of these four styles are your dominant tendencies? Which of these styles would improve the relationships with people you interact with in work contexts? For instance, lab studies found support for the hypothesis that individuals who observe self-deprecating humor experience higher levels of creativity. By contrast, the participants who experienced ridicule type of humor were more inclined to conform and afraid of failing.[16]

In organizational settings, leaders' use of self-enhancing humor can increase the employees' individual creativity provided there's an existing trust in leaders.[17] Moreover, in one to one conversations, leaders' use of aggressive humor leads to lowering the perceived trust and performance of the employees, irrespective of the employee's levels of self-esteem

---

[16] Janes, L. and Olson, J., (2015), Humor as an abrasive or a lubricant in social situations: Martineau revisited, *Humor*, Vol. 28, no. 2, pp. 271–288. https://doi.org/10.1515/humor-2015-0021

[17] Lee, D-R, (2015), The Impact of Leader's Humor on Employees' Creativity: The Moderating Role of Trust in Leader, *Seoul Journal of Business*, Vol.21 No.1, pp. 59–86.

and self-efficacy.[18] By contrast, when leaders use affiliative humor, they signal humility – reducing the status difference between leaders and their teams – and integrity – behaving in a way that is consistent with the organizational values.

To conclude, irrespective of your sense of humor with family members and friends or your job status, the affiliative and self-deprecating styles are more empathetic and safer choices in conversations where the goal is to broaden people's thinking. The rule of thumb is, *"Laugh at yourself, not at others."*

The affiliative and self-defeating styles can become powerful communicators to increase creative problem-solving abilities, trust, and prosocial behaviors – qualities you want from the people who evaluate your original ideas. Laugh with others, not at others.

Is This a Good Moment for Improvised Humor?

It takes two to laugh. So, you want to become savvy at fishing for the moods suitable for smiles and laughter. Humor can sometimes be perceived as beneficial or harmful when the listener is not in the right mood.

Your playfulness triggers a humorous moment. Yet, the interpretation of the person at the receiving end can make or break the joke. Should the interlocutor be fixated on hearing a serious reply, the opportunity for laughter will be wasted. Responding with humor when the listener doesn't expect it may temporarily affect your credibility. We have two alternatives

---

[18] Neves, P. and Karagonlar, G., (2020), Does leader humor style matter and to whom?, *Journal of Managerial Psychology*, Vol. 35, No. 2, pp. 115–128. https://doi.org/10.1108/JMP-12-2018-0552.
Gkorezis, P. and Bellou, V., (2016), The relationship between leader self-deprecating humor and perceived effectiveness: Trust in leader as a mediator, *Leadership & Organization Development Journal*, Vol. 37 No. 7, pp. 882–898. https://doi.org/10.1108/LODJ-11-2014-0231.

to prevent this risk and reap the benefits of connection, vitality, and creativity through humor:

(1) How can you tell when the interlocutor looks available for a joke? To probe their openness toward a moment of laughter, you can choose to pay attention to two kinds of behaviors in the conversation:

- Is this a moment when you feel psychologically safe around the evaluator?

- How often has the listener been asking interesting questions?

The more friendly and the higher the level of engagement, the more likely they are ready for a laugh.

(2) You can prepare the interlocutor by notifying a lighthearted statement, as follows. *"Let me tell you something funny," "There's a funny twist in this idea...," "I'm amused to realize...,"* etc.

These anticipatory statements can diminish the comic impact but compensate by framing the expectations. The worst that can happen is that the interlocutor will ignore them and move on to other ideas.

Of course, you can be wrong about people's emotions and the level of responsibility they take in offering feedback. Therefore, the decisive factor in taking a moment to speak with humor is the extent to which you feel a temporary connection between you and the evaluator. When in tune, be ready to joke.

How to Manage the Situations When the Interlocutor Is Not Amused

When was the last time you tried to make someone smile only to fail? You must know it feels humiliating or embarrassing.[20] When you take the lead to initiate laughter, there is an implicit invitation for human connection and solidarity in face of a present challenge. Therefore, you become vulnerable by assuming the risk that they will not accept the invitation. Should the risk become reality, bugger! Poor choice of joke.

---

[19] Inspired by www.balls.ie/the-rewind/13-bad-joke-memes-to-get-you-through-the-lockdown-433123

[20] Bell, N.D., (2015), We are not amused, Failed Humour in Interaction, Walter De Gruyter. https://library.oapen.org/bitstream/handle/20.500.12657/25216/1004877.pdf?sequence=1
Bell, N.D., (2009), Impolite responses to failed humor, published in: Humor in Interaction, Edited by Neal R. Norrick and Delia Chiaro, pp. 143–164. https://doi.org/10.1016/j.pragma.2008.10.010

At the same time, listening to humor feels like a test of intelligence. When the listener realizes they didn't get the joke, they can feel uncomfortable. *"Why did I not get it?"* Or they may be judgmental. *"You little smart aleck…,"* interpreting your humor as an intention to place yourself in a superior position or, even worse, as a verbal attack.

How can you handle the situations when the receiver deals with a sense of failure in making sense of humor? There can be various reasons for which humor is misinterpreted – refusal to enter a playful mood, lack of familiarity with the words and experiences, loss of attention to the information flow, etc. The unavoidable outcome is a momentary loss of connection between you and the interlocutor. When you sense that your humor didn't sit well with the listener, apologizing or offering an additional explanation of the joke would only worsen the conversational disruption.

The crux is to reestablish the interlocutor's sense of psychological status. To this view, you can start by summarizing what was agreed upon up until that point in the discussion, and the topics left uncovered. It is important to help the interlocutor regain a sense of control and perceive you as harmless. To this view, you can allow the interlocutor to decide what ideas are worth focusing on next.

Using humor and listening to humor is not so much a test of common knowledge but more like a test of willingness to be momentarily playful. Luckily, in a relationship where there's a foundation of trust to start with, a conversation consists of ebbs and flows of emotional connection. So sooner or later, the dynamics will be restored.

In the following sections, we'll look into how you could rev up the listener's engagement in the conversation through analogies and imaginative thinking.

CHAPTER 18

Listen for Inspiration

What Is an Attitude of Inspiration?

A new indoor playground opened in Helsinki. It offered educational playrooms for the babies' and toddlers' creative thinking. It was distinctive from the sporty playgrounds existing then in the market. It had the soul of the designer imprinted in every room.

I took my sons to this place for a couple of visits. Once, as we were about to leave, the owner approached us to inquire about our experience. Her eyes were shining with pride. For a few seconds, I hesitated. *"Should I tell her what she wants to hear or what I have to say?"*

I started telling what I loved about the space. The instant I mentioned that, in my opinion, the entry ticket was too highly-priced, her face turned into a black cloud. She entered into a lecture mode about family budgets and cost-savings that parents can make to afford to pay for the entrance to the playground.

A fruitful way to think about a feedback conversation is as an opportunity to collect more information than you would otherwise be exposed to. Instead of taking a defensive attitude, ready to fire counterarguments, you can choose an attitude of inspiration. The goal is to identify probable courses of action and maybe some moments of spontaneous humor, based on the interlocutor's raised concerns. But what is inspiration?

One of the meanings described in the Merriam-Webster dictionary is *"a divine influence or action on a person believed to qualify him or her to receive and communicate sacred revelation."* In this definition, there are embedded

© Oana Velcu-Laitinen 2022
O. Velcu-Laitinen, *How to Develop Your Creative Identity at Work*,
https://doi.org/10.1007/978-1-4842-8680-7_18

three characteristics: (1) there is an external source that communicates a message, (2) the message is acknowledged by the receiver who is moved to take an action which was inconceivable before the strike of inspiration, and (3) the increase in the sense of worthiness of the individual.

Indeed, the Ancient Greeks thought that inspiration comes not when you need it but when the Muses grant permission.[1] The nine daughters of Zeus and Mnemosyne would allow access to divine thoughts for some chosen mortals with talent in poetry, music, dance, history, astronomy, etc. For instance, if you wanted to be funnier, Thalia, the muse of comedy, was the one to implore for an abundance of humorous ideas. If you were interested in history, Clio would be guiding your learning.

On a scale of 1 (*like a dull pencil*) to 5(*like a babbling brook*), how inspired do you feel daily? A dream, a book, a song, a coincidence or a planned meeting with a special person (i.e., boss, teacher, mentor, influencer) can fuel the determination to take new action. Some psychologists and neuroscientists who study creativity view inspiration as a motivational state of being, preceding the creative idea, in artistic and non-artistic domains, which moves you to information seeking and knowledge acquisition.[2]

Inspiration takes you by surprise, and it mobilizes you. It makes you feel uplifted and enthusiastic about deliberate change. These positive emotions transform into a heightened and sustained commitment to getting involved with the subject of inspiration – a new idea or question. So, inspiration is like the wind in your sails that carries you from the beginning to the end of the creative process.

---

[1] www.britannica.com/topic/Muse-Greek-mythology

[2] Thrash, T.M., et al., (2010), Mediating Between the Muse and the Masses: Inspiration and the Actualization of Creative Ideas, Journal of Personality and Social Psychology, Vol. 98, No. 3, pp. 469–487.

Thrash, T.M., and Elliot, A.J., (2003), Inspiration as a psychological construct, Journal of Personality and Social Psychology, 84(4), pp. 871–889.

What does it mean to be chosen by the Muse? The qualities of the person who can hear the message from the external source are the third defining characteristic of inspiration according to the Merriam-Webster definition. If inspiration is not an act of will, what do you need to do to get into the favor of the Muse?

You may not be able to control when inspiration strikes, but you can do something to lure it into your life. You can stimulate your thoughts by being open to new experiences like visiting a museum or taking on skills in new areas. The more you allow yourself to be exposed to unfamiliar ideas and experiences, the higher your likelihood to get inspired and express new ideas.[3] However, inspiration doesn't happen if new experiences are like water off a duck's back to you. You need to allow yourself to be receptive to novelty, even when it's not love at first sight or hearing. In particular, in feedback conversations, you may want to train the ability to explore others' ideas, withholding the need to reject them.[4]

You may be thinking, *"Hold on! If I am less judgmental with the others' comments, how can I discern what is relevant for developing my original idea?"* Postponing your judgment now and then during dialogue is like the tiny pause between your breaths, enabling you to continue taking the next breath. Being less judgmental allows you to revisit your ideas from an enriched perspective provided by the evaluator's experience and knowledge.

The first step in making yourself more receptive to inspiration is to observe your emotions and reactions when you listen. Whenever you realize you have a strong reaction toward someone's opinions, count 1, 2, 3 and sigh. *"Thalia, please help me hold the rumbling judgement!"* Give your inspiration a name – *"Buddy," "Precious," "Hey you,"* etc., – that has a meaning to you and can soften your temptation to deny the criticism.

---

[3] Epstein, R. and Phan, V., (2012), Which Competencies Are Most Important for Creative Expression?, Creativity Research Journal, Vol. 24, Issue 4, pp. 278–282.
[4] Shelley Carson, (2010), Your Creative Brain, Harvard Health Publications.

If inspiration is the wind in your sails, you need to know how to steer the boat – your thoughts – to make the most of the ideas that arise in the discussion. You want to make it to the end of the conversation, as you intended at the outset: as a creator with a receptive mind.

The Ancient Greeks got it right again when they believed that Mnemosyne, the goddess of memory, was the Muses' mother. The more you regulate the level of judgment in a conversation, the more likely you will make surprising connections between what you hear and the knowledge or personal events in your memory.

The second step in making you more receptive to inspiration is the ability to make remote associations. Inspiration may not be an act of will, but it can be an act of activation of memory through the use of language. To this view, in the next session, you find out how to appeal more often to analogies when you express more complex thoughts.

The playground with a soul went into bankruptcy in the first year after its opening. We enjoyed each visit when we felt like kings in a large space of colored floors, detailed walls and miniature landscapes. Of course, it is hard to tell what went wrong, but one thing is certain: if you truly care to develop your creative products, enter feedback conversations committed to an attitude of inspiration.

Use Analogies to Sort Out Difficult Concepts and Ideas

"I tried to explain as much as I could," Poppet says. *"I think I made an analogy about cake."*

"Well, that must have worked," Widget says. *"Who doesn't like a good cake analogy?"*

—Erin Morgenstern, The Night Circus[5]

---

[5] www.goodreads.com/quotes/tag/analogy

An analogy is a creative thinking ability that enables the comparison of two concepts, **A** and **B**, to explain an idea. **A** is the **principal concept** that is new to the listener and needs to be explained. **B** is the **model**, which is familiar to both the speaker and the listener.

Here we can see two examples of analogies:

"A good speech should be like a woman's skirt; long enough to cover the subject and short enough to create interest." Winston S. Churchill

"I like to imagine that the world is one big machine. You know, machines never have any extra parts. They have the exact number and type of parts they need. So I figure if the entire world is a big machine, I have to be here for some reason. And that means you have to be here for some reason, too." Brian Selznick, The Invention of Hugo Cabret

In Churchill's analogy, the aim is to emphasize the key functions of a memorable rhetoric by comparing A (a good speech) with B(a woman's skirt). In Selznick's analogy on the purpose of life, an individual's life (A) is likened to a machine part (B).

An analogy is a communication tool which works well when you know the literal message you want to convey. The analogous thinking starts from inferences from previous knowledge and experiences, resulting in more accessible explanations to present to the listener. The challenge is that faulty analogies can cause more confusion than the clarification of an idea. So, let's look into three requirements for a good analogy, shall we?

Choose Familiar Models of Reference

First, to make a good analogy, beforehand, you want to have some essential details about the person you are having a dialogue with. What can be told about the listeners addressed by Churchill's and Selznick's analogies?

Winston Churchill talks to an audience of men interested in public speaking. Women may or may not be amused by the analogy. Yet, their male counterparts are the ones who get it the best. As for Selznick, he reaches out to people who are looking for their purpose in life. Therefore, when using an analogy, it's good to select a particular knowledge, experience, or life circumstance to which the listener can relate.

"Who doesn't like a good cake analogy?" Everyone ate a good cake at least once in their lifetime. Even people who are not the sugar type. **Familiarity** needs to be the criteria for choosing the model (B) with which you compare the original (A). Then, the listener needs to be well acquainted with the role and functions of **B** to gain deeper insight into those of **A**.

In a way, analogies are similar to inside jokes where the humor is understood by the members of a particular group or community with shared knowledge. In the same way, analogies require a common understanding of the model to gain insight into the original, which the speaker chooses to describe through analogy.

In addition to politicians and writers, scientists too use familiar analogue models to elaborate ideas. In *"The Meaning of Relativity,"* Einstein expressed his view on how phenomena which cannot be directly observed are shaped by the experiencer, as follows, *"The universe of ideas is just as little independent of the nature of our experiences as clothes are of the form of the human body."*

To sum up, rule #1 of making good analogies is to choose your models from daily life objects or from an area of knowledge and experiences you have in common with the listener.

Optional exercise 4: *Change in the audience, change in analogy*

Think of the official title you currently have. Imagine you want to describe it to a 4-year-old. What would you compare it with so that your little listener understands what you do?

Being a _____ is like _____ .

What if you wanted your grandfather to understand what you do?

Being a _____ is like _____ .

How about talking to a cave person?

Being a _____ is like _____ .

For instance, to cave people, professional roles can be likened to small gods. For instance, programmers could be explained like demigods that make inanimate objects think for themselves. Leaders are like fallen gods who look for redemption. Politicians are like god's helpers who dream of omnipotence.

Check the Internal Consistency of A and B

Comparing apples with oranges? The second requirement for a good analogy is to make sure that **the similarities between the original concept (A) and the model (B) hold.**

Let's make the implicit explicit. A generalized analogous statement would sound like this, "**A with feature A1 is like B with feature B1.**" and "**A with feature A2 is like B with feature B2.**"

For this analogy to be internally consistent, there must be a similar relation between the features and the concept, that is, A and A1 must be related in the same way as B and B1. If we deconstruct the implicit meaning of the previous statement, it sounds as follows, "**A1 and A2 have a relation with A which is similar to the relation of B1 and B2 with B.**"

Let's get back to Churchill's analogy, which illustrates a simple analogy. *"A good speech should be like a woman's skirt; long enough to cover the subject and short enough to create interest."* Here, the attributes of the original concept (good speech) are A1 (long speech) and A2 (short speech). The attributes of the model concept (woman's skirt) are B1 (long skirt) and B2 (short skirt). What makes it a good analogy is that the attributes of the original and model objects have in common two functions – to cover the key points and to raise interest.

In the realms of science, technology, and other domains of specialization, most often, it takes effort to understand, visualize, and relate yourself to the essence of abstract ideas. To this view, there's the need for more **explanatory and enriched analogies**. Differently, the more complex the original concept is, the more crucial it is to create a strong analogy.

The attributes of both the target and the original need to be selected based on the **consistency in the shared relations** with the target object and the original concept respectively.[6] The principal (A) and the model (B) must have at least one shared function and at least one different feature. The larger the number of shared relations and the smaller the number of shared attributes, the more useful the analogy is.

This aspect of consistency is exemplified in the structure of the following analogy, *"The human cell is like a university."* This is an explanatory and enriched analogy with five different shared functions.

- A university has the purpose to develop and disseminate knowledge to young adults so they can contribute to a well-functioning society. The human cell has the purpose to grow and make more of itself to keep you alive.

- Like universities, each body cell has a specialization: neurons, red blood cells, immune cells, etc.

- Universities have leadership teams which have the instructions about what information the students need to acquire before graduation. Cells have a nucleus that houses your DNA, the genetic code, which has the essential information for your height, hair, etc., and the normal mechanisms of your body.

[6] Brown, S., and Salter, S., (2010), Analogies in science and science teaching, Advances in Physiology Education, Vol. 34, Issue 4, pp. 167–169.

Aubusson, P.J., and Fogwill, S., (2006), Role Play as Analogical Modelling in Science. In: Aubusson, P.J., Harrison, A.G., Ritchie, S.M. (eds) Metaphor and Analogy in Science Education. Science & Technology Education Library, Vol 30. Springer, Dordrecht. https://doi.org/10.1007/1-4020-3830-5_8

Richard K. Coll, Bev France, and Ian Taylor, 2005, The role of models/and analogies in science education: implications from research, International Journal of Science Education, 27:2, pp. 183–198, DOI: https://doi.org/10.1080/0950069042000276712

- Universities have highly trained educators who transfer to students the master knowledge of their domain. A cell has special proteins that read the information on the DNA string and convert it into a special molecule called mRNA which is then transported to another "organ" of the cell, the ribosome. The ribosome reads the mRNA and produces a protein as instructed.[7]

- The ribosome is similar to the collection of teaching materials, instructions and implicit knowledge that teachers share with their students. In the same way, as students graduate and go out in society to do the work they were trained to do, proteins start wiggling around and interacting with other proteins in the cell to keep up the functioning of the body part they are in charge with.

The five functions are related to one explanatory goal – the property of the cell to create and share information needed for survival. Thus, they fulfill the consistency criteria.

In brief, considering the concept you want to explain, anything from a good cake to life's purpose, it's important to **consciously choose the underlying principle** you want to shed light on through analogy. Extended analogies, with more shared functions between the original and model, are useful when dealing with complex concepts.

Optional exercise 5: Describe a particular work challenge

Think of a recent work experience that was challenging, but you managed successfully. What analogy would you use to emphasize both its level of complexity but also the joy of figuring it out?

Optional exercise 6: Use an analogy to communicate the feeling of being creative

---

[7] Dettmer, P., (2021), Immune, Random House, New York.

Imagine a journalist invites you to an interview and asks you, "What does it feel like to be creative?"

"To me, to be creative is like _____."

To me, to be creative is like drinking a mojito on a hot Summer day. It's refreshing and it brings a sense of freedom.

Ensure That the Comparison Between A and B Is Valid

Last, there are **three types of analogy relations** between the **features and the model/original concept** that ensure the validity of the comparison between the known and the less known concept.

The other day, my son asked, *"Mom, what is a CPU?"* Instead of defining the central processing component of a computer, I used an analogy. *"A CPU is to a computer what the brain is to your body."* Both the CPU and the brain process information, which results in actions.

Every relation A:A1 has a function which you choose to communicate. For the remainder of this section, let's unravel **the types of relations between the feature and the original/model** in the analogies given as examples.

1. The unknown concept (A), the CPU, and the larger system, the computer (A1), have a **part-to-whole relation**. A is a part of A1. The CPU is a part of the structure of a computer.

In Selznick's life purpose analogy, there is the same part-to-whole relation between the explained concept, your life (A) and the environment, the world (A1). Your life is a part of the social collective. It has a purpose, uniquely designed for a particular community.

In the human cell-university analogy, there is a reversed relation, **whole-to-part,** between the principal object, the cell, and its features. The nucleus, DNA, mRNA, and ribosome are components of the cell structure.

2. In the good speech analogy, the feature (A1) –
    length – is **a property** of the explained concept (A) –
    a good speech. A good discourse must not be too
    long but not too short either.

3. And last, in Einstein's analogy, there's a **dependence
    relation.** The principal concept (A) depends on
    the attribute (A1). Our direct experiences shape the
    ideas that form in our minds.

In case you completed exercises 4, 5, and 6, what type of relations do
the original and the model have with their features?

So far, we have elaborated on analogies where the model is **"like"** the
original concept. In addition, there can be analogies where the analogue
is **"unlike"** the target of the communication. Here is an example written
by author John Green in Looking for Alaska: *"If people were like rain, I was
like drizzle and she was a hurricane."*

Here, the focus is on differentiation to emphasize what's special about
the concept you want to describe. Therefore, the relation between the
principal and its features is opposite to the relation between the model and
its features.

The drizzle is a light precipitation, coming in smaller water drops
than those of rain. It implies a gentle and accommodating presence. The
hurricane is a storm of strong winds and heavy rain, over a smaller area.
It's a phenomenon you want to watch from a distance.

Why is comparing apples with oranges considered a faulty analogy?
They are both part of the fruit category but not the same family. Apples
belong to the Rosaceae and oranges belong to the Rutaceae family. The
features, taste, feel, looks, and scents make them incomparable.

Despite their innate dissimilarities, oranges and apples could be
used in a good analogy to express differences in personal preferences, in
knowledge acquisition, for instance. *"Just like some people like apples and*

others oranges, some people like statistics and others like anecdotes." Both apples and oranges can satisfy hunger, in the same way as stories and data satisfy the curiosity for information.

In brief, you can think of a new concept that you want to describe as a system of elements or a part of a network of objects and events. And it has some functions.[8] To this view, you start by selecting the principle of the unknown concept that you want to explain through analogy (see Figure 18-1). You'll then identify the elements or objects that fulfil a harmonic function for the respective principle.

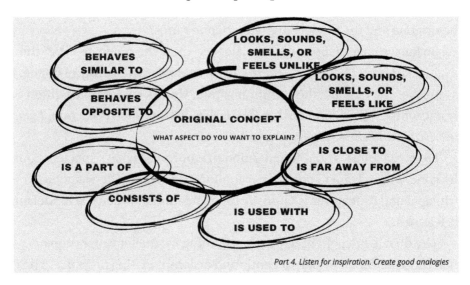

Part 4. Listen for inspiration. Create good analogies

Figure 18-1. *Good analogies*

_____

[8] Han, J., Shi, F., Chen, L., and Childs, P., (2018). A computational tool for creative idea generation based on analogical reasoning and ontology. *Artificial Intelligence for Engineering Design, Analysis and Manufacturing, 32*(4), pp. 462–477. doi:10.1017/S0890060418000082.
Gentner, D., (1983), Structure-mapping: a theoretical framework for analogy, Cognitive Science, 7, pp. 155–170.

Using analogies requires a good memory and empathetic and critical thinking to appeal to familiar "likes" and "unlikes" when introducing new ideas. It can help to come to feedback conversations prepared with analogies that describe the core concepts. Expressions such as *"Let me give you an analogy...," "It's just like...," "It's the same as...," "It's no different than...,"* are great openings.

The owner of the indoor playground could have taken the feedback dialogue as an exploration of viable services from the client's perspective. For example, they could have asked, *"Think of this playground as a gym for your kids' minds. What would be the services and how much would you be willing to pay for?"*

To conclude, whenever there's a chance to clarify or explore challenging ideas, dare to use analogies to help others understand you better and make them collaborators to your product development.

Optional exercise 7*: Master analogies*

Think of three major concepts in your line of work. Is it an object, an activity, or a process? What are the top characteristics/functions? What would be an everyday object, activity, or process you can compare them to?

What would be the next scheduled meeting when would be a good time to introduce your master analogies?

CHAPTER 19

Listen for Imagination

My imagination functions much better when I don't have to speak to people.

—Novelist Patricia Highsmith

Most often, we think of imagination as an activity of the mind which flows unhampered when you are alone with your thoughts. This section discusses how to make our imagination work during feedback conversations. Speaking in analogies is based on associating what you hear with what you already know to explain a present idea better. Listening for imagination is about transforming what you hear into a possibility. It's about using a trigger to ask "What if" questions, opening the mind to future scenarios.

What Is Imagination?

"All the world's a stage," wrote Shakespeare, "And all the men and women merely players."[1] Moreover, every man and woman has an inner life where they invent their preferred stages, with players, conflicts, resources, and desired outcomes.

---

[1] www.shakespeare.org.uk/explore-shakespeare/shakespedia/shakespeares-plays/as-you-like-it/

© Oana Velcu-Laitinen 2022
O. Velcu-Laitinen, *How to Develop Your Creative Identity at Work,*
https://doi.org/10.1007/978-1-4842-8680-7_19

Studies in comparative psychology have identified a few cognitive abilities that human beings and animals have in common, such as memory, social reasoning, physical reasoning, communication, and empathy.[2] Yet, the ability to form alternative scenarios, to envision and speculate future situations, is one of the distinctive features that sets us apart from the animal species and is generally known as imagination.

Let's take as an example of the ability to form alternative scenarios the act of looking at this photo.

[3]

You can "see" what else could be happening rather than what is in fact the case. How about seeing yourself taking a bite from this cake? What might the flavors be? Answering these questions makes you consider courses of action which you have not yet experienced.

In addition, you can anticipate the consequences that would come from those actions. What if you tasted a cherry cake with meringue? How would you like the contrast between the softness of the dough and the crisp of the meringue? Thanks to imaginative thinking you can engage in mental simulation, entertaining the cause and effect of likely events. Are

---

[2] Suddendorf, T., Two Key Features Created the Human Mind, 2018, Scientific American, pp. 35-39.

[3] www.canva.com/

you salivating? You have eaten the cake in your imagination or as they say, with your eyes. Enjoy the sensation. If you're unimpressed by the image of this cake, the flavors imagined are not to your taste.

Imagination does not emerge out of nothing. Imagination is triggered by internal or external factors that have significance for you. It draws upon previous experiences and knowledge, and it is motivated by the desire to change, discover, or invent in the physical world.[4] Are you now thinking about baking a cake to your liking? Once you identify a future scenario that resonates with you, you get motivated to turn it into reality.

Peeking into the anatomy of the human brain, we can notice the traces of imagination in the default mode network, a brain network connecting both hemispheres that is used to encode and retrieve personal information and hypothetical events. Once you project yourself into a future scenario, it becomes part of you, your episodic foresight. It adds to your portfolio of inner theater plays that make you hope or fear the future. Therefore, you can revisit a preferred envisioned future and improve it when you decide to turn it into reality. What if you added some liquor to the cake?

---

[4] Jung, R. E., Flores, R. A., and Hunter, D., (2016), A New Measure of Imagination Ability: Anatomical Brain Imaging Correlates, Frontiers in Psychology, Vol. 7, www.frontiersin.org/article/10.3389/fpsyg.2016.00496, DOI=10.3389/fpsyg.2016.00496

In addition to remembering the past and envisioning the future, imagination has the third key aspect evidenced in the default mode network, which is considering the thoughts and perspectives of other people.[5] Should there be any kids who want a piece of the cake, can you add the liquor?

Summing up, we define imagination as the ability to break free from what has been done in the past and take a stand in the present in order to play with probable futures that benefit a group of people.

Is Imagination the Same As Fantasy?

For Goethe, the German poet, philosopher, and scientist, fantasy was a precondition for intuitively experiencing the world and observing nature's hidden mechanisms. So, let's address the elephant in the room. When you think of imagination, what synonyms come to your mind? To what extent are imagination and fantasy interchangeable?

From the perspective of the final outcome, imagination is based on the ability to think of something – an event, concept, product – which is not yet real, in a particular space and time, but it has the potential to become a reality. When an imagined event, like a societal change, becomes a trend, followers will experience it directly. An imagined product can become a prototype or innovation that will be used by audiences.

---

[5] Buckner, R. L., Andrews-Hanna, J.R., Schacter, D-L., (2008), The Brain's Default Network
Anatomy, Function, and Relevance to Disease, Annals of the New York Academy of Sciences, Vol. 1124, Issue 1, pp. 1-38.
Suddendorf, T., and Redshaw, J., (2013), The development of mental scenario building and episodic foresight, Annals of the New York Academy of Sciences, Vol. 1296, Issue 1, pp. 135-153.
Crespi, B., Leach, E., Dinsdale, N., Mokkonen, M., and Hurd, P., (2016), Imagination in human social cognition, autism, and psychotic-affective conditions, Cognition, Vol. 150, pp. 181-199, https://doi.org/10.1016/j.cognition.2016.02.001.

Fantasy is what fiction writers excel at through their craft to invent stories and characters that make readers relate to and project themselves in the respective world for as long as the book is read. Therefore, fantasy results from the ability to think of something – an event, object, person – that feels real. Still, it does not have a physical representation in a particular space and time. The feeling of reality arises from the mental images and emotions evoked in the creator's and reader's minds.

When the reader finishes reading a fiction book, the story and characters remain words on paper. Some may linger in the reader's memory for a while longer, but sooner or later, they will be replaced by flesh and blood people in real interactions. As for the writer, new fantasies are awaiting.

Therefore, fantasy is a form of imagination, a crucial type of thinking in some professions, like the arts. As a kid, artist Dasha Pears was drawing worlds of elves and weird creatures. She was not interested in landscapes or anything else she would see from her window. As an adult, she recovered her childhood interest through surreal fine art photography, where not only does she capture the world as she sees it but she also wants to invite people into her surreal worlds.

"Surreal fine art photography means that what you can see in my art is not what you can see in the objective reality around you," says Dasha. *"Basically my art sort of surprises people. There's always this surreal element there."*

To enjoy the versatile benefits of the imaginative mind in your non-artistic domain, you shouldn't mistakenly take fantasy for imagination.[6] Yet, you shouldn't refrain from fantasizing either, provided this is natural thinking to you. For example, if you're a game programmer, you can fantasize all you can to come up with a compelling vision for a product.

---

[6] Thompson, N.A., (2018), Creativity and imagination in organizations, Organization Studies, Vol. 39, Issue 2-3, pp. 229–250. https://journals.sagepub.com/doi/full/10.1177/0170840617736939).

Suppose you're a researcher with some suppositions about the concepts of investigation. In that case, sooner or later, those relations need to prove themselves valid in a universe governed by the principles of physics and human cultures.

To conclude, fantasy is a type of imagination that is beneficial in the ideation stage in artistic and non-artistic domains.[7] Furthermore, there are other forms of imagination.[8] What do you need to know about the different types of imagination that boost your potential to create in the physical world?

Three Imagination Activities That Lead to New Ideas

There are two types of imaginative thinking that take us beyond "what is" to "what might be": **mental imagery** – imagining in images, body movement, or other sensory modes, like smell or sound – and **counterfactual thinking** – contrasting an event that took place with a hypothetical one. These thinking patterns are activated during one of the three mental activities: **daydreaming, mind wandering, and perspective-taking**.

---

[7] Glăveanu, V.P., Karwowski, M., Jankowska, D.M., and de Saint-Laurent, C., (2017), Creative Imagination, Published in T. Zittoun, V. P. Glăveanu (Eds.), 1 Handbook of imagination and culture, pp. 1-39.
Cornejo, C., (2015), From Fantasy to Imagination: A Cultural History and a Moral for Cultural Psychology, Published in Wagoner, B., Bresco de Luna, I., and Awad, S.H. (Eds.). The Psychology of Imagination: History, Theory and New Research Horizons, Information Age Publishing, pp. 3-44.
[8] Gotlieb, R., Hyde, E., Immordino-Yang, M.H., and Kaufman, S.B., (2018), Imagination is the Seed of Creativity, Published in J.C. Kaufman and R.J. Sternberg (Eds.). The Cambridge Handbook of Creativity. New York, NY: Cambridge University Press, pp. 1-36.

As a side note, there are other kinds of imagination activities that involve altered mental states, out of which some are functional – dreaming, meditation, the use of psychedelics – and others are less functional – hallucinations, delusions, out-of-body experiences.[9] This section does not discuss these types of altered states of imagination.

Daydreaming

Think of a place you like. Think of a person you love. Think of a recent happy memory. These are examples of daydreaming, which is a type of imagination that can evoke feelings, physical sensations, sounds, or tastes. It can be performed both on your own and in a group. For instance, you can decide to daydream alone, in your office, as a break from work tasks. Or, you can daydream in a workshop, where the facilitator guides you toward enriched sensory experiences.

In daydreaming, the attention directs inwardly and entails spontaneous thoughts that are unrelated to one's current context (i.e., stimulus-independent). Your mood, intentionality, and attentional focus are essential elements of daydreaming that can benefit the creative process.[10]

---

[9] Abraham, A., (2016), The imaginative mind, Human Brain Mapping, Vol. 37, pp. 4197–4211. https://onlinelibrary.wiley.com/doi/epdf/10.1002/hbm.23300.

[10] Zedelius, C.M., and Schooler, J.M., (2016), The Richness of Inner Experience: Relating Sytles of Daydreaming to Creative Processes, Vol. 6, https://doi.org/10.3389/fpsyg.2015.02063

A common way of daydreaming starts from spontaneously choosing a particular place, where you feel relaxed, safe, or joyful. You imagine yourself attending an event where you expect a positive outcome. You see yourself talking with people. From this moment on, your imagination is the limit. You engage in inventing actions – yours and others' – and details conducive to desired consequences.

For instance, before a feedback session, you could play in your mind with different scenarios about how to open the dialogue. Next, you can simulate the questions that you might be asked and the answers you could provide. Also, you could rehearse in front of the mirror how you would react when you hear something less optimistic than you expected. Finally, you can imagine the good feelings when your ideas get validated.

Mind Wandering

Mind wandering is similar to daydreaming because it requires internally focused attention. But, unlike daydreaming, zoning out is always a solitary and spontaneous activity. It's not like you get to decide, *"Ok, now it looks like a perfect time to do some mind wandering."* And you sit down on your sofa, purposefully engaging in specific thoughts.

For creative people, zoning out can happen after an intense period of knowledge acquisition around a question of interest. You don't get to choose mind wandering. Mind wandering chooses you. Uncontrollably, your attention escapes to personally significant thoughts, as you are involved in less demanding tasks, like cleaning your home. However, mind wandering is a frequent mental state and can also happen when you're involved in more demanding but less interesting tasks, such as reading a boring work report.[11] Out of the blue, your mind decides that understanding what you're reading is less important.

From what you presently do to topics your mind decides of utmost relevance in the respective moment, this automatic switch entails a state of temporary failure in meta-awareness. You lose track of what you are thinking or doing. On the one hand, you may miss out on some dust here and there in your house or some pieces of information in the report. On the other hand, you may sort out some issues about the salient concerns where your mind unintentionally goes.

Summing up, mind wandering springs from the desire to solve personally significant events, like a challenging creative problem. It provides an incubation stage preceding the "Aha" moment.

As a fun fact, when I wrote this book, my son would ask quite frequently, *"Mom, are you upset with me?"* Every time, I replied, *"No. I'm just thinking."* I thus know what my mind face looks like. Also can't say I'm proud of being mentally absent around my child. But that's how mind-wandering is. It's irresistible.

---

[11] Smallwood, J., and Schooler, J. W. (2006). The restless mind. *Psychological Bulletin, 132*(6), pp. 946–958. https://doi.org/10.1037/0033-2909.132.6.946
Salvi, C., and Bowden, E. M., (2016), Looking for Creativity: Where Do We Look When We Look for New Ideas? Frontiers in Psychology, Vol. 7, www.frontiersin.org/article/10.3389/fpsyg.2016.00161, DOI=10.3389/fpsyg.2016.00161.
Schooler, J. W., (2002), Re-representing consciousness: dissociations between experience and meta-consciousness. Trends in Cognitive Science, Vol. 6, pp. 339–344. doi: 10.1016/S1364-6613(02)01949-6.
Benedek, M., and Jauk, E., (2018), Spontaneous and controlled processes in creative cognition. In K.C.R. Fox, and K. Christoff (eds.), The Oxford handbook of spontaneous thought: mindwandering, creativity, dreaming, and clinical conditions, pp. 1-35, New York: Oxford University Press.

Perspective-taking

Perspective-taking is about the ability to think about a particular concept or situation through different lenses, like someone else's view, time, or different representations of truths. Taking others' perspectives, known also as cognitive empathy, involves the ability to understand what someone else might know about the concept or situation in focus – their experiences, emotions, and knowledge. Taking the time and underlying assumptions, perspective requires flexibility in changing mental frames, placing yourself in a situation in the distant past or far ahead in the future ruled by different rules.

Perspective-taking can be carried out on your own or in dialogue. It can happen involuntarily. Other times, it can be planned to occur in the company of another individual.

These three imagination activities – daydreaming, mind wandering, and perspective-taking – can be distinguished based on three defining elements:

(1) How is the act of imagination initiated in the mind? We can have **spontaneous** or **deliberate** episodes of imagination that take place without or with our conscious direction.

(2) What are the social surroundings of the individual who engages in imagination? We can engage in **solitary** or **social imagining**, which occur without or with the active involvement of other people.

(3) What are **the stimuli** of the imaginative act? We can experience **sensory acts of imagination**, which are based on the ability to perceive something in the absence of the right stimuli, like imagining to hear the sounds of a tune when there's silence around you. Or we can experience episodes of **creative imagination,** which consist of spontaneous combinations of ideas through associations or dissociations, purposefully denying at least one aspect of what is commonly believed to be real.

The following extract from Marcel Proust's *Remembrance of Things Past* illustrates how a present sensory stimulus – a familiar flavor – involuntarily triggers the character's childhood memories.

And once I had recognized the taste of the crumb of madeleine soaked in her decoction of lime-flowers which my aunt used to give me (although I did not yet know and must long postpone the discovery of why this memory made me so happy) immediately the old grey house upon the street, where her room was, rose up like the scenery of a theatre to attach itself to the little pavilion, opening on to the garden, which had been built out behind it for my parents ... And just as the Japanese amuse themselves by filling a porcelain bowl with water and steeping in it little crumbs of paper which until then are without character or form, but, the moment they become wet, stretch themselves and bend, take on colour and distinctive shape, become flowers or houses or people, permanent and recognisable, so in that moment all the flowers in our garden and in M. Swann's park, and the water-lilies on the Vivonne and the good folk of the village and their little dwellings and the parish church and the whole of Combray and of its surroundings, taking their proper shapes and growing solid, sprang into being, town and gardens alike, all from my cup of tea.

Moreover, an intense sensation – visual, auditory, motor, or olfactory – combined with a past experience can result in the desire for new action. Just as the taste of madeleine brings back vivid details of the town and people during childhood, it could have given rise to a glimpse of the future, like living in a new home or reconnecting with a long-lost friend. Thus, the novel would have had a different plot and character development.

Other than sensory triggers, an act of imagination can be triggered by the sudden identification of hidden assumptions about accepted truths. This surprising discovery motivates the creator to go through the effort to introduce a new idea in a community or domain of knowledge.[12] The following photos are two examples of creative imagining that delivers humorous ideas.

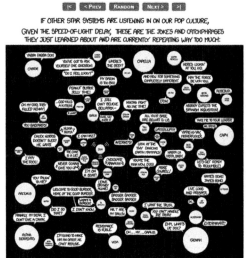 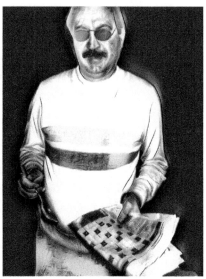

On the left, we can see the xkcd comic, Interstellar Memes, where in each of the star systems, there are some inhabitants, who pick up the pop culture phrases, of different years, on Earth. In terms of the reality shared by most astronomers, for now, it is believed that Earth is the only inhabited planet.

On the right, we can see an instance where the protagonist pretends to be a blind man filling a crosswords puzzle when in fact, he wasn't. Did you notice "the pen" with which he was planning to fill in the puzzle?

---

[12] Liao, S.-Y., and Gendler, T., (2020). Imagination. In E. N. Zalta (Ed.), The Stanford encyclopedia of philosophy. (Summer Edition). https://plato.stanford.edu/archives/sum2020/entries/imagination/
Carson, S., (2010), Your Creative Brain, Harvard Health Publications.
Currie, G. and Ravenscroft, I., (2002), Recreative Minds, Clarendon Press. Oxford.

To recap, if sounds, body movements, or a madeleine crumb trigger the sensory imagination, distorted rules of reality trigger the creative imagining. Ultimately, both categories of stimuli can lead to creative ideas. Spontaneous versus deliberate, solitary versus social, and sensory versus creative imagining describe when and how the three forms of imagination occur: daydreaming, mind wandering, and perspective-taking. Which one comes more naturally to you?

Daydreaming and mind wandering activities are predominantly sensory imagery activities. On the other hand, perspective-taking is mainly a counterfactual thinking type of imagination. In the next section, we'll discuss how perspective-taking can feed the imagination of those partaking in a feedback conversation.

Conversed Imagination

In this section, we are not going to dwell on daydreaming and mind wandering, which can be powerful exercises to fuel creativity throughout the creative process. In exchange, we want to understand how we can stimulate imaginative thinking by influencing shifts in the participants' mental frames. Hence, we elaborate on "conversed imagination," which we define as the ability to generate spontaneous counterfactual questions that nudge the conversation at a hypothetical level, where both you and your interlocutor entertain possible futures that challenge the current understanding about the topics of discussion.

From the neurocognitive standpoint, the conversed imagination requires an interplay between the default mode network, cognitive control network, and the semantic cognition network. Put differently, when you listen to feedback on your original work, you unconsciously compare what you hear with what you know, what you did, and what you plan to do in the future. Such comparisons can result in new visions or modifications to the current implementation strategies.

Mental time travel, **role play**, **contrasting beliefs,** and **falsifying assumptions** are tactics through which you can effectively process what you know and change the outlook on the talking points.

The Time Perspective

Mentally traveling in time is a good tactic to remind us that what is taken for granted today was considered a revolutionary idea or object yesterday. Let's consider the following riddle:

"There is an ancient invention still used in many parts of the world today that allows people to go through the walls. What is it?"

When was the last time you took a close look at a door and thought, *"Wow, this is an amazing door."* Daily, we hastily open and close so many hinged or sliding doors that we hardly ever think about the times when they didn't exist. It's more likely that you use or hear metaphoric expressions like, *"In every relationship, I'll leave an open door,"* or *"You never know what happens behind closed doors."*

In every other aspect of life, the past and future are connected by the creative imagination of the present. Here are some examples of conversed imagination that could provoke habitual thinking around the following question, "What are the strengths of my product?"

- "If I had asked you this question one year ago, what would you have answered?"

- "If I had asked you this question ten years ago, what would you have answered?"

- "If I ask you this question in five years, what would be a likely answer?"

- "If I ask you this question fifteen years from now, what would be a likely answer?"

You're not expecting a right or wrong answer from the interlocutor. Instead, the goal is to loosen up the attachment to experiences and knowledge, to avoid getting fixated either on what you know or on the evaluator's standpoint, so you can make room for new possibilities of actions in your creative project.

Everyone can "see" future possibilities, provided one takes time to reflect on questions such as "What did I find impossible ten years ago and nowadays it is part of my everyday life?"

Engage in Role-Play

Impersonating someone else could free you from being stuck with a point of view. Role-play – the flexibility to step into someone else's shoes and act as if you were that person – is a useful exercise to generate new explanations and perspectives related to the themes of concern.

In a feedback dialogue, a role play can be initiated through "What if" questions. Assuming you converse with a person with an entrepreneurial background, you could ask, "What if Arianna Huffington were here. What would she be doing?" or "What if Elon Musk were here. What would he be thinking?" Should the evaluator be a physicist, you could ask, "If Stephen Hawking were here, what would he be thinking?" or "If Richard Feynman were here, what would he be thinking?"

It can be that none of the aforementioned names ring a bell to you, and that's fine. The preceding examples underline the quintessential aspect of the personal significance of the role models. When you want to inspire someone to think differently about an issue, the role models need to be picked from domains of expertise shared by the speaker and listener. They need to be relatable to stimulate out-of-box thinking.

Effective engagement in role play leads to a change in the frames of thinking. This means that you start thinking in terms of *"What is the sum of 2+2?"* and end up contemplating, *"What are the numbers that add up to 4?"* Can it be $-1000 + 1004$, $1 + 1 + 2$, $-1 + 5 + 0$, or $1/2 + 7/2$?

Contrasting Beliefs

When a trusted person evaluates your creative work, a space of possibilities opens from their observations. What if the interlocutor spotted a detail that provides the key to successfully completing your project? Of course, in reality, nobody, not even the oracle, would have all the answers for you. However, to broaden your awareness of the status quo of the project, you may want to consider others' inputs as a game of contrasts.

When the evaluator's beliefs are in dissonance with your beliefs about what is true, you can opt to access a thinking mode where you take the interlocutor's statements as hypotheses. What if the interlocutor's observation is right, even if you doubt it? What then? *"If… then"* thinking opens up the mental space to investigate further issues that otherwise wouldn't cross your mind. (See Figure 19-1.)

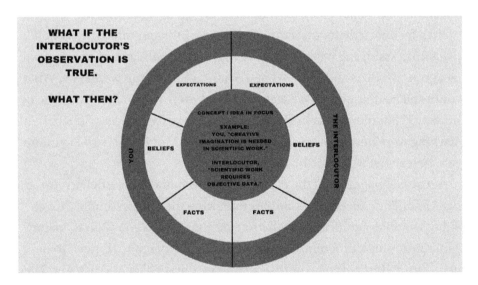

Figure 19-1. *If-then thinking*

As a role-play, let's pretend you are a young scientist in astronomy. After work, you go for a beer with another fellow researcher. At one point, the following question arises, *"How much of your imagination is required in the work that you do?"*

Behind any opinion related to this question, there is an unwieldy collection of (1) beliefs about what is morally right scientific thinking, (2) expectations about actions that are conducive to research ideas, and (3) facts or experiences that confirm the validity of the beliefs and expectations.

Your friend is adamant. Using your imagination in research is blasphemy. As the discussion unfolds, they relate the experience when they indulged in imaginative thinking to write a research proposal. Sadly, it led to a wild-goose chase and the loss of a funding opportunity.

How do you respond? This is a good moment for "If … then" thinking. If their interpretation is accurate, that research proposals require data that can be validated, then what are the consequences for your belief that imagination is important for astronomy researchers?

"If … then" thinking leads to more questions. If it's true that scientific work delivers objective data. If it's also true that, for you, imaginative thinking is a natural ability, then this question follows. *"At what point in the research process do the imagined possibilities need to be converted into mathematical formulas that describe the mechanisms of the cosmos?"* The implication is that whatever imaginative ideas you may want to test in research, in the end, the findings need to be backed by mathematically sound formulas.

This scenario illustrates that the more you allow yourself to flex your mind with another person's views, the more questions form in your mind about your project. At this point in the conversation, the ability to ask questions without knowing the answer is more important than already having an answer. What if your research project in astronomy would be turned into a science fiction book? Then, what kind of truths would your imagination have to be faithful to?

The takeaway is that in any domain of creation, taking in the evaluator's beliefs and merging them with your beliefs result in conceptual expansion. You'll raise questions that bring forth unexpected twists in your viewpoints. They will go through the reality filter should you decide to seek for the answers.

Optional exercise: Think of a recent discussion where you had diverging points of view with someone else. What was the main argument that the interlocutor used?

For the duration of the exercise, try to withhold your judgment. Start from that hypothesis and complete the sentence, "If this is true, this changes what I think about _____."

"If this change is true, then it changes _____."

Kindly repeat this exercise three more times. What does the fifth hypothesis look like? Next, what would you be interested in most? To revisit some of your initial beliefs? Or to read more some information that strengthens some of those beliefs?

In this exercise, you can verify what beliefs are paramount for you and what beliefs you are willing to reconsider.

Falsifying Constraints

> *I can do anything I can imagine and I think it would deliver the best value for the audience.*
>
> —Solopreneur and author, Peter Ivanov

The fourth and last tactic to stimulate imaginative thinking during dialogue is falsifying constraints, which is about the ability to notice and negate fundamental facts. Is this really so? Creating and innovating in the physical world is based on constraints. Constraints, like what the customer needs or what the competition offers, are anchors for the applied imagination of creators, especially in the business, technology, health, and science fields.

Constraints are built on assumptions. For instance, when an entrepreneur thinks of delivering the best value for the audience, an implied assumption is that the audience knows what they need or desire. Is it really so that the customer knows what they need? "What if" questions can transform an assumption about what is real into an alternative scenario exercise.

"What if the customer does not know? What if I created a product that this customer would find surprisingly useful? What would that product be?"

"What if the value of my existing products could be extended to customer segments or geographical regions I haven't worked with so far?"

So it happens that for Peter, the Covid-19 outbreak opened up opportunities for a larger portfolio of customers. Considering his expertise in managing virtual remote teams, when companies worldwide started working from home, he was ready to provide the solutions to help them navigate their collaborations in new virtual environments.

"What if this constraint is not a constraint?" These kinds of questions can stimulate your thinking, provided you can put aside existing plans for a few minutes.[13] Further prospective questions enable mental simulations starting from the ability to identify and stretch assumptions about the key end users, knowledge, skills, available resources, or anticipated events – political, social, technological, and economical.

What might be a noteworthy societal change on the horizon?

What possible solutions can you create?

Who might they be for?

---

[13] Abraham, A., (2018), The forest versus the trees: Creativity, cognition and imagination. In R. E. Jung and O. Vartanian (Eds.), *The Cambridge handbook of the neuroscience of creativity*, pp. 195–210, Cambridge University Press. https://doi.org/10.1017/9781316556238.012
Abraham, A. and Bubic, A., (2015), Semantic memory as the root of imagination, Frontiers in Psychology, www.frontiersin.org/articles/10.3389/fpsyg.2015.00325/full

Where would the beneficiary enjoy the new product? At work or in their free time? When they are sick or when they learn? When they travel to space? etc.

What kind of interaction product-user would be needed? Physical, digital, or hybrid?

When would the product be ready? This year, in two years, etc.

What are the resources needed to develop such a product?

In what environment will you be working? Physical, online, or both?

The answers to the preceding questions have fundamental assumptions embedded in them. Let's take resources as an illustration. What resources would you use to develop a new product?

There can be two assumptions. You can think you have all the resources in-house, or you count on signing agreements with external contractors or experts that could provide the missing resources. In any free market, there's competition. A typical business thinking is that the competition needs to be outsmarted, right? And yet, can there be any ways in which this principle could be bent?

What if one of the competitors could help with some of the resources or work required in developing the new product? Who and why would they be interested?

The answers could generate new solutions and actions, unusual from the ones taken in the past, toward innovative products.

In a feedback dialogue, you may experience situations when the interlocutor raises some concerns. For example, there can be issues related to the methodology, forecasting, clients' acceptance, etc. These concerns are the constraints to work with.

First, single out the underlying facts. Then, invite the evaluator to hypothetically explore it together. *"I can see that you base your concern on this fact. What if the opposite were true?"*

Discussing alternative realities can deepen the metacognition about affordances and contingencies, in your creative process. Counterfactual thinking is to your creative mind what seeds are to the fertile soil. They will spawn a realistic course of action when the time is right.

In brief, the fourth way to imagine tomorrow's reality is to poke into the facts and information you and your interlocutor take as constraints. And you don't have to wait for the next COVID-like crisis to imagine what might be. Only for the following conversation with the right person.

The Humor of an Imagination Gap Can Save the Conversation

In 2001, the experimental psychologist Richard Wiseman collaborated with the British Science Association to carry out a scientific search for the world's funniest joke.[14] After receiving 40,000 jokes, which were rated by 350,000 people from 70 countries, the following joke ranked the top funniest:

"Two hunters are out in the woods when one of them collapses. He doesn't seem to be breathing and his eyes are glazed. The other guy whips out his phone and calls the emergency services.

He gasps, 'My friend is dead! What can I do?'

The operator says 'Calm down. I can help. First, let's make sure he's dead.'

There is silence, then a shot is heard.

Back on the phone, the guy says 'OK, now what?'"

A British psychiatrist submitted this joke. When Wiseman contacted him, the psychiatrist explained that he'd tell the joke to cheer up his patients. People feel better when they hear that someone is always doing more stupid things than themselves.

---

[14] https://richardwiseman.wordpress.com/research/laughlab/

The two hunters' joke illustrates how imagination in the form of misunderstood assumptions can drive us to action without doubting whether what we heard was correct for a split second.

Let's take a look at another winning joke in Wiseman's search for the funniest joke, this time in the category *"best joke submitted by a well-known scientist."* The joke was submitted by Nobel laureate and professor of chemistry, Sir Harry Kroto:

"A man walking down the street sees another man with a very big dog. The man says: 'Does your dog bite?'

The other man replies: 'No, my dog doesn't bite.'

The first man then pats the dog, has his hand bitten off, and shouts; 'I thought you said your dog didn't bite.'

The other man replies: 'That's not my dog.'"

The two men were talking about two different dogs. In the same way, the operator and hunter have a diametric understanding of the statement, *"First, let's make sure he's dead."*

These two jokes spill the beans about how the imagined understanding of others' statements results in humor: when the imagined perspective is contradicted by the accurate perspective of what is actually meant. Humor starts with an initial understanding of an event or stimulus, followed by a conflicting reinterpretation of the event or stimulus in the punchline.[15] In the same way imagination works for us to create humor, in everyday conversations, imagined understandings can push us toward constructive or less constructive consequences in everyday conversations.

In dialogues, when you misinterpret an initial stimulus, your mind concocts a narrative that will confuse you as you listen to the speaker. This is the imagination gap, the story that your mind artfully invents

---

[15] Martin, R.A., and Ford, T.E., (2018), The Psychology of Humour, Second Edition, Academic Press.

when you have failed to listen actively.[16] The quality of the conversation is compromised. When was the last time this happened to you? What did you do?

In Romanian culture, there's this saying, *"A deaf person hears what suits them."* It's easy to mishear a word and give it an imagined meaning in the context. Filling in what the other is saying is done in accordance with what fits with your past experiences, knowledge, or personal expectations. This phenomenon of the human mind became known by the name *mondegreen* in American culture in 1954.

Writer Sylvia Wright invented the word *mondegreen* in an essay in *Harper's Magazine*. She described how she misheard a line from a 17th-century ballad, "The Bonnie Earl of Moray."[17] *"They have slain the Earl o'Moray, and laid him on the green."* and *"They have slain the Earl o'Moray, and Lady Mondegreen."* . These two sentences give rise to two different mental images, isn't it? The former was the actual line, and the latter was what Sylvia heard.

To the extent that you start suspecting that you either misheard or misinterpreted a comment in a conversation, this realization has a mirthfulness potential. Should you bring it up, you take the opportunity to replace a misunderstanding with a bit of laughter and alignment in ideas.

A feedback conversation is about assessing the level of completeness of a creative project. A lax but candid attitude toward mistakes reminds us that the focus is on being merciful on what could have been done better and daring to search for what could be done differently.

---

[16] Pelaprat, E., and Cole, M. (2011). "Minding the Gap": Imagination, Creativity and Human Cognition, Integr Psych Behav, 45, pp. 397–418, DOI 10.1007/s12124-011-9176-5.

Nichols, R. G. (1955). Ten components of effective listening. *Education, 75,* pp. 292–302.

Nichols, R.G. and Stevens, L.A. (1957). Listening to people, *Harvard Business Review,* pp. 85-92.

[17] Seelig, T., (2015), Insight Out, HarperOne.

"My imagination functions much better when I don't have to speak to people," writes novelist Patricia Highsmith. However, when you talk with people, the conversed imagination leads to unexpected ideas, which cannot occur in solitude.

Part 4 Summary

This fourth and last part of the book is based on the presumption that in the first two stages of development as a creator, you may have not fully acquired the sense of balancing what is interesting for you and what is useful for your audiences. To this view, you may want to initiate one-to-one conversations with trusted peers, mentors, and possible end users to test their view of the expected utility of your creative products. Whether you're an entrepreneur, researcher, or innovation expert, your creative integrity is a guiding principle for the quality of feedback conversations.

Listening with creative integrity means spotting opportunities for inspiration and imaginative thinking. At the same time, listening with creative integrity involves speaking with humor to create a playful attitude around serious ideas. Speaking with humor is not going to undermine the importance of dialogue. Quite the opposite, it will enable a refreshing break to reassess the perspective on the details that matter.

Momentary exposure to humorous comments enhances creative thinking. The use of humor is not only an indicator but also a stimulator of out-of-the-box thinking. The better the humor comprehension, the higher the receiver's creativity. Therefore, humor is a form of creative thinking that can boost problem-solving during dialogue.

About 70% of the humor that we experience daily comes from spontaneous conversational humor. It consists of telling funny comments or anecdotes about what happened to you. In this book, we discussed the essential components for creating humor, which is humorless per se, but when put in practice, they harness your potential to produce witty remarks.

There are people – stand-up comedians, actors, writers – who have a knack for making large audiences laugh. There are folks around whom family, friends, and coworkers gravitate due to their talent for seeing and expressing the funny side of boring events. And there you are. You're a creator. Your aim is to improve your verbal humor to maintain an open-minded attitude throughout feedback conversations. You can do that in three steps: get playful, get ready, and be flexible in seeing and taking the time to say something funny.

First, develop a joyful spontaneity that helps you reframe daily experiences in an entertaining way. Second, mark the transitions in a conversation with humor: when you define a concept, when you rephrase, or when you summarize an idea. Third, learn to be sensitive to how your sense of humor is received. Humor can connect and disconnect people. We highly value the individuals who are good at making us laugh, but we also withdraw from those whose wit can hurt us.

What sense of humor is more likely to be perceived as harmless? Irrespective of your joking style with family members and friends or your job status, using humor that boosts the value of a relationship with another person or lowers your value is an empathetic choice in conversations. The rule of thumb is, *"Laugh **at** yourself, not **at** others."*

A feedback conversation is an opportunity to collect more information than you would have otherwise been exposed to. The more open to ideas both you and your interlocutor are, the higher the output of constructive ideas. There are moments in discourse when being open to ideas happens naturally. Yet, there are times when you, as the conversation leader, need to make an effort to maintain the open-mindedness of the dialogue.

Speaking in analogies can help you communicate abstract, complex, or poorly understood concepts with enhanced clarity. Yet, it's important to make sure you don't compare apples with oranges to further confuse the listener. The more complex the idea, the more important it is to make a solid analogy. We looked at three rules for creating effective analogies:

choosing familiar domains for the model concept, checking the internal consistency of each of the two compared concepts, and the validity of the comparison.

From the point of view of the brain processes, using analogies triggers the associations between what you hear and what you already know. On the other hand, listening for imagination is about transforming what you hear into a possibility which is not yet perceived in the immediate surroundings.

Out of all the imagination forms, we focused on conversed imagination, defined as the ability to generate spontaneous counterfactual questions that take the discussion to a hypothetical level. The aim is to change the perspective on what are the possible, plausible, or impossible futures before choosing a likely scenario to transform into reality. Mental time travel, role play, contrasting beliefs, and falsifying assumptions are four tactics through which you can take the discussion to a hypothetical level.

Mental time travel can remind us that what is taken for granted today – a door – was a revolutionary object in the past. Through role-play, we can impersonate other people with relevant backgrounds and experiences. Contrasting the evaluator's beliefs with your beliefs about what is the underlying truth about an idea can result in a conceptual expansion, opening the mind toward unanticipated possible actions. Is this really so?

Falsifying assumptions is the fourth method of conversed imagination which sheds light on the constraints of the existing project. An entrepreneur can build a product based on what the customer wants. What if the customer does not know what they want? "What if" questions can transform a fact into an alternative scenario exercise. If not the customer, then who else can more accurately anticipate societal changes?

Challenging assumptions about what is possible in your time can open your eyes to alternative future scenarios. In the worst case, they can validate your future plans. In the best case, such exercises of imagination can enable the next innovative product.

The imagination gap, such as the "Does your dog bite?" or mondegreen experiences, concludes this last part of the book. The irony of dialogue is that we misunderstand others more often than we think. Hence, when you become aware that your mind coined a different story than what the speaker said, it can be useful to bring it up in the conversation.

When you dare to speak up about the funny side of the discrepancy between what you believed they said and what they really said, you show that you care to listen carefully. When you laugh together, you co-create new ideas. And if nothing else, you'll gain points from the listener for transparency, which maintains the trust in the relationship.

Conclusions

The Evolving Creator – Mind the Insight and Get to Work

How to conclude a book about creative self-development? For a while, I thought about leaving an open ending. The book can be boiled down to one sentence: when you commit to exploring your creative potential, you manage a personal goal which becomes a life's mission. What is a more conclusive message than keeping your mind in shape for creative insight and ready to work on it? But there was something that didn't give me peace until I sat down to write the afterword.

Creative self-awareness can be defined as alertness to new insights. As I could see from my own experiences and the stories of the interviewed professionals, every now and then, a new day can bring a surprising twist which deepens your insight about what else you might create. Are you ready to catch it?

"If you think about your development, in what ways has it changed your understanding of who a creative person is?" I asked sales engineer and author Oscar Santolalla.

"I guess my first impressions were that there's just the artist. My impression for quite a long time. But then I mentioned other activities, like advertising and writing speeches, that require creativity. Yeah, another thing is that many people believe that the genius, like DaVinci or Gaudi, are these guys who have done a lot alone. I also thought that one person did everything, which is not true. Definitely, it was a team effort. The guy who had the biggest creativity, the biggest genius and he managed to inspire others. And that really happens. But one genius who does everything, that's not true."

© Oana Velcu-Laitinen 2022
O. Velcu-Laitinen, *How to Develop Your Creative Identity at Work*,
https://doi.org/10.1007/978-1-4842-8680-7

Oscar reconsidered two beliefs about the creative person: the image of the artist and the contribution of the individual creator. What did you learn about yourself that you didn't know before reading this book? If there's one thing I hope you take with you is that you belong to one of the four types of creators: the expressive ones, the healers, the change makers, or the abstract thinkers. The expressive types focus on transforming their emotions and experiences into works of art that touch the audiences. The healer types care about uplifting others. The change makers take initiative to build momentum for movements in civic or business communities. And last, the abstract thinkers feel a deep affinity toward figuring out problems in domains of science, technology, or economy.

Moreover, you can be a combination of two types of creators, or even three in some cases. However, to become a recognized creator, it's not enough that you get an insight about your type. You also need to be willing to take action. The Romanian sculptor Constantin Brâncuşi said, *"Things are not difficult to make; what is difficult is putting ourselves in the state of mind to make them."* The second thing that I hope it sticks with you is that a day in a creator's life means habits of curiosity and observation that get you inspired to labor away on each creative idea that wants to become objective reality through you.

Without an Audience, There's No Purpose to Create Anything

Joel was the most senior member of the writer's club I attended more than a decade ago. He used to spend his retirement days in one of the libraries in Helsinki, writing short-stories inspired from the time he spent in the USA. With a smile of satisfaction and a trembling hand, he would take meticulous notes about the comments that the other participants would have about his stories. The club disintegrated when its enthusiasts got carried away with other priorities. Years later, when I heard that Joel had gotten over a severe illness, I invited him for dinner with my family. At one point, I asked him, "So, what are you writing about nowadays?" "I stopped writing," he replied in a low tone. "There's no one to write for." For all those years, I had lived with the impression that one day Joel would publish his short-stories. The truth was that we, the members of the writing club, were his audience.

The third and last idea that I would like to leave as food for thought is the importance of balancing what you're interested in creating with the audience you intend to serve at different stages of development. To create is not an act of selfishness, quite the contrary, it's an act of humble generosity, of offering an improved experience of life to fellow human beings.

Oana: Considering everything you've achieved in your career so far, what would you say were the happiest thoughts?

This was the last question in the interviews with the ten professional creators mentioned throughout the book. Here's what they answered.

Composer Matias Kupiainen: *"It's a really good question. Of course, I had many good moments. The funniest thing, I was laughing on stage like in this super weird mental state almost ten years ago. The first really big show that I played was when you have 75,000 people in front of you. Then you put your hand like this (fist up in the air) and everybody does it after you. That's a weird feeling. You actually have power, you put your hand up and 75,000 people follow you. The first ten minutes I wasn't able to play guitar because I was laughing. It was so funny. That's a really odd situation. I don't know if it's a happy moment but it's like something I remember because it was so weird.*

And then of course in these kinds of moments when you think you have been working on a song or album for a long time and finally you get it ready, it's super big relief. Finally it's done! I calculated a few years ago that making an album it's basically 10,000 working hours. So, for me it means I have to work constantly for almost 18 months. 24/7 working 18 months. That's the time it takes."

Dasha Pears, Surreal Fine Art Photographer: *"I'm happy that I decided to pursue it (the artistic career), very much, because I wasn't for a long time sure why I'm here and that's when you kind of, you don't have a meaning in your life it's really hard to live, I think, for many people. Well, some people maybe don't need that, but I was struggling for a long time, even when I chose to be a photographer. I was like, 'what do I want?,' and the only answer that came to my mind was 'I want to become famous.' Okay, what kind of a dream is that? And why do I want to become famous? Do I want to have houses and cars and stuff? No, and why? And now, now I know.*

So that's the happy thought, that I can encourage people, I can share my view of the world with people and maybe through this make the world a bit better. Because, well, again, not very long I came up with this idea for myself that, when I encourage people to create something, they are focused on creation and not destruction. They would be more on the constructive side, on the positive side and that's kind of my contribution into making the world a better place. Of course it won't change the world like, 'Ah, just Dasha came and changed the world,' but this is what I can do and what I'm doing."

John Bates, Leadership Communication Expert: *"There are a couple of highlights you know. I got to train all the NASA active astronauts, about a year ago. That was absolutely a bucket list, you know. I never thought I would do that in my lifetime. And I did and they actually really liked it.*

And then I got to Dolph Lundgren, you know from Rocky. What was fulfilling about that is that he came in really ready to tell a really vulnerable story about his life that was gonna make a difference for people and I got to help him unpack that and create it for maximum impact. And now that talk has I think over a million views. And it is really beautiful, Dolph Lundgren being vulnerable and authentic. And he gets stopped, a guy stopped him a while ago, 'Hey Dolph, I love your movies but I love your Ted talk more.' And he had a glint of tears in the corner of his eye and Dolph said, 'I know how he was raised. 'I know what he went through.' Amazing. That kind of stuff, that's so fulfilling.

And even if the talk doesn't get a million views. I got to work with hundreds, maybe thousands of people on their most meaningful message. That's fabulous. Whether it has 100 views or a million, they put it out there, and people are seeing it and getting it and that's really fulfilling."

Helder Santos, Professor in Biomedical Engineering, whose published research is in the top 1% of highly cited works from European institutions according to the Royal Society of Chemistry[1]: *"Oh... that's a very tough question. A happy thought. I think a happy thought in my career is if I can help the new generation of whatever career they will have. So it makes me very happy if someone comes to work with me, gets their degree, goes and gets their job, and many years [later] we find [each other] again and they say 'Thank you very much for what you taught me because that has helped me, first of all to grow as a man or as a woman, and I learned some values, I learned some ways how to do things that I didn't have before....' So I think that I get a bit of a tear in the corner of the eye, because I think this is the most important thing.*

Basically, what I'm saying is that a happy thought in my career is making sure that we are somehow contributing to the happiness of others, one way or the other. Either by teaching them something, by interacting with them and giving them new knowledge, or by what we do. Maybe someday we could help them to treat something."

Professor Vincenzo Cerullo, Finland's #1 and Europe's top #4 scientist specializing in oncolytic virotherapy, according to Expertscape[2]: *"Actually I have two, two things that come right away, or probably three. The first one is the thought of having helped even a single person. Sometimes I say, imagine how great it would be, the idea of whatever we have thought in this small*

[1] www.rsc.org/
www.linkedin.com/posts/h%C3%A9lder-a-santos-10a630a_thank-you-to-the-royal-society-of-chemistry-activity-6939622284982706176-gNzU?utm_source=linkedin_share&utm_medium=member_desktop_web

[2] https://expertscape.com/ex/oncolytic+virotherapy/c/fi
https://expertscape.com/ex/oncolytic+virotherapy/c/eur

lab if in 5-6 years, has helped a single person. I'm not saying here "save" word (sounds like save the world) because that's stupid, but even a single person. That is probably my top thought. The second top is the possibility of making enough money to build up a children's hospital or something like that so that you can really see the thing. And then, third thought is to donate the University of Helsinki 100 million, I said it once for, as a joke, 'Don't worry, I'll give you 100 million euros,' but I'm thinking now, I don't know why this thought doesn't go away, so that one day it will happen. But those are the top three. But the very first one is the one that really puts me like wow, then I would consider it a merit."

Tulia Lopes, Confident Communication Architect: *"My happy thoughts, and I have many, is when I see in a masterclass, a two day event, that someone is coming. I know how they come. I see how they come. I see their bodies. I hear how they communicate. And then after two days, the revelations that they have, that they have already in two days improved a little bit, or I would say changed and transformed for their own best, in only two days. And for me it's always the big happy thought and the motivator for me to do what I do because I know I start with one person, and then, the next day, at the end of the day, it's not a different person, but is this person showing, blossoming more and then there's so much more for the person to blossom. And that for me is the big gratification I have in everything I do."*

Pamela Thompson, Leadership Coach and Consultant: *"Yes, one was, actually before I head to Afghanistan, I was taking a body-centric coaching course and the facilitator/coach asked for somebody to demo the process. This was a body-centered decision-making process. No one else was volunteering, so I volunteered and she said, 'find a line and a floor.' And so I found a line and a floor in my office and she said, 'imagine something that you really want, just like imagine it and feel it in your body. Now notice if any fears or negative beliefs come up for you, and imagine each one of those as rocks in a rucksack on your back, just feel them weighing you down. Now imagine releasing them all, just letting them go and drop to the ground.' Then she said 'Now cross that line and say aloud whatever you want, and*

*you can shout it, you can speak it, you can cross the line however you want,'
so I leapt across the line and I said 'I wanna play big!'*

*Within two weeks I got an email inviting me to throw my hat in the ring
for one of three senior positions in Afghanistan and one of them had my
name written over, it was senior technical advisor – strategic planning and
performance measurement, and I've been wanting to go to Afghanistan for
a number of years and I thought this is the universe telling me, it's offering
me to play big. So two weeks after that, I got the email, I made the decision,
talking to my husband, to throw my hat in the ring. Two weeks later I was
part of the interview process. A month later I was on the ground in Kabul,
I signed a 9-month contract which extended to 13. Yeah, it was one of those
things where, I said, I didn't even know what playing big was gonna look
like but it brought all or many of my skills together, my creative side, my love
of cross-cultural work, helping people from different tribes. In Afghanistan,
creating conditions, giving them skills so that they can work collaboratively
together, it was really fun. It can be a very stressful environment, I was very
close to a suicide bomb attack, that said it was very rewarding."*

Peter Ivanov, Virtual Teams Expert and Author: *"This is the quote that
I'm ending with my keynotes and it goes like this. If you dream alone, this
is just a dream. If we people dream together, this is the beginning of a new
reality. It is from John Lennon and I believe it has to do with imagination
and the creative process. And I believe we have to nurture our creativity
but if we do it as a group, the multiplying effect would really create a new
reality."*

Entrepreneur Harriet Fagerholm, Evolutionary Co-Creative Guide and
Leadership Coach: *"All the encounterings I've had with all the people here
[in this room]. I've been able to serve their deepest healing, their deepest
emotional wounds that are blocking their creativity and joy of life, you
know? Those moments are the happiest ones because you're feeling that you
are contributing to something valuable."*

Oscar Santolalla, Sales Engineer and Author: *"One happy thought is, for instance, about my podcast* Time to Shine. *I started from being completely unknown and people gradually started to know about the podcast. The first times that people tell you, 'Oh, I've been following you for one, two years.' Sometimes, the praise comes from people who are definitely more capable than me in this field. So yeah, you feel good, that's validation."*

All in all, the answers show that the role of a creator comes with the power to do good for others. The reward for being a creator comes from seeing the impact you seek to make.

What is one of your happiest thoughts? If you put it in action, what kind of a project would it materialize in? When would you be ready to start it?

Index

© Oana Velcu-Laitinen 2022
O. Velcu-Laitinen, *How to Develop Your Creative Identity at Work*,
https://doi.org/10.1007/978-1-4842-8680-7

Printed by Printforce, the Netherlands